PATRIOTS AND WARLORDS

Brothers' Journey
towards Republican China

EDWARD D. WANG

ISBN -10: 069202672X
ISBN -13: 978-0692026724
Library of Congress Control Number: 2014937516
Qilin Publishing, Evanston, IL 60202

CONTENTS

Maps:

Administrative Divisions of the
People's Republic of China (PRC)

Map of People's Republic of China, 1913

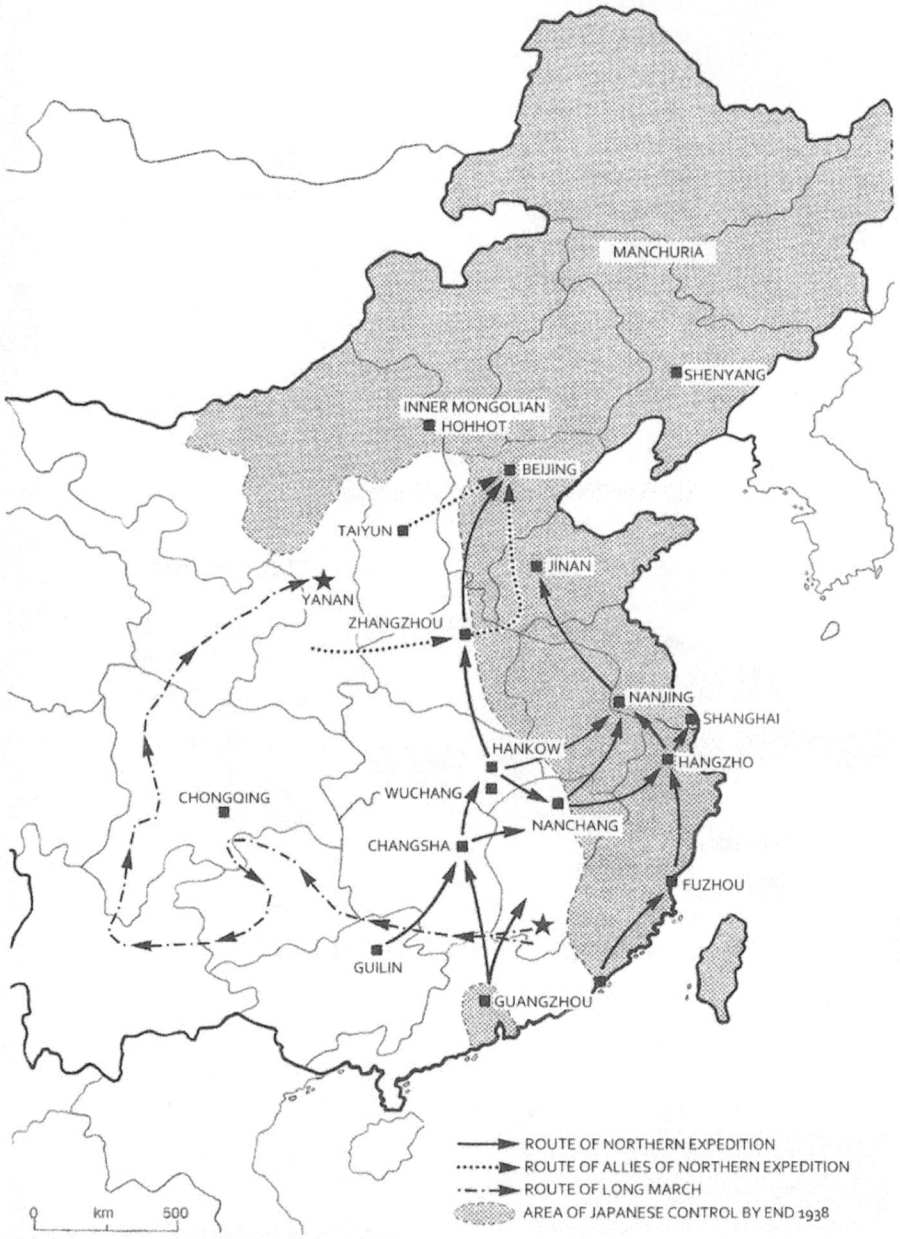

Map of Northern Expedition, Long March, Japanese Occupation

MANCHURIA

SHENYANG

INNER MONGOLIAN
HOHHOT

BEIJING

TAIYUN

JINAN

YANAN
ZHANGZHOU

NANJING
SHANGHAI
HANKOW
HANGZHO
CHONGQING
WUCHANG
NANCHANG
CHANGSHA
FUZHOU
GUILIN
GUANGZHOU

ROUTE OF NORTHERN EXPEDITION
ROUTE OF ALLIES OF NORTHERN EXPEDITION
ROUTE OF LONG MARCH
AREA OF JAPANESE CONTROL BY END 1938

km 500

CHARACTERS

The Wang (王) Family

Qiyuan (起元, 1863–1904): Boqun's father, militia leader, head of Wang clan, scholar

Liu Xianqing (刘显情, 1863–1934): Boqun's mother, elder sister of Liu Xianshi

Boqun (伯群, 1885–1944): Revolutionary, official, educator

Bao Zhining (保志宁, 1909–1999): Wife of Boqun, social worker

Dilun (电轮, 1888–1921): Boqun's brother, Revolutionary, General. Married Liu Xianshi's niece (刘从淑, 1886–1919)

Wenbi (文碧, 1882–1936): Boqun's older sister, married Lo Pei (罗培).

Wenxiao (文萧, 1895–19XX): Boqun's younger sister, married Zhao Shouyuan (赵守垣, 1894–1937).

Wenxiang (文相, 1897–1978): Boqun's youngest sister, married He Yingqin (何应钦, 1890–1987), General and principal associate of Jiang Jieshi

The Liu (刘) Family

Guanli (官礼, 1840–1908): Liu Xianqian's father, Xingyi warlord, head of Liu clan

Xianshi (显世, 1870–1927): Liu Guanli's eldest son, Guizhou warlord

Xianqian (显潜, 1865–1838): Liu Xianshi's cousin, Xingyi warlord

Xianzhi (显治, 1879–19xx): Liu Xianshi's younger brother

The Bao (保) Family

Zhang Jian (张謇, 1853–1926): Zhining's maternal grandfather, imperial examination winner, chair of provincial parliament, ministerial official, educator, and business innovator

Shaopu (召葡, 1857 – 1932): Zhining's grandfather, diplomat, and educator

Junhao (君嗥, 1885–1942): Zhining's father, diplomat, married to Zhang Jian's daughter.

Junzheng (君征, 1887–1943): Junhao's brother, graduate of Beijing University, government financial official. Wife's name Luo Pei (罗培).

Junjian (君建, 1898–1970): known as CJ, Junhao's brother, graduate of Beijing University, Columbia University master's degree and PhD, educator, and ambassador. Married an American, Editha, graduate of Barnard College.

Johnson (骏迪, Jundi, 1914–2011): Brother of Zhining, educator, diplomat, married Ye Meizhou (叶美妯, May), Canadian.

Channing (祥麟, Xianglin, 1919): Brother of Zhining, doctor, civil engineering, Cornell University, educator, government research, married Eleanor Marks (1923–2011), American, PhD, Cornell University, government research.

Gerson (紫宸, Zichen, 1921–2009): Brother of Zhining, Great China University graduate, army officer, diplomat, officer of UN Economic Commission, married Zou Zhaomei (邹兆美, Soumy, 1922 – 2013`), a Guangdong native.

The Revolutionaries

Chen Qimei (陈其美, 1878–1916), Cheng Biguang (程璧光, 1861–1918), Cai E (蔡锷, 1882–1916)

Dai Kan (戴戡, 1880–1917)

Huang Xing (黄兴, 1874–1916), Hu Hanmin (胡汉民, 1879–1939)

Kang Youwei (康有為, 1858–1927), Kung Hsianghsi (孔祥熙, 1881–1967)

Li Yuanhong (黎元洪, 1864–1928), Liang Qichao (梁启超, 1873–1929), Liao Zongkai (廖仲恺, 1877–1925)

Mao Zedong (毛泽东, 1893–1976)

Soong Chingling (宋庆龄, 1893–1981), Soong Jiaoren (宋教仁, 1882–1913), Sun Yatsen (孫逸仙, 1855–1925)

Wang Jingwei (汪精卫, 1883–1944)

Zhang Bailin (張百麟, 1878–1919), Zhang Guotao (张国焘, 1897–1979), Zheng Taiyan (章太炎, 1868–1936), Zhou Enlai (周恩来, 1898–1976), Zou Rong (鄒容, 1885–1905)

The Warlords

Bai Chongxi (白崇禧, 1893–1966)

Cao Kun (曹锟, 1862–1938), Chen Jiongming (陈炯明, 1878–1933)

Duan Qirui (段祺瑞, 1865–1936)

Feng Guozhang (冯国璋, 1859–1919), Feng Yuxiang (冯玉祥, 1882–1948).

Li Zongren (李宗仁, 1890–1969), Liu Xiang (刘湘, 1888–1938), Liu Wenhui (刘文辉, 1895–1976), Long Yun (龙云, 1884–1967)

Sun Chuanfang (孙传芳, 1885 – 1935)

Tang Jiyao (唐继尧, 1883–1927), Tang Jiyu (唐繼虞, 1890–19xx) Tang Shengzhi (唐生智, 1889–1970)

Wu Peifu (吴佩孚, 1874–1939)

Xu Shichang (徐世昌, 1855–1939) Xu Shuzheng (徐树铮, 1880–1925)

Yan Xishan, (阎锡山, 1883–1960) Yuan Shikai (袁世凯, 1859–1916) Yuan Zuming (袁祖铭, 1889–1927)

Zhang Xueliang (張學良, 1901–2001), Zhang Zuolin (张作霖, 1875–1928)

The Officials

Soong Meiling (宋美龄, 1898–2003), Soong Tseven (宋子文, 1891–1971), Sun Fo (孫科 , 1895–1973)

The Military

Chen Cheng (陈诚, 1897–1965)

Jiang Jieshi (蒋介石, 1887–1975)

Lin Biao (林彪, 1907–1971)

Sun Liren (孙立人, 1900–1990)

Xue Yue (薛岳, 1896–1998)

Zhu De (朱德, 1986–1966)

INTRODUCTION

This book was written at the urging of my family, particularly my children, for the sake of keeping in memory the history and the stories of the Wang family. I left China on the eve of the defeat of the nationalists by the communists in 1949 at the age of fifteen with my mother and four sisters to go to Taiwan. We then traveled through Hong Kong, Bangkok, Manila, and Lima and finally landed in the United States in 1951. Our family, like many other Chinese before us, transplanted ourselves into a different world. Like those before me, I tried to assimilate myself into the American culture. My Chinese education stopped at age fifteen, and for the rest of my life, I was educated in the United States. In writing this book, I have come to appreciate the Chinese culture and history, which gave me a better understanding of the persona, motivations, and eventually the path each character in my book has chosen and how the results of their choices impacted their respective lives. Thus I have tried to articulate what I believe to be the most salient aspects of the Chinese culture and history and where she found herself in the mid-nineteenth century as my book begins.

Chinese culture can be traced back as far as 7000 BCE but only reasonably documented when the Yellow Emperor—the legendary founder of the culture and ancestor of the Han people reigned in 2700 to 2600 BCE. Modern Chinese written language can trace its beginning back to the second millennium BCE and hence its culture and history continuously from that time. Its long history consists of cycles of natural disaster, war, and civil strife to relative peace and harmony. The collapse of each dynasty is followed by an emergence of another, which reconstituted under a new leader with the old governance, with little effect on the general populace. Such collapses and reformations repeated in cycles lasting some hundreds of years from the beginning of Chinese history.

At its zenith, all Chinese considered China to be the center of the world. Its culture extended from the steppes of the north into Siberia to the lowlands of the Indochina in the south to the west into Tibet, Xinjiang, and beyond to the Himalayas and to the east into the Gobi Deserts of Mongolia. China has been the source of many inventions, including the so-called four great inventions: papermaking, the compass, gunpowder, and printing. The Chinese developed technologies involving mechanics, hydraulics, and mathematics applied to horology, metallurgy, astronomy, agriculture, engineering, music theory, craftsmanship, nautics, and warfare. In the period of 400 till 220 BCE, they included advanced metallurgic technology: the blast and cupola furnaces, forging, and pudding processes. A sophisticated economic system gave birth to inventions such as paper money before 950. The invention of gunpowder by the tenth century led to an array weapons, such as the fire lance, land mine, naval mine, hand cannon, exploding cannonballs, multistage rocket, and rocket bombs with aerodynamic wings and explosive payloads. The eleventh-century invention of the compass allowed Chinese sailors to sail as far as East Africa and Egypt. In water-powered clockworks, the Chinese had used the escapement mechanism since the eighth century and the endless power-transmitting chain drive in the eleventh century. Large mechanical puppet theaters driven by waterwheels and carriage wheels and wine-serving automatons driven by paddle-wheel boats were developed at about the same time.

The Chinese economy during the Song dynasty (960–1279) accounted for 80 percent of the world's GDP, and even as late as 1820, it still produced over 30 percent of the worldwide GDP. Thus it is not surprising that by the European middle ages, China considered itself to be at the center of world given its geographic location, its history of inventions, and a flourishing economy based on abundant natural resources. China had led the world in nautical technology since 1000, yet its fleet has never ventured in exploration or conquest or in spreading the Chinese virtues to those beyond its immediate coast.

The only exception was in the reign of third emperor of the Ming dynasty's (1368–1644) Yongle emperor (1360–1424), who sent Zheng He (1371–1433), a Mongolian Muslim eunuch who was conscripted into the Emperor's service as a child, on seven expeditions from 1405 till 1433, which were stuff of legend with astounding technologies and skills. The larger so-called treasure ships were ten times the size of the *Santa Maria* sailed by Columbus to America in 1492. Zheng's first trip in 1405 consisted of twenty thousand eight hundred men and a fleet of sixty-two such large treasure ships supported by about a hundred and ninety smaller ships. The fleet included: equine ships carrying horses and tribute goods and repair material for the fleet, supply ships containing staples for the crew, troop transports, warships, patrol boats, and fresh water tankers.

The fleet visited Brunei, Thailand and Southeast Asia, India, the Horn of Africa, Arabia, and even America, dispensing and receiving goods along the way. Zheng He presented gifts of gold, silver, porcelain, and silk; in return, China received such novelties as ostriches, zebras, camels, and ivory for the emperor. While the size of Zheng He's fleet was unprecedented, the routes were not. The fleet followed long-established, well-mapped routes of trade between China and the Arabian Peninsula since at least the Han dynasty (206–220 BCE). Prior missions were recorded that in the Three Kingdoms (220–280 BCE) period, Chinese ships sailed along the coast of Asia and reached as far as the Eastern Roman Empire. In the Song dynasty, China had conducted large-scale maritime trade in the South Pacific and Indian Oceans, reaching as far as the Arabian Peninsula, India, and East Africa. Zheng He generally sought to establish good relationship and spread Chinese culture. His large army awed most would-be enemies into submission. He, however, did ruthlessly suppress pirates and other known enemies of China who had long plagued Chinese and southeast Asian waters.

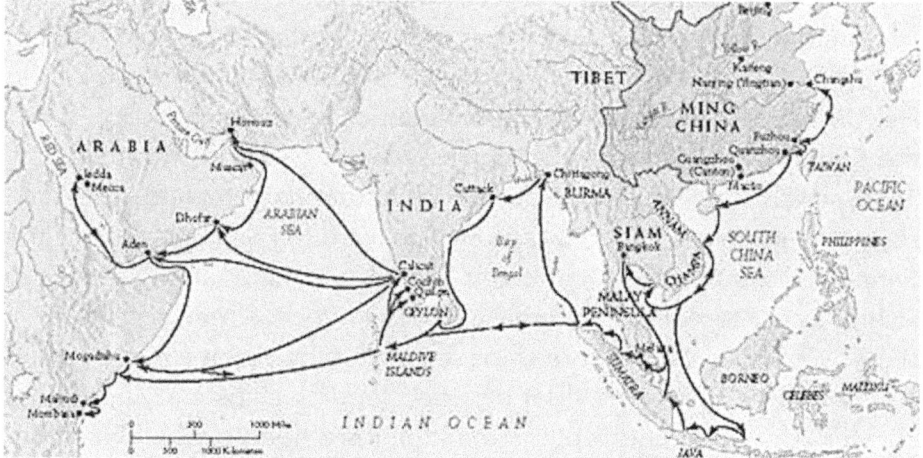

Zheng He's Voyages, 1405–1433

The purpose of Zheng's expeditions was not historically clear, but it was the Yongle Emperor's intent to demonstrate imperial superiority to the world and to spread the Chinese culture. He had no desire to colonize others but wished to establish his "mandate from heaven," which would facilitate the traditional tributaries system of trade whereby the other nations would recognize the superior position of the Chinese emperor and send various indigenous gifts and treasures for his pleasure in order to trade for Chinese goods they desired. Those bordering and near the Chinese coast, such as Korea, Vietnam, Burma, Thailand, etc., were considered tributaries, except for Japan, which China considered an inferior offspring that had acquired a barbarian nature. The next Ming emperor, who believed the superiority of the Chinese culture and the mandate of its emperor were well established, stopped the expeditions in 1433.

This China's self-centered isolation developed and nurtured a particular Chinese self-perception that China was, indeed, the Middle

Kingdom or the center of the world and its culture the most advanced civilization of humanity. This worldview was not overreaching in the eyes and minds of the Chinese since by most measurements of human culture development, whether in technology, sciences, or economy, China had frequently outperformed western European, Indian, African, and Arab nations. Though China traded with foreigners occasionally and at time even adapted ideas and inventions from them, the Chinese view of trade has never changed from others paying tribute to its superiority instead of a mere normal exchange of goods as trade is traditionally understood by the rest of the world.

To understand this view of the Chinese, one also needs to understand the unique structure and values of its society. Unlike the Western world where religious values became the center of the community, China has been essentially secular in its culture values. There are no creation theories, life after death promises, etc., but a set of rules of conduct prescribed by Confucius (551–479 BCE), who lived in a most-chaotic period of history when greed and ambition turned into violence and rebellion in the Warring State Period (475–221 BCE). Confucius, like Socrates, Plato, Aristotle, and later Machiavelli, was a philosopher who offered his advice to princes and kings contending for dominances in his time. He was not successful in his lifetime in helping to structure a government of a harmonious community based on his principles of compassionate rule, filial piety, and righteous individual behavior. However, his teachings lived on through his writings and his disciples till the Han dynasty, when his writings were adapted as the state creed akin to a combination of a religious doctrine and a state constitution. Learning is the key to a Chinese society, according to Confucius, and the lack of it can turn the positive human nature into negative conduct.

The imperial examination system established in 605 was the major mechanism by which the central government obtained and held the loyalty of local elites. Their loyalty ensured the integration of the Chinese state and countered tendencies toward regional autonomy.

The system distributed its prizes according to provincial and prefectural quotas in numbers roughly proportional to each province's population. Thus, it promoted stability, social mobility, and a self-conscious national identity that underlies nationalism. The uniformity of the content of the examinations meant that the local elites and scholars across the whole of China were taught the same values. Even though only a small fraction, about 5 percent, of those who attempted the examinations actually passed them and even fewer received office ranks, the hope of eventual success sustained their commitment. Those who failed to pass after several tries did not lose wealth or local social standing; as dedicated believers in Confucian orthodoxy, they served, without the benefit of state appointments, as teachers, patrons of the arts, and managers of local projects for public works, schools, or charitable foundations. Most importantly, over time it fostered a tremendous emphasis on education of the populace and encouraged local investment in learning. It became the mainstay of the family values of each Chinese family, be it rich or poor. Yet the system also promoted resistance to change, since limiting the topics to Chinese classics based on Confucius's teachings in the examination system removed the incentives for Chinese to learn sciences and mathematics or to conduct research, which over time caused China's scientific and economic development to fall behind Europe.

All of the aforementioned culture differences have given the Chinese a mind-set or paradigm different from that of the Western world. Their long history of wars, natural disasters, and chaos has taught the Chinese there is always a solution to every potential problem as long as the objective is clear, and patience and compromise are part of the solution. This is shown by comparing the games of chess and Wei Qi, the original Chinese version of the Japanese Go that originated twenty-five hundred years ago. Chess victory results from deposing the king through decisive moves. However, Wei Qi is based on surrounding your opponent's pieces by incrementally building up strategic positions. The win is relative, and the margin is usually slim.

This concept is also the way the Chinese conducted warfare and diplomacy with foreigners. Twice the native Han emperors of China were defeated and China taken over by the barbarians Mongol Yuan (1271–1368) dynasty and the Manchu Qing (1644–1912) dynasty. Yet China absorbed these conquerors into the Chinese culture since they were convinced such a vast and unique nation could only be ruled by the established Chinese methods and language. Eventually these conquerors were assimilated as Chinese, and their original land became part of

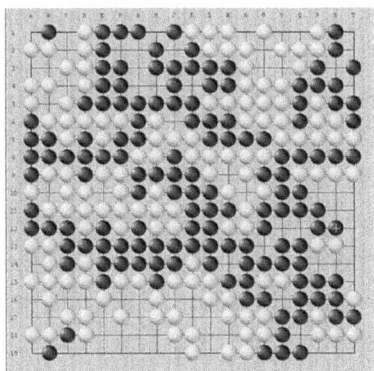

Wei Qi Win

China, albeit it took tens or hundreds years to do so. This is remarkable in human history since most vanquished were assimilated into the conquerors' culture and methods, but the Mongol and Manchu conquerors were integrated into the culture of the vanquished Chinese.

By the late eighteenth century, however, China faced accelerated expansion of its population. Having remained at 100 million through much of history under the Qing dynasty, the population doubled from 150 million in 1650 to 300 million by 1800, and reached 450 million by the late nineteenth century. By then there was no longer any land in China's southern and central provinces available for migration. The introduction of New World crops such as sweet potatoes, peanuts, and tobacco, which required different growing conditions than rice and wheat, had already claimed available land. This shortage of resources was exacerbated by the decrease of the state's political control as the size of the central government remained the same while the population grew. By the nineteenth century, control and responsibility for government was increasingly left in the hands of local leaders whose allegiances were to their localities, clans, and families rather than to the state.

At the end of the eighteen century, China, to the outside world, was at the zenith of its wealth, attracting the attention of the foreign powers that had developed industry and scientific advances enabling tremendous increase in productivity and trade. They envisioned China as a huge market in a new world order, unbeknownst to the Chinese, for they considered the foreigners to be, as always, barbarians and treated them as such. Thus, the rights of free trade, embassy representation, equality of nations, etc., established in the rest of the world did not apply in China. The barbarians could live in the assigned coastal areas and conduct trade only in one port. Such unequal treatment by the Qing court particularly upset the British since they enjoyed trade advantages throughout the rest of the world, including Japan. More specifically, the Europeans had low Chinese demand for their goods and high demand for Chinese goods, including tea, silk, and porcelain. European merchants had to purchase these goods with silver, the only acceptable currency to the Chinese. In the mid-seventeenth century, China received around thirty million kilograms of silver, principally from European powers, in exchange for Chinese goods. British trade had been using the gold standard and therefore had to purchase silver, incurring an additional cost. The British and other Europeans tried to reduce the trade deficit by importing tea from British India and other places, and the Germans managed to reverse engineer porcelain production, but the deficit remained and the British turned to opium as the main trade product to China. In the eighteenth century, against Chinese law and protests from the Qing government, British traders began importing opium from India. The British exported a large quantity of silver for Chinese tea. With India and its poppy fields under British control, it was the logical option to fix the imbalance of trade.

British opium was an instant success by the addiction of thousands of Chinese and reversed the flow of silver. A porous Chinese border and rampant local demand only encouraged the all-too-eager British, and the Qing government was unable to halt opium smuggling in the southern provinces. By the 1820s China was importing nine hundred tons of opium annually. In the 1830s, negotiations between Britain and China came to no avail, and in 1839 war broke out. The Chinese were no match for the British, and after it had occupied Guangzhou in 1842, the Qing court sued for peace, which concluded with the Treaty of Nanjing negotiated in August of that year and was ratified in 1843. In the treaty, China paid an indemnity to Britain, opened four ports to Britain, and ceded Hong Kong as well, most humiliating to the Chinese, who had recognized the British as equals and granted them extraterritorial rights in the treaty ports.

In 1844, the United States and France concluded similar treaties with China respectively. A second Opium War started in 1856 with Britain and France joining forces. They occupied Tianjin, reached the wall of Beijing, and burned the old summer palace before the Qing court agreed to all terms demanded by the foreigners. Ten new treaty ports, including Tianjin, opened to trade with the Western powers, they allowed foreign diplomats in Beijing, and the Chinese government legalized and regulated the opium trade. China also ceded to Britain Kowloon, on the mainland opposite Hong Kong. Permission was granted for foreigners, including missionaries, to travel throughout the country. An indemnity of three million ounces of silver was paid to Great Britain and two million to France. Other foreign powers were pleased with the outcome too, since they hoped to take advantage of the opening up of China. Russia soon extorted the Maritime Provinces from China and founded the port of Vladivostok.

To make matters worse, in the late nineteenth century, a series of drought and famine, corruption, and an inept Qing government generated unprecedented chaos in China. The foreigners' presence as imposed by the unequal treaties weakened the Qing court and the economy, which left China unable to provide for its huge population. A series of rebellions then occurred across the country. The Taiping (1851–1864), Nian (1853–1868), Moslem (1855–1873), and Boxer (1898–1901) rebellions all took place in the latter part of the century. Although the Qing court prevailed over these rebellions, it needed the help of foreign troops and firepower for which it had to pay repeatedly dearly in both money and exterritorial rights. Through it all, the central government had lost much of its control and had to relegate the authority to the provinces.

The ability of the Western nations and later Japan to impose their economic demands on China by force of arms was jarring to the Chinese view of themselves as a highly developed civilization. Moreover, the Western notion of a system of international relations conducted among sovereign nations challenged Chinese singularity as the most advanced and universalistic civilization. It was also difficult for the Chinese, whose emperor had been recognized as the supreme authority by countries bearing tribute to the Chinese court, to adapt to the system that had evolved in Europe by the 1800s whereby sovereign nation interacted as equals. This had become the most contentious issue in negotiation with the foreign powers since it was the foundation of the Chinese worldview. Initially the Chinese responded to the foreign powers by their age-proved strategy of ceding territories and money to soothe the barbarians and trying to absorb them into the Chinese culture as well as playing one foreign nation against another. The foreigners, on the other hand, considered themselves more culturally advanced and militarily superior. Their interest was to exploit China for economic gains, and they had no interest in adapting to the Chinese culture. Furthermore, the personal relationships of the leaders had always been at the basis of the Chinese diplomacy. This was not a factor since the foreign decision makers were oceans away and not part of any negotiation between the parties.

As shown by the book title—*Patriots and Warlords*—the main timeline of this book is the Warlord Era (1916–1928). For centuries, soldiers were at the bottom of the Chinese social ladder. There is a Chinese saying, "Don't use the best iron to make nail; don't take the best person to make soldier!" Such prejudice extended to lower-level officers and even generals without a classical education. This changed in the period covered by this book. A warlord is someone with an army that is willing to follow him into battle with whomever he chooses for whatever purpose. A typical warlord's officers and troops must be personally loyal to him; such loyalty is expected all the way down the chain of command. It is a feudal structure that once existed in every part of the world. Such personal loyalty can be as strong as national or institutional loyalty, but if the warlord dies or retires, his army will usually be absorbed by another usually the enemy. It is not adaptable to the modern organization of promotion or rotation of officers based on rank, experience, education, and merit, for loyalty is above all.

A warlord maintained his army usually at the expense of the people of the territory he controlled. Over time it became difficult for a warlord to establish an effective and stable political structure. This became particularly acute in the beginning of the twentieth century in China. The Qing court, due its own military weakness, had to rely on the local warlords to maintain order. The warlords had to expand their sphere of control to support their armies. They engaged in fighting each other to maintain or expand their territory. The warlords of this era were a mixed lot. They ranged from Zhang Zuolin, the illiterate bandit who became the warlord of Manchuria, to others who were wellborn and educated and trained in Japan or Europe as professionals, such as Duan Qirui, the onetime premier and president of the Republic of China. It becomes extremely difficult to judge the characters in this book to decide whether they are patriots or despots.

At the start of the twentieth century, China was in a crisis like a melon being carved up. Its economy was stagnant, its territory was being usurped by the foreign powers, and internal rebellions threatened its stability. Among the Chinese elites there were many ideas and as many courses of action on how to survive as a sovereign nation and change its path in history. This is the story of my father, Wang Boqun, and his younger brother, Wang Dilun, in their quest for a republican China; they were at the leading edge of change that eventually brought about the China of today. It is about the journey of two brothers from a relatively lesser warlord family of one of the poorest provinces at the beginning of a remarkable period of transition of China. It relates how they channeled their upbringing and experiences into contributions and sacrifices for their belief that China could overcome the foreign colonization and find a path toward its glorious past. The Wang brothers were at the beginning of a tumultuous change that led to the China of today. It is no less than miraculous and speaks to the resilience of the Chinese culture and the spirit of its people that China survived and now in 2014 is becoming one of the world's most-powerful nations.

I have described the salient historical background and listed the names in both Chinese and English. Thus readers with more interest in details can look them up on the Internet or peruse through the references section of the book. I have decided to use the current Pinyin method of spelling for Chinese names, people, places, and events, instead of the older Wade-Giles method developed by the British and exclusively used till 1980s. Also for the Chinese written characters, I have chosen to use the simplified version promulgated by the People's Republic of China since 1960s. It is now taught and used by an overwhelmingly larger percentage of Chinese around the world.

Finally about source material I used for the book. Most of the personal events and quotes are from conversations with relatives and friends, my mother's yearly summary, and letters written by the principals, particularly the Wang brothers and their maternal uncle, Liu Xianshi. I have read many books, journals, and articles in both Chinese and English written about this period. I have not attempted to footnote any of the knowledge I have acquired. This book is not about historical facts but the principal characters and their respective roles in history, as I understood them. It's basically a family story rather than historical record. In some incidents, due to lack of records, I had to extrapolate the thinking behind the actions of different individuals by only what I knew to be their backgrounds and beliefs. I have attempted to list all the articles and books I have read in the Reference section, and of course, I used the internet as secondary verification sources for dates, events, and maps.

CHAPTER 1

BEFORE 1906
FAMILIES LIU AND WANG

Xiawutun, Xingyi, Guizhou

It is in Xingyi before daybreak. It is the hour of the hare. Pale light from the opening sky begins to reveal the shape of the Wang family estate. Set off by a high brick wall, a large enclosure rises from the early light atop of a plateau between limestone Karsts Mountains and rice terraces, revealing wooden pavilions with scarlet columns and green, tubular roof tiles. Wang Boqun awoke early on this very special day of his young life with many thoughts racing in his head so he had to rise and start his tai chi exercises way before the usual hour. Today he would begin his long journey to Japan to attend the Chuo University in Tokyo for the next three or more years, only three years

1

after his father's death in 1902. He was very proud and gratified by his selection from the hundreds who applied to study in Japan at the government's expense. He had implored the prefect, Liu Xianshi, his uncle by marriage, to be impartial about his selection. Liu had assured him, "Boqun, you were among the top four out of fifteen selected by the committee of your teachers, and I am merely the rubber stamp. I was not even afforded a vote in this." Yet he could not stop thinking about how much he was going to miss his family, teachers, and friends to be so far away for such a long time.

Xingyi is located on the border where Guizhou meets Yunnan and Guangxi Provinces, and it was at the time the wild west of China, surrounded by uninhabited, rugged mountains and unnavigable, fast rapids. The Xingyi county seat was located on a richly irrigated plateau, probably the largest piece of level land in the entire province, at the juncture of two important trade routes that linked the provincial capital of Guiyang to the capital of Yunnan, Kunming, where it reached to the French colony of Vietnam. It also had access to the river transport systems of Guangxi to the city of Guangzhou in Guangdong Province.

In the eighteenth century, Xingyi was an established marketing center for forest and mining products from southwestern Guizhou and eastern Yunnan. Cotton was imported to be weaved into all types of clothing products. Opium was introduced into the region in the beginning of the century and rapidly became the main export item. In spite of the trade routes, Xingyi remained a wild, unregulated, and chaotic city with no banks, and most transactions were conducted by barter, with opium most frequently used as the means of exchange. Up until the late eighteenth century, non-Han tribes, particularly the Miao, inhabited most of Guizhou's southwestern areas. Due to the increasing importance of trade routes, more and more Hans chose to settle in the area and resulted in numerous clashes between the Han settlers and the indigenous minority tribes led by the Miao.

The Wang family had come to Xingyi in the 1700s as part of a group of Hans sent by the Ming emperor with the mandate to secure

2

the trade routes and to pacify the periodic uprisings of the Miao. The Wangs were natives of the Yangtze Delta in eastern China, which provided the troops led by the Marquis Jing Shangding. In late 1790s Jing and his Han compatriots fought many battles with the Miao lead rebels. In 1797 they finally defeated the rebels, established a firm control over southwest Guizhou, and set up a county government to administer tax collection, security, healthcare, and education. The Wang family settled into an area known as Jingjiatun (Jing family compound) in Xingyi County and gradually moved away from their military and bureaucratic background into farming of the land given to them by the Ming emperor as compensation for the expedition. By the early 1800s, the family had a large land holding and a substantial income from it and enjoyed the life of typical upper gentry of that time. The Wang clan had replaced the Jing clan in Jingjiatun as the most important family in the village, and several of its members had held the provincial degree of the examination administered at the provincial level every three years to qualify for official posts. It was the only means to enter the gentry class regardless of wealth. The Wang clan earned their leadership position by merit and enjoyed the respect of their peers and loyalty of the peasants and other gentries in the county.

The most important family in Xingyi County at the beginning of the twentieth century was the Liu family based in Xiawutun. At the end of the eighteenth century, Liu Taiyuan from Hunan, a traveling peddler of literary supplies, had moved his family to Xingyi and started a tung oil–extraction business in a remote part of Xingyi county. Liu, attracted by the available land in the county, started the oil business just to make money to invest in the land, for he foresaw the importance of the trade routes. His son, Liu Yanshan, moved the family business from the county seat to Xiawutun, a village in a fertile irrigated valley only two miles from Xingyi, to gain close access. The business flourished so much that Liu became the richest clan in the county by the mid-1800s.

In the first half of 1800s, China, under the Manchu Qing, had survived through a number of rebellions; the most significant was the

Taiping rebellion, which began in Guangxi and eventually controlled most of south China by 1851. It took the combined efforts of the Qing government with the help of the British and the French to suppress the Taiping rebels by the late 1860s. The weakened Qing court, however, had lost effective control of the provinces, especially those far from Beijing.

In Guizhou bandits and minority tribes caused great havoc among the people and the local authorities, and the Qing Army was ineffective in quelling these insurgences. The Qing government decided to enlist the local gentry in the pacification of the region. With the mandate from the emperor—"Root out the rebels to defend the nation and pacify the homeland of the citizens"—the local gentry formed militias from the populace of the towns and villages who had the stakes to protect their family and landholdings. The various villages, such as Jinjatun and Xiawutun, had to fend for themselves by organizing the local militia under the leadership of the local landowners for self-defense against the rebels. The Wangs and the Lius both assumed such leadership in their respective villages. The Lius, however, were much more active and aggressive in this regard. The Liu family built a stone-walled fortress to protect the family compound in Xiawutun and collected taxes and provisions to support their militia and to fund community construction and education projects. They also built the largest militia of the county.

In 1858, along the Guizhou-Yunnan border, a minority tribe, the Muslim Hui, led several ethnic and secret society uprisings, which eventually occupied a substantial part of Xingyi County, including the county seat. The Liu family, then headed by Liu Yanshan, at the urging of the Xingyi local government, had recruited a militia, which by the early 1860s had reached over ten thousand men. In campaigns waged in 1864, 1866, and 1868, with the help other family militias, including those under the Wang family, they had defeated the Hui rebels and pacified and recovered the rebel-held parts of southwest Guizhou.

4

The Lius has thus become the most powerful family in the region but they had also suffered considerable loss. The older two of Liu Yanshan's four sons died in battle in 1863 and 1865 respectively. In 1867 Liu Yanshan died of natural causes, and the third son, Liu Guanli, took over the family leadership, assisted by his young brother, Liu Guande. They led efforts to build ten more forts in the neighboring areas and reinforced the wall of the county seat. Liu even built a loyalty temple to commemorate the deaths of his brothers and other local heroes. The Qing government had recognized the Liu family's contribution by awarding Liu Guanli the rank of major of the army. Liu Guanli, as the head of the family, became the head of all the militia in Xingyi in addition to holding the rank of the county prefect, which in effect placed him in charge of the entire region.

The Liu family took advantage of their position by vastly expanding their land holdings in the province and collecting a great amount of funds to support their militia and to augment their wealth. They were also ruthless against other militia leaders in the region, who from time to time challenged their authority. In such power struggles, the Liu would adapt the scorched earth tactics of attacking the opposition's forces, pillaging and burning their villages, and killing their families. Such actions allowed the Liu family to eliminate many enemies and expand their own forces by absorbing the rival militia into their own and taking over their land holdings. In early 1870, this abuse of power by the Liu family had prompted the Qing court to order the governor general of Yunnan in Kunming, who oversaw Guizhou, to conduct an investigation. Liu Guanli was cleared of any wrongdoing and also managed to enhance his position by using his political connections and bribery. In addition, Liu served on the Yunnan governor general's staff in Kunming until 1875.

When Liu Guanli returned to Xingyi, the combination of Qing government forces and the local militia had quelled the rebellion, and conditions in southwest Guizhou were substantially improved. The government had moved to strengthen its military forces around the country and looked upon the militia as a potential threat. Many of the gentry's militia leaders around the country, such as the Lius, had gained substantial wealth and political powers so that a large militia became an unnecessary financial strain. Liu Guanli also understood that military power had brought the family to its powerful position; political and financial power would maintain it in a time of relative peace. Thus he joined many like minds, such as the Wang family, who had decided to disband the family militia. Liu announced that he would retire from government service and devote himself to taking care of his ailing mother.

The Jingjatun militia, throughout the first half of 1800, under Wang Peixian was the second-most-powerful military force in the region. The Wangs were the Liu family's closest ally throughout their rise to power in the previous tumultuous period. Wang Peixian, however, did not harbor the ambition of the Lius to dominate the region for wealth and power. He saw the need for military force strictly for the self-defense of his home community and the improvement of lives of the peasants. He continued to hold that the role of the gentry was to serve the peasants, not to take advantage of them. He was also a realist, however, and appreciated that the Liu family's rise to power had brought better community services, particularly education and health care, to the general population, and more importantly, the peasants were substantially better protected from rebel and bandit attacks. Thus he supported them through all their struggles against the rebels, bandits, and other militia. In 1875 Wang Peixian died at the age of only thirty-five, leaving five young children. The oldest, Qiyuan, a son was only eleven. On his deathbed, surrounded by family and the heads of his ally families, he said to Liu Guanli:

> The Wangs have always supported the Lius in your family's many trials and tribulations. Unlike you Lius, we Wangs are more interested in the security of our clan,

history, arts, and philosophy. Thus, please protect the Wang offspring with your martial prowess and political connections. You will be repaid many times through our combined families' achievements for the welfare of our people andt country.

In front of the elders of all clans, Liu had answered, "Big brother, go in peace, for the Liu will always stand together with the Wang, come what may." In the coming years, many would use these words often to quell disagreement between the clans; but in the end, it would be to no avail.

After the end of the rebellions and the disbandment of the militia, the Liu clan continued to be the dominant force in southwest Guizhou. The local government officials seldom made any important appointments, funded any significant activities, or forwarded any recommendations to the provincial government without the approval of Liu Guanli. Liu Guanli astutely concluded that the power and influence of the family would be better served in education and through education by connecting to the provincial, national, and international elites of the time. He established and funded the first library of the county, provided scholarships for local talents, and financed the import of prominent scholars from Kunming and the provincial capital, Guiyang, to Xingyi as lecturers or as permanent teachers. As a result, Xingyi became known as an educational center, second only to Guiyang in the province. The education level in Xingyi improved dramatically, and the Lius continued to improve their social and political influence through the late 1800s. The Liu gained further prestige as an elite or gentry family when in the mid-1800s Liu Guanli's second born and first son, Liu Xianshi, and his nephew, Liu Xianqian, both earned the degree of Shenyang in the first-level examination.

Liu Xianshi as a youth did not have the volatile nature of his father, who had an explosive temper and was prone to impulsive actions, but gave an outward impression of softness. Inwardly he exhibited the same ruthlessness of his father and was even more cunning in his nature. He had earned the nickname of "Smiling Tiger Face" from friends and enemies alike. Although his father had pushed him to study for the examination, but his passion was for martial arts. He applied himself enough to pass the first level of examination, after which he spent most of his time recruiting and training a core group of militia. His younger brother's conviction of the reform movement and connection to its members throughout the region also affected his attitude toward reform.

Wang Qiyuan by 1882 had become the head of the Wang clan in Jingjatun. His uncle had taken over the family since Wang Peixian's death in 1875. He was a scholar and had earned the degree of Shenyang in the examination, and he went on to earn the degree of Gongseng (region level), the highest achieved by anyone in his generation in the county. He gave up his pursuit of the higher examination to take over the family's affairs when his uncle died. In 1884 Liu Grandli had recognized his capability both as an intellectual and as an administrator, and Liu arranged the marriage of the oldest of his five children, Liu Xianqian, to Wang Qiyuan. This further cemented the relationship between the families and fulfilled the promise he had made to Wang Peixian on his deathbed.

Wang Qiyuan, 1901

Wang Qiyuan was a believer of the system of governance put forth by Hong Xiuquan, the founder of the Taiping rebellion and the self-proclaimed younger brother of Christ. In spite of his disagreement with Hong's attacks on Confucianism, he found Hong's ideas on reform and government highly appealing. He had implemented such reform of land holdings in Jingjatun, which entailed the division of all farmable land to all the families in the clan and their supporters according to family size, with men and women receiving equal shares. All produce left after each family's need became part of a common pool for medical, education, and security expenses. Such reform gained high praises for Wang Qiyuan from the peasants and gentry alike and bound the clan together as it had never been previously.

In 1895 China lost the first Sino-Japanese war over a dispute over Korea, which resulted in the ceding of Korea, Taiwan, the Pescadores, and parts of Manchuria, in addition to more trading ports and a large amount of money to Japan. In 1896 the Guangxu emperor tried to establish a constitutional monarchy with basic changes in the structure of the government and the economy, including the elimination of the examination system and the reorganization of the military. Manchu elites led by Empress Dowager Cixi, the emperor's aunt, opposed the reform, and usurped the emperor. In 1898 Cixi took over power and put the emperor under virtual house arrest. China again faced with civil unrest and rebellion throughout the provinces. In this period Cixi executed many of the stalwarts of the reform movement, who supported the emperor, and the rest were exiled to Europe, America, and Japan.

In late 1897, as part of the reform promulgated by the Guangxu emperor, an eminent scholar with ties to reform movement became Guizhou's education commissioner, who then established a State Craft Academy in Guiyang, which introduced Western studies into its curriculum for the first time. Liu Xianzhi, the younger brother of Liu Xianshi, was among forty some Guizhou students selected to enroll there. Subsequently he went to Japan to do further study, and he joined the constitutional monarchy movement. Li Xianzhi return to Xingyi in 1900 and brought back with him ideas of reform and a lot of reform connections, particularly in neighboring Yunnan, Hunan, Sichuan, and Guangxi Provinces. The Lius realized that these new reform programs were creating new areas for the family to gain power and wealth. Thus they quickly moved to confirm and enhance their leadership by introducing such reforms in the Xingyi area.

In the midst of the struggle for control in Beijing, Xingyi faced numerous rebel and bandit actions in the late 1800s. The most serious was on the border with Guangxi, where major rebellions had been raging for some time. By 1897 Liu Guanli was no longer able to mount his horse due to the rheumatism he had suffered with for over twenty years. Liu Xianshi interrupted his study and took up the position of commander of the newly reconstituted Xingyi militia. He stated, "I much preferred action over study." In 1901 he was soundly defeated when he ventured to occupy the city of Xingyi and lost several hundred of his militia. In 1902 a large rebel army from Guangxi crossed the river and advanced toward the county seat while the government garrison was in Yunnan for another rebellion. Without the Qing troops, Liu's militia was outnumbered and overwhelmed at Xingyi, and they had to retreat hastily to Xiawutun. The rebels massacred over four hundred officers and men of Liu's rear guard, and their bodies were stacked up in a place now known as "white bone pagoda." Xiawutun was besieged for six days until the government garrison returned and attacked the rebels from the rear. The militia and garrison joined forces and were successful in pushing the rebels back to Guangxi. As a result, the militia became the border pacification regiment of the Guizhou army. Liu Guanli was appointed as the commander-in-chief, and his son, Li Xianshi, and his nephew, Xianqian, became commanders of two of the battalions. The governor of Guangxi later selected Liu Xianqian as the commander of his personal guard battalion. Liu Xianshi's battalion was renamed the second battalion of the western defense army, and he remain its commander and thus renewed the Liu family's former military power base. Liu's reputation as a military commander, however, was not sterling among those who were knowledgeable.

After the rebellion was quelled, the Lius turned to the reforms promulgated by the Qing government. The first priority was to implement the modern educational system to replace the examination system. Due to his ill health, Liu Guanli turned over the family affairs to Liu Xianshi at age thirty-five. Liu Xianshi became the most powerful man in southwest Guizhou, in spite of his militia defeats. He was also responsible for the many advances in educational reforms in Xingyi and surrounding counties, such as establishing more than twenty lower-level primary schools and converted the private upper-level academy into a public school. In addition he headed up an education department he had set up. He also estab-

Liu Xianshi, 1910

lished a girls' school, a military school, a teaching institute, and public reading rooms and a library. He also promoted the idea of sending the best students for advanced studies oversea, mostly to Japan, for both political-economic and military studies. Liu as the head of the regional education department did not have much use for Western ideas. He had stated, "Study of foreign books makes for belief of foreign ways. Belief in foreign ways makes dust of ancestry." The Lius by a combination of financial cunning, military power, and political expediency had become the most powerful and wealthy family in Guizhou. The family land holdings alone exceeded four thousand hectares or over ten thousand acres, which was astonishing for the time.

Wang Qiyuan died in 1904 at forty-one. He left his wife, Liu Xianqian, to raise five children: two boys, Boqun, nineteen, and Dilun, fifteen; and three girls, Wenbi, twenty, Wenxiao, ten, and Wenxiang, only seven. Although Wang Qiyuan's younger brother, Wang Qixian, took over as the head of the family, he consulted Liu Xianqian on every issue and decision in family and clan affairs. When he died in 1905, Liu Xianqian became the dominant force in the Wang family's affairs.

Her keen mind and charismatic presence was a constant reminder that she had the power of the Liu family behind her, yet she never compromised the welfare of the Wang clan for her own benefit. She had indeed became the matriarch of the Wang clan first and a member of her own Liu family a distant second. Her husband had told her many times:

> My dearest wife, you have done more for our clan than I could. You have given me two sons. Boqun has fulfilled my wishes for filial piety and for his passion for the classics and Dilun for his keen interest in military strategy and leadership of men demonstrated at an incredibly early age. I am truly blessed, and the clan will be well regarded in the future with our sons at its helm.

He did not mention his three daughters, but deep down he loved them all equally, as his wife knew well. Boqun remembered his father well, particularly during the times they spent together each day for an hour going over the teaching of Laozi, Confucius, and Mencius. At ten, he studied with a group of three famous teachers who had only taken a handful of students they considered worthy. At time of his father's death, Boqun was the most accomplished of all their students.

❖ ❖ ❖

Boqun walked out of his bedroom around the corridor to the door of the central courtyard, where he had begun practicing Chen-style tai chi since he was five. As flagstones struck by the beginning rays of sunlight, Boqun started the usual preparation of quieting his mind so his body could move without the encumbrance of distractions. He was not able to unwind and to disengage his mind about the events of his life in spite of his usual fine control of his breathing rhythm. His mind continued to whirl about his family and what had brought him to this particular point of his life.

As Boqun began his usual sequence of the tai chi form of Buddha warrior attendant pounds mortar, he reflected on the now-famous statement of Mencius, which had become his own essence for an educated life:

> Benevolence is man's mind, and righteousness is man's path.
> How lamentable is it to neglect the path, and not pursue it?
> To lose this state of mind and not wise enough to seek it again!
> When men's fowls and dogs are lost, they know how to find them again,
> However, when they lose their mind and do not know to seek for it.
> The great end of learning is nothing else but the quest for the lost mind.

As he moved through the form, his mind became more meditative, and he heard his father's words in his mind:

> Boqun, always remember that benevolence is only second to filial piety in a learned life. Once you have taken care of your responsibilities of filial piety, you must exercise what Mencius has taught

us. *Noblesse oblige* is your obligation to the country, the clan, and its serfs, and benevolence must be your path.

Wang Boqun had never ceased to be surprised by his father's gentle manners since his grandfather had a reputation as brave a militia commander as any who fought shoulder to shoulder with Liu Guanli and his men. Yet deep down he knew that unlike the Lius, his grandfather only fought hard to protect his own, and by nature he was a gentle intellectual, as was his father.

Boqun was now fully into his routine forms of white crane spread wings, six sealings and four closings, and a single whip. His mind continued its own contemplation of those closest to his life and those he must now leave for a seemly indefinite period of time. He realized that, of course, he did not really have a choice. Filial piety demanded that he follow his mother's instructions to avail himself of this opportunity. His mother, matriarch of his clan and first daughter of the ruling family of Xingyi, was a very formidable person indeed. She was small in stature and had bound feet, but when she entered a room, her dominant presence was evident to all. She moved with those bound feet as though she was floating on a cloud with unencumbered grace.

Just three months earlier Boqun had married the second daughter, Qungao, of the head of the Zhou clan, as arranged by his parents since childhood. He hardly knew her at all and was not particularly distressed about leaving her. He was glad, however, that Qungao seemed to have established a good relationship with his mother and would be there to keep her company and provide some help with his two younger sisters. Boqun started the last of his closing forms, and he heard Dilun's, voice calling from the balcony: "Elder brother, please finish your exercises and prepare for the departure."

❖ ❖ ❖

Dilun, his only brother, was three years younger at seventeen. He was the one person Boqun realized would miss the most of all those dear to him. Dilun was a most prodigious of all the siblings. It was told that on the fifth night of the seventh month in the fifteenth year of the Guangxu Emperor, when Dilun was born, lightning ran across the roof as though it was a wheel of fire, thus the name Dilun, which meant "electric wheel." He was very different from his elder brother in many respects of personality and interests. He was impatient and volatile, while Boqun was thoughtful and contemplative. He was as passionate about martial arts and military strategy as Boqun was about political theory, arts, and philosophy. Yet they both shared their father's legacy of *noblesse oblige* and the need for China to rise from the oppression of the foreign powers and the corruption of the Manchu Qing court. It was common knowledge in the county that the Wang clan was indeed fortunate to have two such young men borne by marriage to a powerful Liu.

Liu Xianshi, prefect of Xingyi and younger brother of their mother, had lamented many times to her, "My dear sister, you have two sons. I wish they were Lius. There is no one in our clan who will be able to match them in capabilities, particularly when they are operating as a team. Please ensure they will take care of our clan in the future as we Lius have taken care of the Wangs."

His sister replied, "Little brother, I will certainly try, but remember that I am now a Wang. Hopefully we two clans will always work together, but there should be no doubt which side I will be on in a dispute."

Liu was silent, knowing his sister was utterly earnest in her loyalty to the Wang clan and particularly to her sons.

❖ ❖ ❖

Boqun acknowledged Dilun. "I have finished, and we can depart in an hour." He started to walk back and wondered how Dilun could always speak at the top of his voice without concern for waking up anyone, especially their mother, who had a habit of sleeping late. He said to himself *sotto voce*, "He seems to have the ability to get away with everything." On the short walk back to his room, he noticed the fine floral details of the ceiling on the walkway, the fragrance of the plum blossoms amid the bamboo trees lining the path, and the brilliant sunrise in the distant sky. He sighed to himself. "I shall be back."

CHAPTER 2

1906

BOQUN'S JOURNEY TO TOKYO

In 1895, when Boqun reached the age of ten, China was at a historical watershed. Foreign incursions had brought three defeats from three major wars. The last, in 1895, was at the hands of the upstart Japanese over the control of Korea and was the most humiliating. The Opium Wars against Britain, France, Russia, and the United States resulted in crippling concessions in 1842 and 1860. Most distressingly, the wars exposed the undeniable foreign technological superiority in life and war. All of those who were educated and informed, such as the thousands of scholars assembled in Beijing for the triennial examination in 1895, realized something was fundamentally amiss in China. As a result, scholars and Qing officials alike initiated numerous reform movements. Most notably was the 1898 effort of Kang Youwei and Liang Qichao approved by the idealistic young Guangxu emperor, who reigned nominally under his aunt, the empress dowager, Cixi. Unfortunately, the reform promulgated by Guangxu lasted for just a hundred days before Cixi removed him. It became very clear that the Qing court would not change China through any meaningful reform. Many reformers lost their lives; Kang and Liang were able to escape to Japan and continued to organize support for a constitutional monarchy.

In 1900, in reaction to the reform movement and amid drought and famine, the Boxer Rebellion originated to address rising frustration and suffering endured by the masses at the hands of the foreigner powers. The Qing court encouraged the rebellion, mistakenly thinking it would lead to the foreigners' departure. Instead, the war ended with heavier punitive payments and secession of more territories and treaty rights than any previous war. In essence, by 1901 China had become a colony of foreign powers.

By stark contrast and during the same period, Japan had progressed enviably toward modernization and had risen to become a world power. Though archeological studies established that the islands of Japan were inhabited several millennia before Christ, the country had remained a closed and tightly controlled feudal country since its unification in 1603. A closed-door policy in 1639 imposed a total ban on contact with the outside world. Japan remained isolated, save for closely monitored transactions with Chinese and Dutch traders. Following its turbulent feudal past, the country welcomed a period of peace and prosperity. By the mid-eighteenth century, over a million people, exceeding both London and Paris in population and land area, inhabited its capital, Tokyo. Though the imperial court continued to reside in Kyoto, Tokyo gradually evolved into a bustling center of commerce and industry.

In the latter half of the nineteenth century, the Western powers were increasingly calling on Japan to open its doors to trade. The crucial turning point came when the American black ships of Commodore Mathew Perry arrived in 1853. Not only did it open Japan to external trade, but it also ushered in the country's rapid modernization. The whole country, headed by the reformed-minded Emperor Meiji, plunged into a frantic drive to catch up with the West. The court moved from Kyoto to Tokyo, making Tokyo the official capital of the country. Even today, vestiges remain of the Meiji Restoration (1868–1912). The reforms introduced during that period initiated the present education system. Both the Diet (parliament) and the Bank of Japan were established during this period, and today these two institutions continue to dictate the political and financial affairs of the country. Even baseball, the most popular sport in Japan today, dated back to the mid-1800s. In the Meiji Restoration, one can clearly see the seeds of today's Japan.

Cultural exchanges between China and Japan existed since the sixth century. Although Japan was never officially part of the Middle Kingdom, Chinese and Japanese alike considered the Japanese, at least partly, to belong to the Chinese diaspora. Chinese who traveled to Japan, such as the Buddhist monks of the Tang dynasty or the Confucian loyalists of the late Ming dynasty, came as purveyors of higher civilization and as teachers to the provincial Japanese. Therefore, it was a major reversal in the historic relations between the two countries when, in the dawn of the twentieth century, Chinese students flocked to Japan to learn how the Japanese had so quickly mastered the secrets of Western "wealth and power."

The repeated defeats and humiliations of the late nineteenth century, with the Boxer Rebellion at its climax, had shown that China's traditions alone were no longer able to provide the guideposts for survival in the new world of imperialistic and international power politics. This awareness was especially acute for the young intellectuals who realized the solution was more in Western learning rather than Confucian texts. Study abroad suddenly seemed the quickest and most effective way to accomplish that. Japan was not only closer and more affordable than Western nations, but it also it had successfully absorbed Western knowledge without losing its distinctive native identity. Moreover, the Japanese culture and language seemed less remote for young Chinese contemplating study abroad. In the aftermath of Japan's startling victory over China in the Sino-Japanese War of 1894 to 1895, there were only two hundred Chinese students in Japan; by 1900, the number had doubled. After the Japanese victory over Russia in 1905, the number jumped to five thousand, reaching a peak of ten thousand in 1908. Numbers tell only part of the story. For a crucial transitional generation of Chinese intellectuals and political, and military leaders, Japan became the most relevant mentor for how to build China into a modern industrialized nation-state.

❖ ❖ ❖

Boqun's upbringing was similar to that of many gentry Chinese of his age. Under his father's direction, his education began at the age of six with the Confucius's *Book of Filial Piety*. He completed the *Four Books* by age ten and the *Five Classics* by fifteen, mostly under his parents' guidance. He then continued to study under three famous teachers in the region who helped to prepare him for the first level of examination, Shengyuan. These teachers, handpicked by his parents, were specialists in Mencius.

Mencius, like Confucius, believed rulers were divinely placed to guarantee peace and maintain order among the people they ruled. Unlike Confucius, Mencius believed the people could justifiably revolt when a ruler failed to bring about peace and order. Several times throughout Chinese history, Mencius was regarded as a potentially dangerous man, leading to the banning of his books. Boqun's father, however, found Mencius's teaching to be a good foundation for drastic changes from rule of the Qing court given the dire state of China at the time. He also agreed with the utopian Taiping philosophy of governance, which stressed equality of life among all, with even the peasants having rights to a decent living through land ownership, education, and hard work. Although the Taiping rebellion failed, it sharply focused on the failure of the Qing court to govern and to make the necessary changes. He often quoted Mencius to Boqun:

> Although a king has presumably higher status than a commoner, he is actually subordinate to the masses of people and the resources of society. Otherwise there would be an implied disregard of the potential of human society heading into the future. One is significant only for what one gives, not for what one takes.

In late 1898 Guizhou established a State Craft Academy in Guizhou at its capital, Guiyang, which introduced Western studies into its curriculum for the first time. Liu Xianzhi, the younger brother of Liu Xianshi, enrolled there, and after graduation he went to Tokyo for further study. There he joined Kang's Reform Party and served on the staff of Liang Qichao, the young protégé of Kang who became the key political thinker and promoter of a constitutional monarchy. Li Xianzhi return to Xingyi in 1900 and brought back with him the ideas of reform and numerous reform connections, particularly in neighboring Yunnan, Hunan, Sichuan, and Guangxi Provinces. The Lius realized that these new reform programs were creating new areas for the family to gain power and wealth. Thus they quickly moved to confirm and enhance their leadership by introducing these reforms in the Xingyi County.

In 1901, when Boqun reached the age of sixteen, his father and his uncles, the brothers Liu, decided that instead of Boqun continuing his education on the traditional examination tract, he should instead pursue his education at the more modern State Craft Academy in Guiyang. Over the next four years, Boqun studied math, science, and world history, along with Western philosophy and political science in Guiyang. He was greatly impressed with the translation of such books as Edward Bellamy's *Looking Backward*, Etienne Cabet's *Voyage to Icaria*, and John Fryers's *Homely Words to Aid Governments*. Through family connections and proximity to Kunming, the provincial capital of Yunnan bordering on French Indochina, Boqun was also able to read the work of the Chinese revolutionary and reform writers, such as Zon Rong, Kang Youwei, and Liang Qichao. By the time he was selected to go to Tokyo, Boqun had established a political belief similar to the revolutionaries of his time. He hoped to meet some of the leading revolutionaries and be among his kindred spirits in Japan.

Boqun joined a group of seven students from all over Guizhou who gathered and embarked from Xingyi on a sunlit day in early September 1906. Almost two-thirds of the group was destined for military schools, and the rest, including Boqun, were to study Western sciences and economics. They were mostly from gentry families or the cream of the Guizhou intelligentsia. It is interesting to note that most of them did not come from military schools and neither had they served in the military, but most were from the best and most prestigious modern schools, and many of them had passed at least the lowest level of the examination.

Boqun found himself in a like-minded group and made friends easily for the long journey. The group, including bodyguards and attendants, traveled mostly by pack horses and river transports, following the trade route to Nanning in Guangxi Province and then continuing another five hundred some miles to Hong Kong via Guangzhou. In Hong Kong they had booked steam ship passages to Yokohoma, a trip that would take several months of arduous travel. Boqun had accompanied his uncles to both Kunming and Guiyang, both of which are about two hundred kilometers away each, taking a week to travel. The journey to Tokyo would be over ten times the distance, with half of it on the high seas. Nevertheless, he was extremely excited and looking forward to this watershed moment of his young life.

The students arrived in Guangzhou after five weeks of exhausting travel. Guangzhou, the capital of Guangdong Province, was already a city bustling with trade and Western influence. They stopped only for a night and then pushed on to British-controlled Kowloon after saying good-bye to their escorts. As they approached the British passport control at the border, a sense of humiliation welled up within Boqun. He noted that most of his companions had tears in their eyes, and some of them were openly sobbing over the shame of standing on land that had once been Chinese. They vowed to make whatever sacrifices necessary to strengthen the motherland so no such humiliation would ever again befall China.

Dai Kan 1906

The group was met by relatives and family friends who had arranged for lodging and sightseeing until their passage on a Japanese steam ship sailing for

Yokohoma in mid-October. Through the journey, Boqun had become good friends with Dai Kan, five years Boqun's senior.

Dai's background was unique to the group. He came from a relatively poor family. His mother passed away when he was only eleven, and his father was determined for him to have a good education. He was extremely intelligent and mature at an early age; a famous teacher in Guiyang, who held the highest provincial degree, accepted Dai in his school, and he progressively moved up in the academic ranks. In 1904, after only a year of further studies, his teacher recommended him for study in Japan. On this trip with Boqun, he was returning to Tokyo after two months of home leave.

Although Boqun was almost a half-foot taller at six feet tall, he looked up to Dai as an older brother who impressed him by his achievements from such a humble beginning. In fact, Dai was active in Tokyo's student revolution movement and was friends with several senior revolutionaries, including Liang Qichao, whose writing was familiar to Boqun. On the journey they had numerous lengthy conversations and found they were kindred spirits. Boqun was particularly interested to learn more about Liang, who was the most important original thinker of his time. Dai had joined the Protect the Emperor Society formed by Kang Youwei and Liang in 1899. He worked on the staff of several papers and journals founded by Liang, including *Shiwu Bao*, which was widely circulated among revolutionary-minded, such as the Wang brothers.

Over the long journey, Boqun wanted to learn more about Liang from Dai, who was glad to oblige.

> Liang had a humble background, like my own. His father is a farmer by trade but with a well-rounded classics background, which provided an early introduction to various classics and literature to his young son. Did you know he passed the provincial examination at the age

of eleven and the next level at the age of sixteen, the youngest of that time? Yet common knowledge is that he failed the national examination twice in a row! Well, the first was in 1890, when the Qing court decided to flunk his mentor, Kang, for his reform ideas. Kang and Liang both took the exam. Kang disguised his writings in more classic forms, and he passed. Liang's writing was reformative and thought to be that of Kang's and was thus doomed by the examiners to failure. Liang tried again in 1895, when he was already the leader of a well-known organization, Gongche Shangshu, which advocated reform, and he was failed again because of his then well-known politics.

Boqun expressed his disbelief that after enduring such unfair treatment, Liang remained an avid supporter of the constitutional monarchy. Dai continued,

You are probably wondering whether he is just following the lead of his teacher, Kang. After the failure of the reform movement in 1898, Liang escaped to Tokyo and became the leading teacher of the Chinese students there, as well as a publisher of political journals and translator of Western literature. To understand more about the various forms of government, he decided to visit Australia, Canada, and the United States. He visited the United States in 1903 and was received by President Theodore Roosevelt and by J. P. Morgan, but he was disappointed with the political system and concluded it should not be the model for China. Instead, he considered the constitutional monarchies in Japan and Germany would work better for China. Liang based his view of democracy for China on the transformation of the people to become informed, active, and responsible citizens through a necessarily long educational period under the guidance of enlightened elites. This is basically what Plato wrote about in 380 BC as the ideal state in his *Republic*. Liang felt that in such prolonged period of transition without an emperor figure to lead the people, China risks ungovernable chaos.

Boqun fell silent, thinking he must keep an open mind and try to learn more about the different systems of government to form his own opinion about what was best for China.

❖ ❖ ❖

Liu Xianshi had arranged with relatives in Hong Kong to meet and provide lodging for Boqun during the stopover. Boqun asked Dai to come along since he had no family or relatives in the city. At the time Hong Kong society had three distinct groups divided along both racial and class lines: the Chinese elite, consisting primarily of the successful merchant class, not the scholars as in China proper; Chinese workers, who were the majority of the population, ranging from stevedores to rickshaw pullers to domestic servants; and the British community, at first composed mainly of members of the armed forces and scions of the great merchant companies whose fortunes were built on the opium trade. There were other groups, including assorted Europeans and Americans, Sikh policemen imported from British India, and Parse and southeast Asian traders and seamen. Thus the students found themselves very much in a foreign and racially mixed land for the first time in their young lives.

It was common knowledge to the students that the network of connections between Hong Kong and Guangdong ensured that Hong Kong occupied a special position in the unfolding events of late-nineteenth-century Chinese history. Of particular significance was the fact that a number of important Chinese intellectuals and statesmen, including several future leaders, had their first direct encounter with Western society in the colony.

In Hong Kong, the future Taiping rebel leader Hong Rengan, a nephew of the Taiping founder Hong Xiuquan, was baptized into the Christian faith. Qing officials captured Hong, but he managed to escape and flee to Hong Kong in 1853. His account was a principal source of Western knowledge of the Taiping uprising. Many other Chinese gained their first exposure to Western society and culture in Hong Kong. In the atmosphere of rising revolutionary activity around the turn of the century, it offered some a safer haven from the Qing police than the foreign concessions of Shanghai and other treaty ports. Thus, for example, the leading reformer, Kang Youwei, escaped by way of Hong Kong to Japan after the failure of the Hundred Days' Reform movement in 1898.

Most famous among Chinese leaders whose sojourns in Hong Kong affected the Guizhou students' future career was Sun Yatsen, who later became the founder and the first president of the Republic of China. Sun was a Guangzhou native and a Hakka, which means "guest families." The Hakka are a sub-group of the Han people with their own unique language and a population around 80 million. They settled in Southern China and often migrated to various countries throughout the world. It was a source of many revolutionary, government, and military leaders, notably Hong Xiuquan, the Taiping founder. The Hakka significantly influenced the course of Chinese and world history.

Sun Yatsen grew up in Hawaii, became a Christian, and graduated from the Hong Kong College of Medicine in 1892. He organized a failed revolt in Guangdong in 1895 and escaped to London to continue his studies. Qing agents managed to kidnap him in London and held him at the Chinese embassy. It was in part through the help of his former British teachers in Hong Kong that Sun was able to obtain his release. Banned from the colony, Sun went to Japan in 1897 and spent most of the next seven years organizing a series of uprisings against the Qing government. His beliefs were mostly republican and nationalist, with elements of socialism. Sun's hopes to introduce Western production and other technical advances to China without changing fundamental Chinese culture were well known to, and admired by, Boqun and Dai Kan. Most revolutionaries, however, did not believe Sun had the support of the intelligentsia, and his ideas were too drastic compared to others, like Kang Youwei and Liang Qichao, who advocated constitutional monarchy.

❖ ❖ ❖

In Hong Kong Boqun was traveling in a strange and unfamiliar world. In Kowloon, they rode on the widest road they had ever seen, recently built by Matthew Nathan, a Jewish major in the British Royal Engineers. It would later become the sparkling Nathan Road, a major commercial center and "neon capital" of the world. Earlier that year the queen of England had knighted Nathan, who became the first and only Jewish governor of Hong Kong. The Liu relatives' house was a large three-floor Western-style mansion in Kowloon. Boqun and Dai would share a large guest bedroom, attended by a servant to help them clean up and unpack. As soon as they were alone, Boqun became keenly aware that his Manchu hairstyle stood out in his new surroundings. After their conquest in 1644, the Manchus' forced the long pigtail (cue) and shaved forehead hairstyle upon the Chinese, and it became a symbol of shame for most revolution-minded Chinese.

Dai had cut his cue off when he was in Tokyo previously, and Boqun became increasingly embarrassed by his. He said to Dai, "I look like a backward stranger in this place! I have been waiting a long time to cut off my cue. I can no longer contain myself. Please help me remove this symbol of degradation!"

After Dai had complied, Boqun was so full of emotion that he began to expel the humiliations and anger he felt about what the Manchu had done to China. He was now ready to face the foreign devils with his Chinese pride.

For the next several days, their relatives took the young men to Hong Kong for a bit of sightseeing. They traveled by the new Starry ferry to the second-largest port in the world at the time and saw the multitude of magnificent steamer ships, war ships, and Chinese junks where thousands of Chinese lived and called home. They walked the tree-lined avenues of the city and looked upon the Western colonial architecture with curiosity. They marveled at the fine stone steps of Duddell Street built in 1875 to 1889, connecting it with Ice House Street. Large gas lamps mounted on the top of the balustrades and at the foot of the steps provided the most electric light the young men had ever seen. They rode on the street trams, which had just been completed throughout the city, and took the peak tram, built in 1878, to the top of Victoria peak, surveying the city in awe from its highest point. They also visited Chinese temples around the city, particularly the Tin Hau Temple, dedicated to the goddess of the sea and protector of fishermen.

They were impressed by the Western "barbarians'" accomplishments and surprised at how well the two cultures and people mixed and lived in relative harmony. They often ran into some of their fellow Guizhou students around the city, the majority of whom had also cut off their cues. They pointed at each other laughed together about how much they had changed since leaving home. After days of sightseeing and eating substantial meals, the young men recovered from their arduous journey. Boqun wrote letters to his mother and Dilun about the new events and sights he had experienced, but most importantly he wrote of his determination to study hard and his dedication to the rebirth of the motherland as an equal among the rest of the world powers.

On the last day of their stay in Hong Kong, Boqun and Dai's host invited them to a farewell dinner. They hiked to the restaurant through a bamboo forest, stands of which grew eerily inside of abandoned huts and skirted bogs of fragrant wild ginger. The restaurant was located on a ridge, with panoramic views of Hong Kong and the surrounding bays. They were glad their hosts accepted their polite and humane refusal to go to a restaurant that was famous for a local dish of monkey brain, notorious among the rest of mainland Chinese. A live monkey's brain is served while it screams and dies a painful death. Instead, the young men went to a seafood restaurant for a sumptuous banquet of crusty salt and pepper tofu, heaping platters of fish, crabs, and scallops in tangy black bean and chili sauces, and delicately sautéed pea shoots. Both young men had never eaten seafood since there was little available in their home province. After some initial trepidation and much to their surprise, they found it delicious. It was a good thing since they would be on a diet full of seafood once they arrived in Japan. With sincere gratitude, they thanked their hosts profusely for their hospitality and kindness. They had come long way from the backwaters of their isolated home province.

Early on the morning of November 8, 1906, the Guizhou contingent, along with fifty other students from across China, boarded the Japanese steamer ship *Aki Maru* and set sail for Yokohama. Situated on a peninsula facing the western coast of Tokyo Bay, Yokohama is the second-largest city in Japan and lies a mere thirty kilometers from the capital, Tokyo. Since its port opened in 1859, it has served as a window to the world. Japan's first Western-style hotel and restaurant opened in Yokohama, and a railway to Tokyo was completed in 1872. When Sun Yatsen first settled in 1897, there was already a large Chinese community in the bustling port city, which would later become the largest Chinatown in the world. The representatives of their home provinces met the students. Those who planned to study in Yokohama were escorted into the city. Others, like Boqun and Dai, went directly to the central train station for travel to Tokyo.

It was the first time the students traveled by train. Boqun had seen the French in Kunming building the railway from French Indochina, but it would not be completed until 1910. He thought to himself, *We could have saved many days if that railway had been finished by now.* Japan had only completed the railway from Yokohama to Tokyo in 1899, and it was an instant success. While traveling through the countryside, it became clear that rail transport was at the heart of both nation building and the transformation of Japan into a modern state. Along with newspapers and radio, the rail network linked distant parts of Japan into a conveniently traversable nation. Well into the turn of the century, the Japanese people's sense of belonging remained restricted to local geographic and political units, be they former feudal domains, villages, or even dialects.

Dai Kan noted, "It is the railway that supports the development of a metropolitan center, which becomes the site of manufacturing, commerce, politics, and education and the backbone of an industrialized and modern nation."

Boqun replied, "This is the technology that will enable China to join the modern world and help Guizhou become industrialized and economically developed. I would like to make a contribution to bringing the railways to China and in particular to Guizhou."

Several representatives of the various provincial student groups met the students at Tokyo's railway station. They then traveled by trams to their residences. Tokyo had only switched from horse-drawn cars to electric tram cars in 1904. Tramways vastly increased the possibility of encountering strangers, a distinct feature of modern life new to the students. Traveling with strangers in close quarters required an exercise in responsible self-discipline, which was assiduously promoted by the Japanese Meiji government. To Boqun's surprise and shock, a fellow Japanese passenger took off and neatly folded his trousers and then placed them on the overhead rack immediately after taking his seat. He then remained quite unperturbed, sitting in a most dignified manner in only his half-length muslin drawers. As in Hong Kong, the students also noted the prevalence of electric streetlights and the wide availability of electricity. It made the students' hometowns seem to be literally in the dark ages.

After bidding good-bye to Dai Kan, who had returned to his previous lodging, Boqun and the Guizhou contingent arrived at a modest-looking, low, wooden house typical of those found in Tokyo at the turn of the century. Platforms of polished cedar and pine made up the interior of the house. The floors were carpeted with spotless woven matting and walled by delicate *shoji*. There was a scrupulous neatness, exquisite elegance, and dainty aesthetic reserve. Unlike houses in China, there was little ornamentation. Except for the faultless carpentry and vivid walls and paneled ceilings, it seemed comparatively austere. Rooms were assigned to each of two new arrivals with low study tables and bedding of typical Japanese furnishings, as well as sets of plain kimonos. There was also a stack of books by Sun Yatsen and his close associate, Huang Xing, a Hunan native, who passed the national examination and received his Jinshi degree when he was only twenty-two years old. In 1902 Huang went to study abroad in Japan and enrolled in the Tokyo University. While in Japan, Huang developed an appreciation for the study of military affairs and studied modern warfare under Japanese officers in his free time. While living in Japan, Huang practiced horsemanship and shooting every morning. Huang's military training in Japan prepared him for his later role as a Chinese revolutionary. Notable among the revolutionary material was Sun's treaties on the Three Principles of the People and many articles, newspapers, and journals discussing the problems of imperialism in China and the need to establish a republic.

The new students changed into kimonos and joined their compatriots for their first-ever full Japanese meal at the students' favorite restaurant. The new arrivals found the kimonos surprisingly comfortable, practical, and easy to adjust to. An equal number of young Japanese ladies in colorful kimonos greeted the six new students and two hosts at the restaurant entrance. After removing their shoes, the students were led into the dining room, where they sat cross-legged on cushions that lined three sides of the room. A pretty, well-dressed Japanese waitress, with hair that shined like polished black ebony and full of flowers and jeweled pins, tended each guest. Each student started with a cake of sugared confectionery, brightly colored leaf biscuits, and a tiny, transparent porcelain cup of hot tea. Then came the first "honorable" tray—a small lacquered tray with lacquered bowls, a covered basin of clear soup, a little pot of soy sauce, a gilded platter with various sweet and aromatic condiments, and cutlets of salmon encircled by freshly picked vegetables.

The waitress counseled the students on the types and amounts of condiments to use for the different dishes; she filled the sake cup or rearranged the various little bowls and platters. She cleared and brought the next course. There were shrimps pickled with apricots laid in beds of colored rice and chestnuts, wild goose with radish cakes, and hare seasoned with preserved cherries amid little squares of perfumed almond paste and biscuits of persimmon. The main attraction was a glass slab with various strips of fish grouped by hues and colors, reminiscent of a modern masterpiece watercolor painting. There were cuttlefish, crab, mackerel, trout, and sole. Boqun hesitated due to his lack of experience with raw seafood, but after some urging from his convincing waitress, he tasted everything she presented and ended up wondering if boiling and frying everything might not be best after all.

Boqun, 1906

At the far end of the room, the *shoji* were pushed back and three musicians played familiar yet different string instruments. Before them sat the first-ever geishas Boqun had ever seen in person. The geishas performed one of the most famous Japanese dances—the story of a wooden beauty coming to life in a temple. The simple but passionate music accompanied the gilded silken kimonos floating and fluttering about the beautiful geishas. The dance was a piece of choreographic genius, and the students' thunderous applauses brought the evening to a joyous end. It was the first night of many that the students would enjoy during their stay in Tokyo.

The party went on late into the night, with much fellowship and fun sharing a wondrous experience with the newly arrived Chinese. Boqun retired to his room full of enthusiasm and impatient to begin his studies in earnest. Boqun would attend Chuo University, founded in 1885 and one of the most-prestigious universities in Japan. At the suggestion of Liu Xianzhi, Boqun had studied the Japanese language for a year and had already passed a number of proficiency tests before his arrival. His preparation, combined with the Liu connection to the university, allowed him to begin his studies almost immediately while other students had to attend language school for a minimum of three months. Liu Xianzhi, the brother of Liu Xianshi, who had attended the same university and joined the group headed by Kang Youwei and Liang Qichao and later become a close friend of Liang, served as liaison between the group and the university.

❖ ❖ ❖

Intellectuals were not the only Chinese attracted by Japan's success in modernization. Even the Qing government saw the Meiji Japan model as a means of instituting controlled political change and especially after 1900, actively sponsored students going to Japan. Frustratingly, the government found it much easier to encourage students to study in Japan than to control what they learned and how they applied it back home. Many students who went to study Western science ended up in more familiar humanistic subjects; others turned to political organization, military science, and social theory. Often they failed to complete a formal course of studies at a recognized Japanese school, but they did absorb the radical political ideas circulating among overseas students and the general atmosphere of late Meiji Japan. It was, of course, an atmosphere highly charged with the fierce nationalism of a country that had recently overcome threats to its independence and emerged victorious in two wars.

Before 1903, the overseas students were somewhat distrustful of Sun Yatsen and paid no great attention to him. Most had believed Sun's vision of China becoming a republic was too drastic a goal and instead thought the Qing government still had the potential to be reformed and strengthened. Kang Youwei and Liang Qichao were the proponents of a constitutional monarchy instead of a republic. The other students had joined their organization even though their approach was tried and failed in 1898, and they barely escaped with their lives, fleeing to Japan.

Some of the Chinese students in Japan saw evil in modern capitalism and other Western institutions. Others were super-nationalists, believing that what China lacked was identity as a nation, and they wanted a unified state that would give them a sense of patriotism, adding meaning to their lives. Still others leaned toward anarchism, and they admired what they had learned in Japan about Russia's student rebellion, the Narodniks of decades before, whose tactics had been direct action, terrorism, and assassination. Diversity of opinion persisted among the entire range of people opposed to Manchu rule. A few wanted China to copy Western democracy with checks and balances, federalism, and the guar-

Sun Yatsen 1907

antee of human rights. A few Chinese favored exterminating all Manchu, whom they described as incapable of reform and an evil race.

In 1905 there was a decisive, albeit gradual, shift of support to Sun by the students based on several important developments. Sun had connections to powerful secret societies, wealthy overseas Chinese, and international support, especially the Japanese, which the other revolutionaries lacked. He was able to raise money; he had experience in organizing revolutionary activities; and finally, he had an early realization of students as a major component of the revolution and aggressively sought their support. When Boqun and his contingent arrived in Tokyo at the end of 1906, Sun was the head of the Revolution Alliance (RA), formed by the integration of various republican revolutionary and student organizations with the purpose of overthrowing the Manchu Qing Empire and establishing a republic. From 1905 to 1906, about a thousand people joined the RA, 90 percent of whom did so in Japan. Most of the members were students and intellectuals, and nearly all provinces in China were represented in the organization.

By the spring of 1907, most of the Chinese students, including Boqun and Dai Kan, had joined the RA. They joined soon after meeting Sun in person at the end of 1906. Although Sun was only an average size, about five foot six, slight in build, and lacking in the fiery delivery of revolutionary speech, Boqun was struck by his openness and ability to sincerely and eloquently speak about his vision for China. As he got to know Sun better over the years, Boqun came to appreciate not only his vision but also his gracious demeanor, his consideration for others, his courtesy, and his openness to share his experiences and thoughts. Boqun would always remember Sun's words to him at their first meeting that snowy morning in Tokyo. Sun said,

My dearest young Boqun, you are the future of China. Take her and her people to a better place—to a greatness that she deserves.

Boqun replied,

I feel a deep sense of honor and pledge to follow your vision and republican principles: First, drive away the Manchu! Second, recover China for the Chinese! Third, establish a republic! And fourth, equalize land ownership!

CHAPTER 3

1907-1911

BROTHERS WANG AND THE SEEDS OF REVOLUTION

Three years younger than Boqun, Dilun had always looked up to his elder brother for guidance and as role model. As the brothers moved from childhood to young adults, they became more equal rather than the traditional elder to younger brother relationship where the younger would defer to the older brother. They trusted each other implicitly and respected each other's judgment more than any other person. They had come to understand and appreciate their respective strength and weaknesses, and they each accepted that they were better as a team than they were individually. Dilun had the same classics education as Boqun and shared some of the same teachers; but being three years younger, Dilun had more exposure to Western ideas and revolutionary writings earlier in life. Because of this and along with his character, he was impatient to move on from learning to doing.

Dilun, 1904

In 1901, when Dilun had reached the age of thirteen, he passed the entrance examination to the elite middle school in Guiyang, where he studied until he graduated in 1904, when he was only sixteen. He then decided to attend the State Teachers' College in

Guiyang, where he spent the next four years planning a revolution as much as studying. As he explained to his mother and Boqun, "What I find most challenging and interesting is the process of learning and how it can define and change the focus of one's life."

Since childhood, both Dilun and Boqun had studied the traditional four arts: the Qin (Guqin), Shu (calligraphy), Hua (painting), and Wushu (martial arts). Boqun was a lifelong practitioner of Shu and tai chi. Dilun was most passionate about the Qin almost as much as Wushu. He was an expert of Qin. A seven-stringed zither without bridges is considered to be the most classical of Chinese instruments, with over three thousand years of history. It is literally called Qin yet commonly known as Guqin, where "Gu" stands for ancient. Confucius was a master of this instrument. In Imperial China, to learn to play Qin used to be regarded as a very important element for education for the purpose of enriching the heart and elevating human spirit. Dilun's had Wushu expertise in the long fist and five of the eighteen weapons by the age of sixteen. During his school days in Guiyang, Dilun would smuggle forbidden revolutionary material in his beloved two hundred–year-old Qin and transport them back to Xingyi when he traveled back for his monthly visit. While Boqun became deeply engrossed in the writing and philosophy of Mencius, Dilun was equally devoted to the seven military classics, particularly Sun Tzu's *The Art of War.* He actually memorized parts of the thirteen chapters that he quoted often in his teaching and later military careers. The brothers thus were known to complement each other as Boqun represented the Wen (culture) and Dilun the Wu (martial), and it was indeed fortunate for the Wang clan.

While studying in Guiyang, Dilun became well versed in the young revolutionary Zou Rong's well-known work *The Revolutionary Army.* Dilun felt a particular empathy toward Zou, who, like Dilun, received a classical education but refused to sit for the examinations but instead was sent to Japan, where he studied the successful Japanese way of modernization. When he returned to China, he started to write essays on how to free the Chinese nation from the Manchu and foreign incursions. He became interested in Western revolutionary ideas and published his works in Shanghai in 1903. Zou was sent to prison and died there shortly thereafter. Zou's work, however, would stay with Dilun throughout his life as the main tenant of his being. He was struck by the kindred spirit in Zou, who wrote:

> We are slaves of the Manchu and suffering from their tyranny, and externally we are being harassed by the foreign powers. Thus we are doubly enslaved. With the rapid advances in science, the idea that a man becomes an emperor with the mandate from heaven and the human spirits can be subjugated is long proven false. The system of a single man in a despotic form of government ruling over the whole country must be overthrown. With the rapid development in education, everyone, regardless of class or status, will be able to enjoy his or her natural human rights. If today we great Han people are to throw off the yoke of the Manchu, to retrieve all the rights we have lost, and are to take our place among world powers (for we wish to preserve in its entirety our natural equality of status and independence), we cannot avoid carrying out a revolution and safeguarding our right to independence.

On the eve of Boqun's departure for Tokyo, the brothers had a long conversation about their respective aspirations. Even at the young age of seventeen, Dilun spoke with the conviction of a much older and more mature person.

> I am not going to follow you and the others to Japan when I am of age since I would already be involved in

a revolution. I can make a more significant contribution at home than studying abroad. Furthermore, I believe I can learn more by experience rather than studying from the Japanese experience, which may not even apply to China.

Even for Boqun, it was difficult for him to accept that such a young man could be successful without further education and more widened experience, yet he had seen Dilun accomplish some extraordinary things through sheer determination, charisma, and willpower. Thus, he encouraged Dilun to pursue what he considered the best way for his own destiny.

Boqun wrote to Dilun twice monthly while abroad. He shipped to Dilun many of the speeches, newspapers, and articles written by Liang Qichao and Sun Yatsen, among others in the revolutionary movement, together with the various translations of social reforms from Europe and Russia. From these writings Dilun would come to understand the great issues that had dominated the most developed parts of the world in the last half of the nineteenth century. After Boqun had joined the RA in 1906, he wrote to Dilun with unrestrained enthusiasm:

It was a hard decision, for I respect Liang tremendously for his intellect but I have come to believe that China needs to rid of the Manchu and establish a new system of governance. Finally there is an organization and a leader from outside of the traditional elites who has all the right ideals and the necessary attributes to bring China out of the middle age into the modern world!

While studying in Guiyang and with the material sent to him by Boqun, Dilun begun to publish a journal, *Excerpts of Thoughts from the Revolutionaries*, which summarized many articles Boqun sent him and his own commentaries. This was, of course, illegal and had to be distributed surreptitiously on the campus with great care, for being caught would mean jail or death. Dilun had gathered around him a group of several classmates of like mind, and they helped in the writing, printing, and assembly of the journal and took great risks as well.

In 1907, Zhang Bailin, a native of Hunan and a law graduate of Waseda University in Tokyo, organized a branch of the RA in Guiyang responsible for the conference, printing, and publishing of a magazine, the *Southwest Daily*, and provided extensive contact with the military, government, and academic communities. Dilun and his friends joined immediately, and Dilun was made the principal youth recruiter for the organization. Shortly thereafter Dilun wrote to Boqun:

> With my friends, we have cut off our cues, signed our names in blood, and joined the newly formed RA. It is to be the most important decision for a humble eighteen-year-old. I now feel I am a part of a great movement that will free China from the Manchu and deliver our people to a more productive and rewarding life.

After Dilun graduated from the Teachers' College in the spring of 1907, he was appointed as the headmaster of a prefecture academy in Xingyi established by his uncle, the prefect, Liu Xianshi, his mother's younger brother and the most powerful man in southern Guizhou. Dilun was not yet twenty years old. Liu was thirty-seven years old when Dilun returned to Xingyi, and he obviously was very impressed by both of his nephews, Boqun and Dilun. He looked at them to be the next generation leaders of the Liu Clan to replace him, his brother, Liu Xianzhi, and his cousin, Liu Xianqian, since their sons were considered too young or not capable to assume such responsibilities. The Lius were cunning and opportunistic in following in their father's footstep in adapting the reform movement that had allowed them to expanded their power and wealth. Even after the reform-minded Guangxu emperor was placed under house arrest by Empress Dowager Cixi in 1898, the Liu brothers continued to support the reforms. Through Liu Xianshi's contacts in Guizhou and Yunnan, they were both familiar with Sun Yatsen and the RA. They felt a republic would be too drastic and would put their position and wealth into jeopardy. Thus there began to be a fundamental fissure between the Lius and Wangs, unbeknownst to the Lius, since they considered both Wang brothers to be still too young and thought their convictions had not yet taken roots. The Lius believed the Wang brothers could be easily swayed by their older uncles.

Although the Confucian thinking is to rule through persuasion and moral example, it still recognizes that military power and authority must be maintained on equal and complementary footing with civil authority. In the late Qing period, peace and unity had been frequently interrupted by periods of violent uprisings and foreign invasions, placing a premium on military expertise. Liu Xianshi, in his charge to Dilun on the formation of the prefecture academy, said,

> It is the sage who appears when the world follows the Way and retires when it does not. It is the hero who appears when world does not follow the Way and retires when it does. We are now in a period of chaos and crisis, and there is no doubt that the Way has not been followed and it the time for heroes.

Dilun replied,

> Yes, Uncle, it is so, but we must select and train men in
> the traditional background of heroes who are largely
> those who have already established a proper moral
> compass through their studies in Confucian classics
> as clearly declared by the philosopher-general Wang
> Yangming in the fifteenth century. We must modern-
> ize; however, we must include mathematics and sci-
> ences, which are part and parcel of military planning
> and tactics.

Liu agreed. "Let's begin our selection from the top twenty families of Xingyi and neighboring prefectures."

After Dilun returned to Xingyi and made the celebratory rounds of his graduation and appointment, he sat for a long talk with his mother, Liu Xianqing, the elder sister of the three Liu brothers and the only daughter and yet the most capable of the four children of Liu Guanli.

Dilun had made clear his belief that China would not be modern-ized and the lives of her people be improved with a Manchu emperor sitting on the throne. After a lengthy discussion over several hours, Dilun explained and compared for his mother the respective positions of Sun and Kang or republicanism versus constitutional monarchy. She surprised him with her knowledge of the two sides and her under-standing of her sons' position. She said,

> I have already discussed this with Boqun via letters over
> the last few months. We both believe my brothers are
> motivated by the interest of persevering the wealth and

the position of the clan whereas you two are centered on the well-being of our motherland and her people. I know your father and grandfather both fervently believed that our clans' interest is intertwined with the interest of China and her people. The Manchu have not done this, and they will fail. You should work with your uncles on the various reforms since you all agree on them. Your uncles will bend with the wind, and they will come around when you are older and the republican movement will have more grassroots support.

Dilun stayed silent for a long time and realized Boqun had been keeping their mother well informed as well as him.

❖ ❖ ❖

After 1900, China was engulfed by a rising tide of change. Electrified by the anticolonial nationalism for a self-sufficient nation, it searched for a successor authority to replace the Manchu and to modernize the country. Even though since 1750 China had long published books, official documents, and local news, it was strictly limited to the Chinese elites. By 1900, however, translation of Western works and publication of news and commentaries by Chinese and Westerners became widely available. In addition, a new social order began to emerge. Chinese society was now fragmented by an alternative path toward class mobility. Most notably the line between the scholar and gentry to the merchants and the military started to be blurred. In this respect, education became the principal engine for change and modernization. As the new master of the prefecture academy, Dilun had to clarify for himself the purposes and the objectives of education. He was very much influenced by Liang Qichao, even though he did not support Liang's belief in a constitutional monarchy. Dilun had come to accept that the Mencius principle of good governance was based on mutual interest between the ruler and the people, who realized that social order would provide livable lives and disorder would endanger them. Dilun thus believed a proper education should provide both literary and scientific knowledge as well as political and military acumen.

Dilun, 1910

In 1905 the Empress Dowager Cixi had accepted most of the reforms promulgated by the young Guangxu Emperor she had deposed. A new school system was then the official policy for the provinces to replace both the thirteen hundred–year-old examination system and the military examination. Such a system required that each province to establish a military primary school. The master plan called for a three-step system with such primary school in each provincial capital, three regional middle schools, and a Sandhurst (British)-like national military academy in Baoting near Beijing. In the fall of 1906, a Guizhou Army Training School was established in Guiyang. To retain the most promising students, Dilun persuaded Li Xianshi to approve additional funding to the Xingyi Academy for military training, including implements and instructors, for its students so they would become the feeder to the Guiyang school. Upon Liu's approval, Dilun revised and implemented the academy's program to one that followed the German and the Japanese methods for potential military officers. It was a foresight that would serve him well in the years to come.

Liu Xianshi additionally saw an opportunity to modernize the Xingyi military under his control with Qing government funding. He appointed Dilun as a captain of the Xingyi Home Guard Battalion and the commander of the first company, which he himself have been serving on an interim basis in spite of Dilun's lack of military training or experience. Dilun was surprised and honored by the appointment. After some discussion, however, Dilun accepted the position knowing he was the best man for the assignment given the knowledge he has acquired in self-study over the last two years in learning and teaching the students in the academy. Additionally, he knew his uncle trusted him as family, appreciated his capabilities, and knew he would have the trust of the best recruits from his students.

Liu also asked Dilun about his opinion of Yuan Zuming, one of his personal guards, to serve as the commander of the Fourth Company of the Xingyi Home Guard. Yuan, only a year younger than Dilun, came from a relatively poor family in northern Guizhou with impressive physical strength, and he was extremely shrewd. He was also very ambitious and considered the military to be his path to power and glory. He disliked education but managed to graduate from the second session of the Guiyang Army Primary School but was not accepted by Wuchang Army Middle School due to poor eyesight. Yuan joined Liu's militia as a trainer and made a positive impression on Liu as Yuan was as cunning as Liu, and admired Liu's political successes through skillful manipulations. His interest was fueled by personal gain rather than patriotic purposes. Even though Dilun was apprehensive of his motives, he thought his abilities could serve the revolution well and was confident he could be led to achieve nobler purposes. Thus he gave positive feedback to his uncle.

In early 1908 Liu Xianshi also approached Dilun's mother, his elder sister, and Boqun about a marriage between Dilun and one of Liu's favorite nieces, Liu Congshu, to cement further the relationship of the two clans. Liu promised a huge dowry and grand wedding that would put the Wang clan almost on par with the Lius. The family discussed the matter when Boqun returned from Tokyo for a month-long home visit. Their mother liked the girl, whom she knew from childhood, and she was well-bred and beautiful. Boqun deferred the decision to Dilun but said, "I know you want to change our beloved fatherland and to do that you need Uncle Liu's trust and help. He is offering you a chance to ensure that, and you have nothing to lose but everything to gain."

Privately without their mother, however, Boqun and Dilun had several long discussions. Boqun was very impressed with Dilun's accomplishments but warned, "Be careful of the smiling tiger. Even though we are family, he would not hesitate to dispose of us if we became disagreeable to him."

Dilun replied, "I am indeed being very careful not to get into his way, but I believe the day will come that we may be on opposite sides."

Boqun sighed and answered, "I hope not for it would be hard on our dear mother, especially now that you are to be married into the Liu clan."

Dilun commented, "I will try my best; that you know."

Boqun also spent considerable time with his mother, Liu Xianqing, discussing his experience in Tokyo and his commitment to the RA and to the revolution to overthrow the Manchu. His mother's only comments were,

> My son, you need to be extra careful in your dealings with friends and even family in these days of political and economic turmoil, particularly about the revolution, which is not supported by the gentry clans of the province, including most the Liu clan, starting with your uncle Xianshi. He considers such a change to be too drastic and thinks it would bring chaos as we have experienced with the Taipings, where eventually nothing was gained but bloodshed and destruction.

She also reminded him that the Wang family should build a family compound in Guiyang, Guizhou's provincial capital, where both brothers had been and would certainly be spending more and more time in the future. Boqun agreed and discussed this also with Dilun, who was given the task of coming up with a site, a plan, and the funding process, with his mother's supervision in Boqun's absence.

On several occasions Boqun's mother mentioned that his wife, Qungao, had been extremely helpful and attentive to her needs and was a welcome help in the household as well as a companion. On the evening Boqun thanked his wife. "My dear wife, I regret that we have had little time together since our wedding, and I thank you for your contribution in the household management. Most importantly, I appreciate your being an agreeable companion to mother." Qungao replied,

> Dear husband, I do understand your absence is for the good of our motherland and our family. I have dedicated myself to help the Wang family to achieve its goals. I am hoping that I will be able to provide the heir to the Wang clan as your mother has done for your father. As for Mother, I enjoy being her companion and have learned a lot from about many things, including the revolution and the sacrifices all of us must make to bring it about.

Boqun was extremely glad that the matchmaker had done her job well and he could leave for Tokyo with a peace of mind.

❖ ❖ ❖

Yuan Shikai was a Han general born in the northern Henan Province to an affluent family. After he twice failed the imperial examination, he decided on an entry into politics through the Qing Army, where he rose rapidly through the ranks due his cunning nature and political skills. In 1882 he was sent to Korea to help in the training its army for defense again the Japan. Three years later, Yuan was appointed as the imperial resident of Seoul, which meant he had become the supreme adviser on all Korean government policies. He was recalled to Tianjin in July 1894, before the official outbreak of the First Sino-Japanese War over control of Korea, and was appointed the commander of the first modernized army (New Army) in 1895. Yuan gained significant political influence and the loyalty of a nucleus of young officers. By 1901 five of China's seven divisional commanders and all other senior military officers in China were his protégés. The Qing court relied heavily on his army due to the proximity of its garrison to the capital and its effectiveness. Of the new armies that were part of the reform program, Yuan's was the best trained and most effective. During the political power struggle of the hundred-day reform movement in 1898, Yuan had deceived and betrayed the Guangxu Emperor by informing the Empress Dowager Cixi of the Emperor's plan for reform, which resulted in a coup d'état to remove the Emperor from power and virtually imprisoned him for the rest of this life.

In 1899, Yuan was appointed as governor of Shandong Province. During his three-year tenure, the Boxer Rebellion erupted, and he secured the province from the Boxers. Yuan took the side of the pro–foreign faction in the Qing court and refused to side with the Boxers to attack the Eight-Nation Alliance forces, joining with other province governors who commanded substantial modernized armies not participating in the Boxer Rebellion. He ignored Empress Dowager Cixi's declaration of war against the foreign powers and continued to suppress the Boxers. When the Eight-Nation Alliance of Britain, France, Germany, Italy, Austria, Russia, Japan, and the United States mounted their responses to the Boxers, Yuan and his army also helped them massacre tens of thousands Chinese in their anti-Boxer campaign, which ended in 1902.

By the early twentieth century, mass civil disorder had begun and became continuous. To mitigate such problems, Empress Dowager Cixi issued an imperial edict in 1908 ironically calling for reforms along the line of the hundred-day reform proposed by the Guangxu Emperor in 1898 and initiated the era known as the "Late Qing Reform." The edict paved the way for the most far-reaching reforms in terms of their social consequences. Cixi and the Guangxu both died in 1908, succeeded by the boy Emperor Puyi at the age of two with his father, Guangxu's younger brother as regent. In 1909 the Qing court, head by the regent, concerned about Yuan Shikai's growing power, relieved him of his military post and retired to his native village with the official reason of a foot disease.

Upon learning of this news, Dilun asked Liu Xianshi about the power struggles in Beijing and whether he thought such a power vacuum was created as an opportunity for the political change. After some long moments of reflection, Liu responded, "Yuan will not go quietly into retirement. Since the Qing Court is now facing doubtful military support, changes will occur in due course. I think it is a great opportunity for Yuan since he has more military power and the foreigners are behind him."

Dilun couldn't wait till the end of his discussion with his uncle before he put his thoughts down in a letter to Boqun, which in part stated:

> No doubt you are aware about what has occurred in Beijing. Now is the time for the RA to mount some decisive uprisings against the Qing court. I am concerned about Uncle Xianshi's position. He is being an opportunist, as that is his nature, to throw his lot in with Yuan Shikai, who seems to have the upper hand even though he has been exiled. We both know that Yuan is not a republican, and he is by nature just like Uncle Xianshi. I hope we will not have family conflicts on which side we should be on.

❖ ❖ ❖

A chance meeting by Dilun with a young man in late 1909 marked another significant relationship in the lives of the Liu-Wang families. He Yingqin, native of Xingyi and only two years Dilun's junior, was an army cadet selected to go to Japan for further training. He was introduced to Dilun by a family friend when he was on home leave prior to his departure for Japan. He's family operated a successful cloth-dyeing business. He and his brothers learned the values of hard work and frugality, working alongside hired laborers. After beginning his education in a village school, he persuaded his father to send him and two of his younger brothers to the new Xingyi county primary school, which had been reformed to include a Western curriculum. In spite of this humble beginning, He Yingqin was one of the two hundred out of thousands of applicants to enter the first class of the Guiyang Army Primary School in 1907, marking the beginning of his formal military education and exposure to the revolutionary ideas. He graduated at the top of his class and was accepted at the second class of the Wuchang Army No. 3 Middle School in fall of 1908, which was national in scope and much larger and more prestigious than the Guiyang school.

In only his second semester in Wuchang, He Yingqin learned that students from his new school were eligible to test into a study-abroad program in Japan. Admission to a Japanese military academy represented a valuable military training opportunity for a Chinese cadet in the early twentieth century and all but ensured him a prominent position as an instructor upon his return to China. The fact that He Yingqin's name appeared at the top of the list of successful candidates the very next semester, first among all who took the examination, is a testimony to his hard work and academic abilities. In early 1910 he joined a group of twenty Chinese students bound for study in Japan. Having succeeded in military schools in Guiyang and Wuchang and on his way to an elite Japanese military academy, He Yingqin had developed from a country bumpkin from the backward Guizhou Province into a promising young military professional. He had now begun to excel in the classroom, to travel beyond the confines of his home county and province, and to acquire valuable professional experience. His decision to enter the military profession had begun to open up a new world to He Yingqin.

With the recommendation of a close friend prior to He's departure for Japan, Dilun arranged to meet him at a Xingyi teahouse. He arrived in full military dress and sat ramrod straight throughout their meeting of several hours. In spite of Dilun's initial impression that He was rather rigid both in demeanor and in thoughts, he warmed to He after the first hour of exchange of backgrounds. Dilun was impressed that He had learned from his family upbringing, Confucian morality, frugality, and industriousness. He appeared to have a sense of self-discipline, respect for authority, tenacious, and dedicated pursuit of objectives.

Dilun asked, "We agreed that overthrowing the Manchu is the only salvation of our motherland. What you see as your potential contribution to the revolution?"

He answered without hesitation, "For the revolution to succeed, it will require a strong military. I see myself both as a training resource and a leader of military campaigns. My training thus far and the opportunity to study further in Japan will allow me to succeed on both counts."

Dilun came away from the meeting feeling that He was a man who could serve the revolution well and he encouraged He to join him at Xingyi Military Academy after the completion of his Japanese study. He, on the other hand, appreciated and respected Dilun's obvious charisma, leadership, and dedication to the republic cause. Almost immediately after the meeting, Dilun thought a marriage between He and his youngest sister, Wenxiang, would be mutually beneficial for both families. He discussed this with his mother, and she suggested that Boqun should meet this young He and assess his potential for himself. Dilun agreed and wrote Boqun, now already in Shanghai, and asked him for his opinion. Boqun indicated that he would have to meet the young man before forming an opinion. He Yingqin and Boqun would not meet because circumstances put them apart till 1912.

❖ ❖ ❖

Upon Boqun's return from his home leave in mid-1908, he was asked by Zheng Taiyan, editor-in-chief of *Min Bao*, which was the de facto news voice of the RA, to join the paper as his assistant. Zheng was a well-known Chinese philologist and textual critic of his time. He was also a revolutionary jailed numerous times by the Qing court. A friend of Liang Qichao, and a member of the Society for National Strengthening, he had written many articles for Liang's various papers. He joined the RA in Tokyo on June 1906 after his release from a three-year jail sentence. Although they were not close friends, Boqun always admired Zheng for his scholarship as well as his reform and revolutionary efforts. Thus, Boqun accepted Zheng's offer.

"I thank you, elder brother Zheng, for your undeserving trust and your most gracious offer to be your assistant. I will do my utmost to accomplish all my assignments with the hope that I will meet your expectations."

Zheng replied, "Boqun, I think you will do just fine, and I believe we will become good friends in our association."

They shook hands and bowed to each other. Thereupon Boqun spent most of his free time from schoolwork, researching, writing, and editing for *Min Bao* under Zheng's direction, and as part of his work at *Min Bao*, he met and became friends or acquaintances of many reformers and revolutionaries, including Liang Qichao.

In the winter of 1908, Boqun received a wire notice from Dilun that Qungao, his wife, had borne him a son and their mother named him Fuxen and wanted Boqun's approval. Boqun received this auspicious news with extreme glee but much regretted that he would be unable see his family for at least another year. He wired back to Dilun:

Please give my dear wife many thanks for a son and to Mother I wish to express my appreciation for the name she has picked for the boy. As for me, I cannot express the joy I feel for this auspicious news, which has provided the Wang family with the start of the next generation. I just wish that Father would have live long enough to share in the joyous event!

As Boqun continued to work toward his economic and political science degree, his responsibilities at *Min Bao* broadened to the point that Zheng asked him to move upon graduation with the organization back to Shanghai to be close to the revolutionary actions in taking charge of *Great Republic Daily*. On a dreary, misty day in early March 1910, Boqun packed his belongings and bid farewell to his follow revolutionaries and friends at the Tokyo train station. At Yokohoma, he transferred for a steamer to Shanghai. On the long journey, Boqun reflected on his time in Tokyo, where his life had so drastically changed from a country squire to a revolutionary.

Shanghai sits at the mouth of the Yangtze River in the Middle Eastern portion of the Chinese coast. It borders on Jiangsu and Zhejiang Provinces to the west and is bound to the east by the East China Sea. For centuries an administrative, shipping, and trading town, Shanghai grew in importance in the nineteenth century due to European recognition of its favorable port location and economic potential. The city was one of several opened to foreign trade following the British victory over China in the first opium war and the subsequent 1842 Treaty of Nanjing, which allowed the establishment of the Shanghai International Concessions, where the major foreign powers each had their own territory where their respective law governed, and the Chinese needed their approval for business and residence. The city then flourished as a center of commerce between east and west and was known as the Paris of the East.

Even after visiting Hong Kong and living in Tokyo, Boqun was surprised to see such an amassed and modern city upon disembarking in Shanghai's international harbor. He was met by Zheng Taiyan and traveled by tram to a lodging arranged by Zheng in the French Concession where the main office of RA's paper, *Great Republic Daily*, was located. Boqun was appointed as its chief editor. His work with the paper was to gain wide readership and to earn respect for his writing and his political views from the best-known critics, such as Liang Qichao, who had asked Boqun to join him in Beijing as a consultant. Thus, Boqun at age twenty-five had become one of a group of elite literates at the center of the revolutionary movement. He traveled between Shanghai and Beijing on a biweekly basis by train and met with Liang and his wide circle of reformation and revolutionary associates. He impressed them with his intellect and political acumen, and his progress was noted to Liu Xianshi by Liang from time to time through his contacts with Liu's younger brother Xianzhi, who was one of Liang's students.

❖ ❖ ❖

In 1910 on a hot and humid afternoon typical of Shanghai summers, Boqun received a secret wire from his uncle Liu Xianshi urging him to return to Xingyi to take over as his administrative secretary, a highly influential and respected position unusual for a man of Boqun's young age. While he contemplated it, he received a second wire from Dilun, which, in part, stated:

> With revolution uprisings occurring almost in every corner of China, the political situation in Guizhou is extremely fluid, and different factions are poised to assert their influences. Mother and I both believe that you are needed more here than in Shanghai. We beseech you return as soon as possible to take up the position Uncle has offered you.

Boqun, reflecting on this new development, had mixed feelings since he loved his work through the paper and working with Liang in Beijing, which was national and even international in scope. He was meeting many kindred spirits and learning from them. It would be less exciting to go back to Guizhou. Even though it might lead to real political power in the future, that was of little importance to him. Finally, however, family duty and Dilun's pleadings added to his mother's as well persuaded Boqun to accept his uncle's offer.

In the spring of 1911, after less than a year on the job at the paper, Boqun traveled by boat and train for over a week to his beloved Xingyi to the mountains and his loved ones he had missed during the long stay in Tokyo and Shanghai to take on a political assignment in the family business of government. In his first meeting with Liu Xianshi in March 1911, Boqun asked his uncle to define his role in Guizhou's provincial government. Liu explained,

> Guizhou is ripe for a tumultuous change caused by the political struggle of the constitutional monarchy and the republican factions. The political control of our province is up for grabs, and I believe I can do a good job as the governor general and you can help me to achieve that goal. Given your education, experience and contacts, I believe you can best help by serving as my personal representative as well as the representative of the Guizhou provincial government. You can be my eyes and ears at the power centers in Beijing, Shanghai, Nanjing, wherever they maybe. Also, dear, wise Boqun, I am counting on you to council Dilun with the perspective of broad and national political views and the importance of the joint interest of our two families.

Boqun responded in essence that he considered his uncle had just done him great honor and he would endeavor to serve his uncle, their clans, and the Guizhou people to the best of his humble abilities.

In June of 1911, Dilun was married amid the pomp and circumstance the likes of which had not been seen in Xingyi since his mother's wedding to his father. With the family's blessing, Dilun immediately deposited the dowry into the Guiyang Wang family compound fund. The plans called for a compound with three buildings with two identical Western-style structures for Boqun's and Dilun's families, each with its own garden, entrance, and support facilities at separate sides of the compound, and a traditional structure for their mother with enclosed center courtyard in the middle. The two side structures would be connected by a grand causeway, which served to enclose the compound. The compound then had its own outer wall, horse stables, and guardhouse.

Thus, Liu Xianshi had placed both his nephews in key positions of the Xingyi power structure, against the advice of some of his own family. He believed the Wang brothers were the best people for the assignments in the joint Liu-Wang family and he could still influence and direct their paths since they were both still so young and inexperienced.

CHAPTER 4

1911-1914

BIRTH OF THE REPUBLIC AND ITS CHAOTIC AFTERMATH

From 1907 until 1910, Sun Yatsen and his principal associate, Huang Xing, attempted numerous revolts at the Sino-Vietnamese border and Guangdong. Due to lack of financial support and military supplies, all these uprisings were unsuccessful. Finally, in the late summer of 1911, Qing Army units in Hubei Province were ordered to neighboring Sichuan to quell the Railway Protection Movement. A mass protest ensued against the Qing government's seizure and handover of local railway development ventures to foreign powers. These events led to the successful Wuchang Uprising by the combination of various army factions and revolutionary groups headed by Huang Xing that established the military government of the Republic of China on October 11, 1911. This became known as the Xinhai Revolution, and Li Yuanhong was selected as the provisional president.

Li was a native of Hubei and the son of a Qing veteran of the Taiping Rebellion. He graduated from Beiyang Naval Academy in 1889 and served in the First Sino-Japanese War. Li was the Qing governor for Hunan-Hubei Provinces when the revolution broke out. The Wuchang mutineers and revolutionaries needed a visible, high-ranking officer to be their figurehead. Li was well respected, had supported the Railway Protection Movement, and spoke English, which could be useful in dealing with foreign concerns. He was reportedly dragged from hiding and forced at gunpoint to be the new provisional military governor. Though reluctant at first, he embraced the revolution after it became clear its momentum was growing. Qing Premier Yuan Shikai negotiated a truce with Li on December 4, 1911.

Sun Yatsen himself had no direct part in the uprising and was actually traveling in America at the time in an effort to raise more money among overseas Chinese. When he learned of the successful rebellion, he immediately returned to China from the United States in mid-December 1911. After these events, October 10 became known as Double Ten Day in commemoration of the first successful revolution.

In Guizhou Province there has been an antagonistic split in the elites over political control since the start of the Qing reform movement. One faction was the Self-Government Society (SGS) under Zhang Bailin, who started a RA branch in Guiyang. Zhang backed Sun Yatsen's revolution to overthrow the Qing government and form a republic. With the support of military cadets and many of the new Qing Army, the SGS successfully won a majority of the Provincial Assembly in 1909. Their opponent, the Constitution Preparation Association (CPA), favored Liang Qichao's program of constitutional monarchy. Most CPA members were from politically well-connected gentry families and included those who had served in the provincial Qing government. The CPA showed less interest in radical change but instead worked for reform under the existing system. In 1911, when the news of Wuchang's successful revolution reached Guiyang, both factions saw an opportunity to carry out their particular revolution or reform agendas respectively.

In the fall of 1911, the Qing Guizhou governor became concerned about his newly trained Qing army, with its known revolutionary sympathizers connected to the SGS, and he feared they could follow the lead of the Wuchang incident and revolt. At the suggestion of the CPA leaders, he requested that Liu Xianshi bring five hundred of his best militia troops to Guiyang to counter any potential SGS-instigated uprising. In return, the governor promised Liu new weapons from the provincial arsenal for his men. Liu had family connections to the CPA leadership and was sympathetic to their politics. Sensing an opportunity to expand his sphere of influence, Liu decided to lead a Xingyi battalion of some five hundred men started for Guiyang in September 14. Liu had asked Dilun to command the forward company of 150 men consisting mainly of his compatriots. In spite of his own sympathy for Zhang, Dilun saw this as an opportunity for him and Boqun to exert some influence in a fluid political situation and forward their inclinations regarding the revolution.

In southwest China, Yunnan, the province bordering on French Indochina, become the center of republican movement under Cai E. Cai, a Hunan native, who had been a student of Liang Qichao at the prestigious and progressive Shiwu Xuetang (School of Current Affairs) in Hunan and went to Japan to study in 1899 at the Imperial Japanese Army Academy. He returned to China in 1900, when he was only eighteen, and took part in a revolutionary uprising in Hunan. When the rebellion failed, Cai went back to Japan and finished his military education and training. He also joined the RA while there. When he returned to China, Cai had established the Qing New Army officers'

Cai E, 1910

training facilities in Jiangxi, Hunan, and Guangxi Provinces. At the time Yunnan had implemented the military reform in earnest as a new governor took over in 1909. By 1911 Yunnan had recruited and trained twelve thousand five hundred men for its Nineteenth Division of the new Qing army. Its infantry was armed with 6.8mm Mauser rifles and augmented by units with 8mm Maxim machine gun, and its artillery had a full set of forty-five 75mm Krupp howitzers. Cai went to Yunnan and joined the Nineteenth as the commander of the Thirty-Seventh Brigade in mid-1911.

The officers of the Yunnan Nineteenth Army were professionally trained, and many had been received their education and training in Japan. As a result the quality of the military schools was substantially improved after the reform. This cadre of new officers mostly supported the goals of a republican revolution. After the successful October 1911 Wuchang uprising, Cai led his brigade, joined by the other units of the Nineteenth Army, and declared its support for the Republic. The joined forces defeated the resident Qing army and took over the province. Yunnan was a much more developed and richer province than Guizhou, and for most of Chinese history, its governor had great influence over Guizhou if not direct jurisdiction.

In Guiyang Zhang Bailin, encouraged by the situation in Yunnan and learning of Liu's advance toward Guiyang, decided it was the right time for the SGS to initiate its own revolution with the help of parts of the New Army units and student of the Military Middle School. With dubious army support, the Qing governor surrendered on November 2, 1911, and handed power over to the provincial assembly now headed by Zhang without resistance. Zhang then allowed the governor to retire with safe passage to his native village. Thus, the SGS was able to take over in a bloodless coup, and Zhang took control of the provincial cabinet and replaced the CPA members with his own men. The SGS, however, with little administrative and military experience, was struggling to develop a plan for governing. Thus opportunity was presented, as the Wang brothers had foreseen, for political and military control.

At about fifty miles from Guiyang, Liu Xianshi received news of the successful bloodless revolution. His first inclination was to return to Xingyi and wait to see if the revolutionaries' success would not be overturned. Dilun, however, saw an immediate opportunity, and he tried to persuade his uncle to join with Zhang as part of the revolution. He boldly stated, "My dear uncle, you now have the opportunity to gain control of the province. Our force is united under your command while the revolutionaries are still getting organized. We certainly can be the deciding factor while the factions contend for control. Also, we can switch our position anytime when the situation requires."

Liu then sent for Boqun and others and asked them for their opinion. Boqun was irrevocable in his response. "I too believe this is an opportunity for us, even if we are shorthanded. If necessary, I am sure we can count on your friends in Yunnan, who now have firm control of the province."

Liu was thus convinced, and he sent a message to Zhang:

> I congratulate you for the bloodless revolution. Although I have been sent for by former governor, yet for some time my heart has been with the revolution you all support. My nephew, Wang Dilun, has told me that you are a man of honor, and hence, I ask to join you in Guiyang to bolster the revolutionary military position and to assist in any way in the new government that you deem desirable.

Since Liu was known to be sympathetic to the CPA, he asked Dilun to deliver personally his message to Zhang. Liu was well aware of Dilun's connection to Zhang during Dilun's student days in Guiyang, and Liu believed that Dilun could convince Zhang that his intent was sincere and it would be mutually beneficial to cooperate.

The Liu family long had connections to the Yunnan government. Liu Xianshi and his younger brother, Liu Xianzhi, had both served in staff positions in Kunming, and Liu Xianzhi was close to Cai E and Liang Qichao, who had been the teacher of both Cai and the younger Liu. Traditionally under the Qing government, the military governor of Yunnan had general administrative authority for Guizhou as well. Thus the Liu family always made sure they were well connected to the authority in Yunnan for several generations. Because of this, Liu

Xianshi had always been a regional power to be reckoned with. All of Guizhou's political factions wanted him to be on their side.

Upon arrival and briefing by Dilun, Zhang was suspicious of a new declaration of loyalty from the former known constitutional monarchist, but he also had reasons for accepting Liu Xianshi's offer. Zhang realized he needed to bring capable people with military muscle he could count on to help his side to rebuild and manage the affairs of Guizhou. He thought Liu could help unite the SGS, who mostly came from the lower gentry, with the CPA, who tended to have more experience in the government. In addition, of more immediate importance, Liu's five hundred militiamen could either support or oppose the new government. Last, certain weight was carried by Dilun, whom he trusted, even though Dilun had warned him in the past that the smiling tiger face could attack at any moment if it was hungry and even just angry. An eternal optimist, Zhang thus welcomed Liu to Guiyang and even gave him the weapons promised by former governor. Liu was then appointed the minister of military affairs, supposedly lending military backing to the new Guizhou revolutionary government.

Although Zhang and fellow SGS associates were trying to set up a republican government in conjunction with the CPA group in Guiyang, the SGS was continuously outmaneuvered by them. The CPA was more entrenched in the existing government. Liu Xianshi, ever the opportunist, was playing coy as a republican but lining up with the CPA in action since he felt they had the upper hand in the political struggle, and besides, he had doubts about the eventual success of the SGS for establishing such a drastically different republic system of government. The brothers Wang sized up the situation. Dilun said,

Though my heart and mind are with the SGS and Zhang, our sphere of power is so small I am not prepared to choose sides against Uncle's will, which is entirely unpredictable for now. If I had to guess, he is not ready for the radical change of a republic, and I am afraid if rain turns into storm, he will stand by the CPA. What should we do, my big brother?

Boqun replied,

I agree that we cannot afford to challenge Uncle now, and any inkling of our disloyalty will bring great disaster to the family. Be patient and wait for the republic to be more established nationally, and its political influence surely will reach down to Guizhou. As for Zhang, the best you can do for him is to give him fair warning if the tide is turned against him in the meantime.

After Sun arrived in Wuchang, he proposed that the provisional government locate its capital at Nanjing and notify all provinces to send their representatives there for the formation of a parliament and the election of a president. Boqun was nominated by Liu Xianshi to be one of the representatives. Boqun realized Liu's motive for sending him there was to cover all the political bases in a chaotic and fluid power struggle in China. Nevertheless, Boqun considered this to be a great opportunity to participate and to contribute in the formation of a Chinese republic. On December 29, 1911, a meeting of provincial representatives in Nanjing elected Sun as the provisional president on January 1, 1912. It was set as the first day of the first year of the republic. Li Yuanhong was elected as provisional vice president, and Huang Xing became the minister of the army. The new provisional government of the Republic of China was created along with a provisional constitution, which was drafted by a committee of the provincial representatives headed by one of the RA founders, Soong Jiaoren, lifelong friend and Hunan compatriot of Huang Xing.

Boqun was selected to be on the constitution committee for his political scholarship and his revolutionary experiences in Shanghai and Beijing. Sun is credited for the funding of the revolution and for keeping the spirit of revolution alive, even after a series of failed uprisings. His successful merger of minor revolutionary groups to a single political entity provided a better base for all those who shared the same ideals. A number of practices were introduced, from the solar calendar to replace the traditional lunar calendar and to the fashion of the Zhongshan suit, which was particularly favored by Sun.

The Qing court's response to the success of the revolution was to call upon Yuan ShiKai. During his three years of exile, Yuan kept contact with his close allies and through them kept the loyalty of the only combat-ready Qing Beiyang Army. Having this strategic military advantage, Yuan actually held the balance of power between the revolutionaries and the Qing court. Both wanted Yuan on their side. Initially deciding against the possibility of becoming president of a newly proclaimed republic, Yuan also repeatedly declined offers from the Qing court for his return as prime minister of the imperial cabinet. Time was on Yuan's side, and Yuan waited till the Manchu regent and the father of boy Emperor Puyi resigned, allowing him to become the prime minister with the real power of the regent to take over the effective control of the government on November 1, 1911. He then formed a predominantly Han Chinese cabinet of his confidants, consisting of only one Manchu. Yuan thus became the most powerful man in China.

❖ ❖ ❖

While in Nanjing for the provisional parliament meeting, Boqun made a stop at Shanghai to visit some of his friends and to meet with

He Yingqin. He had taken a leave of absence from his study in Tokyo to return to Shanghai with a group of his Chinese schoolmates at the Japanese school led by Chen Qimei. Chen, a Zhejiang native, went to Japan for studies in 1906 and there joined the RA. On November 10, 1915, Chen's forces assassinated the Qing Shanghai army commander and occupied Shanghai. Chen was then made the republic military governor of the region. Boqun met with He Yingqin in his hotel in Shanghai and was immediately impressed by He's earnestness, his obvious military bearing, and all the good points Dilun had sensed in the young man. Boqun had understood that He served in the Third Regiment of the Shanghai Army first as an instructor, actually involved in combat, and was promoted to battalion commander. Boqun congratulated him and asked about his plans for the future. He responded,

Thank you, elder brother, for your kind words. This leave from my study has actually made me realize how much I have to learn from the Japanese. Even though the short time I have spent in Japan only allowed me to learn the Japanese language at the Shimbu Gakko (prep school set up by the Japanese for Chinese students to learn Japanese and to prepare for the entrance into the elite Japanese Imperial Army Academy), I learned that the Japanese military men, senior officers down to common soldiers, all possess discipline, a sense of duty, and strict obedience that are seldom found in our Chinese counterparts. I am certain this kind of military spirit will be required to save our motherland from colonization by the foreign powers. I need to complete my entire study in Japan and then serve in the Japanese Army for the prescribed period as every Japanese officer in the imperial army. Unlike the others who went to Japan to study just so they can join up with the revolution, I had asked for a leave of one year, and if my request was not granted, I would not have left. This is because I really believe the training is the best way for me to serve my country.

Boqun nodded in total agreement and now more than ever thought He would make a fine husband for his youngest sister and a great addition to family. Moreover, Boqun learned that He had already been in touch of some Japanese friends he had made to help with the funding for his education since the Qing court funding he had would no longer be available. Boqun thought about offering He financial support but decided against it since he wanted He to join the Wang brothers out of his own violation.

Thus Boqun said,

I salute your desire to further your education and believe that if I were in your place, I would do the same. Please keep in mind that both Dilun and I believe you have great potential ahead of you, and we would be extremely pleased if you would join us when you complete your education and training. Promise me that you will give us an opportunity to talk to you when you return.

He thanked Boqun and promised he would do so. It would take over a year for He to complete the financing by his Japanese friends and return to Japan in 1913.

❖ ❖ ❖

As Liu Xianshi and his Xingyi group settled in Guiyang, the political struggle between the SGS and CPA intensified. Even with Liu's surreptitious support, the CPA was unable to unseat the SGS government under Zhang by any legal means. In late 1911 an opportunity presented itself for Liu when Zhang and his chief military commander left for Sichuan and Hunan, respectively, to support revolutionary forces fighting against Yuan Shikai's Beiying Army. Each took along substantial numbers of Guizhou troops, thus leaving the new government in a rather vulnerable position. Liu realized this was the opportunity he had been waiting for to improve his own position. He suggested to the leaders of the CPA faction that they seek military assistance from Yunnan's governor, Cai E. With Yunnan's help, Liu argued, the CPA could quickly purge the Guizhou government of SGS supporters and take exclusive control. The CPA leaders agreed since they are well aware of Liu's close relationship with Yunnan.

Liu then decided to ask Cai E to send military help to Guiyang on the pretense of pacifying the infightings between two political factions, the well-known banditry in the province, and various armed bands of secret societies causing general disturbances. Initially Cai, acquainted with Zhang's reputation in the revolutionary movement, resisted interfering with another province's politics. Nevertheless, Cai eventually agreed, at the urging of his second-in-command, Tang Jiyao, along with Guizhou native and Boqun's friend, Dai Kan. Both were constitutional monarchists and supporters of Liang Qichao. Tang, a Yunnan native, studied for the examination but decide on a military career. He went to Japan in 1902 and graduated in the sixth class from the Imperial Japanese Military Academy and joined the RA.

Tang Jiyao, 1911

He returned to Kunming in 1908 and served in new Qing army as the 1th Battalion Commander and later as Cai's adjutant. Tang and Dai both harbored ambitions to be the head of a province and saw Guizhou as that province. In early February 1912, Tang led Yunnan's Second Northern Expedition Army, including Dai Kan, to Guiyang as Liu had requested but with the pretense to relieve other revolutionary forces in Hunan but only travel to Guiyang in transit.

On February 29, 1912, Tang's force arrived in Guiyang, and they were welcomed by the SGS government. On March 2 Tang and Liu joined their forces to carry out a coup. Both Wang brothers had to remain silent even though they realized what was afoot. Dilun in particular was extremely frustrated since his troops had to take part in the disbandment, disarming, and in rare cases, killing of some of his acquaintances serving the SGS forces. Most of the SGS leaders were killed. Zhang Bailin returned to Guiyang but was powerless to counter the combined Tang and Liu forces. He and his family nearly escaped due the warning provided by the Wang brothers. Zhang fled to Shanghai and continued to work for the RA.

Tang Jiyao was appointed as the military governor for the Guizhou Province by a new government controlled by the CPA replacing the SGS members. Liu Xianshi was promoted to major general, Guizhou military affairs director, military affairs secretary, and the Guizhou New Army commander-in-chief of Guizhou's military forces. The Guizhou New Army was reconstituted to include the Xingyi Brigade at its core, under Dilun, now a captain, with Yuan Zuming, also a captain, as his assistant at the suggestion of Liu to keep an eye on his nephew, just in case Dilun might disagree with his policies and politics.

In the winter of 1912, a son was born to Dilun. His mother named him Chongxing, and a Wang family celebration was held to mark the arrival of the second male heir to join Boqun's son, Fuseng, now already four years old. Their mother remarked on how significant this was to the family.

> Your father and my dear husband would be so pleased and proud that you, Boqun and Dilun, have been blessed by our ancestors for each to bring forth a male

heir to assure the continuation of our family bloodline. Now you both respectively and cooperatively have a sacred responsibility to see that your sons are brought up to maintain harmony in the family, prosperity for the clan, and peace in the nation.

❖ ❖ ❖

After the establishment of the republic government in Nanjing, the southern provinces had subsequently declared their independence from the Qing court, but neither the northern provinces nor the Beiyang Army had a clear stance for or against the rebellion. Yuan's strategy as the prime minister was to soften up the republicans so he would be a better negotiating position with Sun Yatsen. He sent his Beiyang Army to recapture Hankow and Hanyang in November 1911. Yuan held his army to regroup in preparation for attacking Wuchang and threatening Nanjing. Yuan became the most important man in China, for he held the most favorable military position.

In early 1912, Sun Yatsen met with Yuan Shikai several times to work out an arrangement between the two sides so no more blood would be spilled. Yuan received and entertained Sun with great respect and sincerity. Sun left these meetings praising Yuan, stating that Yuan wanted the same advancements for China as Sun himself. He announced that Yuan was "beyond suspicion" and he was "a man of great ability." He concluded that to govern the republic, one had to have new ideas and experiences and old-fashioned methods and that President Yuan was "just the right man."

Yuan Shikai 1905

71

Thus, after negotiations between Yuan and Sun, and to avoid further civil war and bloodshed, Sun expressed his willingness to resign his interim presidency to Yuan Shikai should the child Emperor Puyi abdicates and Yuan Shikai would support "a republican nation under its constitution" with its capital in Nanjing. Yuan pressured the Qing court for the abdication of the Emperor on February 12, 1912. Yuan then wired to Sun on February 13 to express his support for "republican government under the constitution" and agreed to move the capital to Nanjing. Sun resigned his post to the interim parliament on the same day. On the fifteenth the parliament declared Yuan as interim president, and Li Yuanhong remained vice president. Yuan then reneged on his promise to move the capital from Beijing to Nanjing in order to preserve his power base in northern China, where the Beiyang army had control over a wide area of the provinces. The revolutionaries compromised again, and the capital of the new republic was established in Beijing. Yuan Shikai was elected as provisional president on February 14, 1912, and sworn in on March 10.

Sun and the other revolutionary leaders' expectation was that Yuan Shikai would share power with a prime minister and a parliament under the new republican constitution. Yuan stated that he supported this structure of the government. He, however, remained commander-in-chief of China's army and navy. While the army he controlled consisted of only eighty thousand men of the Beiyang army, the rest of China's armies were dispersed across China and under the control of various local leaders known as warlords. The Beiyang Army was by far better trained and equipped than any of the other provincial or regional armies, with the exception of the Yunnan Army under Cai E. On September 9, 1912, Sun Yatsen accepted the title of "plenipotentiary" for China's national railroads, with a dream of constructing a hundred thousand kilometers railroad tracks. Sun proclaimed,

> President Yuan Shikai, being a man of great talents, I
> have extraordinary hope that he should be president
> for ten years and China would boast an army of several

millions. At the same time, I would lay a hundred thousand kilometers of railroad tracks, with expected revenues of eight million yuans per year, making China strong enough to be one of the world powers.

On August 25, 1912, the RA and five smaller pro-revolution parties merged as the Guomingdang (GMD), commonly known as the Nationalists, were established in Beijing to contest the first national elections. Sun Yatsen was chosen as the party chairman with Huang Xing as his deputy. The party was organized by Soong Jiaoren, a founder of RA, skillful politician, and lifelong friend and fellow Hunan compatriot of Huang Xing. Soong had become the leader of GMD after the disagreement of Sun Yatsen and Huang Xing on how to deal with Yuan Shikai. Sun and Soong advocated that the GMD should act as a check against Yuan's presidency, while Huang Xing and others tried to enroll Yuan as a member of the GMD. Yuan responded that he would be willing to join GMD if the party would abandon its attempt at parliamentary restraints over the presidency. Huang Xing retired from politics over the dispute. Sun and Soong's main political goal was to ensure that the powers and independence of Parliament would be properly protected from the influence of the office of the president. This was a threat to Yuan Shikai, who by mid-1912 dominated over the provisional cabinet he had named and was clearly demanding absolute executive power.

Meanwhile, the idealism of students was being expressed in agitation for more changes. By the end of 1912, Yuan Shikai was expressing his misgivings with what he described as the unruliness of students. He attacked those who advocated for equality for women, free speech, and the right for assembly and demonstration. He accused them of undermining the family and therefore social order. He suppressed anarchists, whom he accused, with some justification, of preparing for social revolution. He was perplexed by the lack of revenues being collected from the provinces as he tried to bring the provinces under the authority of the central government's rules.

After the Xinhai Revolution, a series of local elections that began on December 1912 with most provinces concluded on January 1913. It was indirect, as voters chose electors who selected the delegates. The parliament was elected by the provincial assemblies. The president had to pick the sixty-four members representing Tibet, Outer Mongolia, and overseas Chinese due to practical reasons. Soong Jiaoren was only thirty years old when he was tasked by Sun Yatsen to organize the GMD for China's first democratic election campaign. Soong proved to be a naturally skilled political organizer but had an arrogant self-confidence that alienated many potential supporters. During Soong's GMD campaign through China in 1912, he had expressed the desire to limit the powers of the president in terms that were often openly critical of Yuan's ambitions. At the end of January 1913, the first comprehensive free election in China resulted in a clear plurality for the GMD with over five hundred of the eight hundred some seats, and the other went to the Republican, Unity, and Democratic Parties, later merged into the Progressive Party under Liang Qichao.

It appeared that Soong would become the prime minister and he would be in a position to exercise a dominant role in selecting the cabinet. GMD could then proceed to push for the election of a future president in a proper parliamentary setting. Boqun joined the GMD, as did most of the RA membership, and served in Beijing as a representative from Guizhou, while Dai Kan remained a member of the Progressive Party and served as a representative as well. Boqun and Dai remained close friends while they both lived in Beijing.

Song Jiaoren was assassinated in Shanghai Central Train Station on his way to Beijing on March 20, 1913. The assassin was apprehended but died in jail before any interrogation could be made. Investigations pointed to Yuan and his prime minister, but it was never proven. In April, Yuan secured a reorganization loan of 25 million pounds sterling from Great Britain, France, Russia, Germany, and Japan without first consulting parliament. The loan was used to finance Yuan's Beiyang Army. On May 20 Yuan concluded a deal with Russia for more money that granted Russia special privileges in Outer Mongolia and restricted

Chinese right to station troops there. GMD members of the parliament accused Yuan of abusing his rights and called for his removal. In July 1913 seven southern provinces rebelled against Yuan, which was known as the Second Revolution. There were several underlying reasons for the Second Revolution besides Yuan's abuse of power. First was that most revolutionary armies from different provinces were disbanded after the establishment of the Republic of China, and officers and soldiers felt they were not compensated for toppling the Qing dynasty, which created much discontent against the new government. Second, many revolutionaries felt Yuan Shikai was undeserving of the post of the presidency since he had obtained it through political maneuvering rather than participation in the revolutionary movement. Last, Yuan's role in Song's assassination dashed any hope of achieving reforms and political goals through electoral means. The Second Revolution, however, did not fare well for the GMD. Yuan's army defeated the various GMD provincial forces, and the rebellion was suppressed. On July 23, 1913, Yuan revoked Sun Yatsen's title of plenipotentiary for Chinese national railroads and declared Huang Xing and others as traitors. Sun left for Japan, where he reorganized GMD to continue anti-Yuan movements. Huang Xing left for the United States to seek financial support.

❖ ❖ ❖

In the fall of 1913, the Wang family compound was ready for move in. Boqun and Dilun had rented relatively small houses in the city, and the rest of the family was still in the family compound in Xingyi. The new compound consisted of three main buildings; the twin Western-style three-floor buildings with dome roofs on the corners of the building for each of the two brothers and a traditional Chinese structure in the middle for their mother. There was an enclosed courtyard facing the middle building with walls and a gallery. There were also large gardens for each of the twin building and a common four-car garage and servant's quarters, a horse barn, and a front entrance with a guardhouse. The entire compound sits atop a hill overlooked the city. It took over a month for the move from Xingyi. The whole family was very excited and happy about the house. Dilun was given the credit for having supervised the design and construction, which turned out to be a great success.

The Wang Family Compound, Guiyang

In October 1913 the parliament members were compromised by threats and bribes from Yuan. He confined them and forced them to elect him formally as president. The major foreign powers extended recognition to his government. President Woodrow Wilson of America was the first to recognize the Yuan Shikai's regime. In November Yuan Shikai, now legally president, ordered the GMD be dissolved and forcefully removed its members from parliament. Since the majority of the parliament members belonged to the GMD, it no longer had a quorum and was legally unable to convene. In January 1914 Yuan formally suspended the parliament, and Boqun returned to Guiyang and was appointed by Liu as the Guizhou National Army counsel and the governor's envoy-at-large.

Upon Boqun's return to Guiyang from the parliamentary debacle in Beijing, he reported to his uncle what had taken place. Liu Xianshi noted to Boqun,

> I always noted that Sun is a dreamer and lacks any experience in realpolitik. He was not suitable for the job of running China. I am glad that Yuan is now taking over, and he will be able to lead the country's progress into a world power.

Though Boqun agreed about Sun's nature of easy trust for others, he had great doubts that Yuan would be the man to lead the republic given his past history. Privately he told Dilun,

> Sun made an honest decision to avoid more military conflict and the bloodshed of a civil war. I think we have to be ever vigilant about the change of political winds from Beijing, for it will not blow for a republic as we had hoped for.

Dilun agreed,

> Yuan is just like the Manchu despots, and his trickery is well documented in history. Sun is naïve, and I believe he will learn by what comes next. I still have faith in him as the leader who can fulfill our hopes.

There was a year of occupation of Guizhou by Tang Jiyao, who drained the Guizhou treasury to fund his Yunnan Army and enrich his own pockets. Liu Xianshi, Dai Kan, and the CPA government joined forces in partitioning Cai E to recall Tang and his army back to Yunnan, reasoning that Tang had accomplished his original objective and the Guizhou government was ready to be completely independent. In September 1913 Cai E was "promoted" to serve as Yuan Shikai's staff officer and transfer to Beijing. Yuan's purpose was to keep Cai close and away from his power base in case he objected to what Yuan had in mind for the future. Yuan then appointed Tang to take his place, thinking Tang, with less political experience, would be more maneuverable, and Tang was not known to be a revolutionary as Cai. Tang immediately led his army back to Kunming and took up Cai's position of Yunnan's all-powerful governorship. Prior to Tang's departure, he recommended to Yuan to appoint Liu Xianshi as the military governor and Dai Kan as the civil governor of Guizhou respectively. Essentially, Liu and Dai were to share the executive power of Guizhou with the CPA administrative government.

An inevitable rift developed between Liu and Dai. Dai considered Liu less qualified to lead the military than him. In confidence he mentioned to Boqun that Liu, having lost so many lives due to his misjudgments and poor leadership in his previous military experiences, was thus was unfit to be the military governor, and he wondered how Boqun and Dilun felt. Boqun responded for both brothers.

> His military record may not be sterling, but the man is shrewd and has developed many close relationships within the Xingyi military, now the core of the Guizhou Army. In addition, as you know, he has a close relationship with Tang Jiyao, which is why he is where he is. As for Dilun, he would agree with what you said, but it would be foolish for him to go against Liu until he has

established himself as a tested leader of the army, and he needs Liu's backing to prove that.

Dai understood from Boqun's comments that Dilun was no position to go against his uncle given his current status and his relationship, not just uncle to nephew but now newly married into the Liu clan as well. Nevertheless, Dai continued his own campaign to strengthen his position in the military and to remove Liu's support from the remnants of the Qing administrative bureaucracy. The rift between Liu and Dai played straight into Yuan Shikai's hands since he wished to have Guizhou firmly in his control. An opportunity availed itself in late 1913 when Liu wired Yuan and stated:

> Given the accomplishments of Dai Kan in the administration of the province and the stability of current political situation, I highly recommend him for a high national position in Beijing. Besides, I would appreciate a clarification of the leadership of the military since much work remains for the new army buildup and training, as you have mandated.

Since Yuan considered Dai to be more capable than Liu and much harder to control due to his association with Liang Qichao and Cai E, he gladly promoted Dai to a staff position in Beijing so Dai could be as closely watched as Cai. Yuan then dispatched one of his trusted men to take Dai's place with the aim of ensuring Liu of his continued support for Yuan and to take charge of the civil administration of the province.

CHAPTER 5

1914-1915

DEMISE OF THE REPUBLIC

The revolution of 1912 had created a power vacuum around the country, and anyone with military support began to assert local, provincial, or regional control. By removing the emperor and the Qing court, the only understood authority of the Chinese people and the military was eliminated, with no unified central authority. Unlike the Russian revolution of 1917, there was a unified military command, which supported the revolutionary government, whereas republican China was made up of separate provinces with their own military under the local strongman or a group of them that generally was more interested in maintenance of the political and economic power than submitting to a central government. As Yuan Shikai took over power with the support the largest military at the time, the Beiyang Army, he understood that he still needed to extend his authority over the rest of the country beyond his immediate control. Far from an idealistic revolutionary like Sun Yatsen, he believed China could only be ruled by dictatorial power, as it had been over the millennia.

After becoming president in April 1912, Yuan started to reduce the national new army of a million men to half but kept his own Beiyang forces intact. This was not successful since none of the provincial governors had followed through on the reduction and some had just began to increase their army size to the new standard as prescribed by the deposed Qing government. Yuan then decided to name the current governor of each province as military governor in charge of the military only, and he added another position equal in rank as

81

the civil governor who would be responsible for the administration of the province. His idea was to move the current military governor gradually out of his influence and replace him with the civil governor, who would be appointed by Yuan. None of Yuan's efforts to control the provinces were successful. In fact one of his fiscal reforms was for the provinces to remit twenty-three million yuan to Beijing, and by the end of 1913, less than three million was received.

In February 14, 1914, Yuan convened a Constitution Revision Conference, which consisted of sixty-six members of the cabinet, other government officials, and provincial representatives for the revision of the provisional constitution of the Republic of China, and Liu Xianshi asked Boqun to represent Guizhou.

> I know you think Yuan will not accept the kind of government you believe we need, but consider that our principal objective of regaining control from the Manchu has been achieved with Yuan's help. I daresay without it we would still be shedding more blood and spending more treasures.

Boqun asked,

> What have you heard from Liang Qichao on his opinion about Yuan's intentions?

Liu replied,

> I have heard from Liang and Cai E, and they both suggested that I convince you to attend, for they believe

we must give Yuan a chance before resorting to a third revolution. Since you were part of the group that help draft the constitution, you would be the best position to do it.

Boqun said,

Of course I will serve my duty, dear uncle, and keep an open mind.

In May, after two months of fruitless debate, the result of the revised constitution was announced. Boqun voted against the revisions, which greatly expanded Yuan's powers, allowing him to declare war, sign treaties, and appoint officials without seeking approval from the parliament. In December 1914 the parliament further revised the law and lengthened the term of the president to ten years, with no term limits. Essentially Yuan was preparing for his ascendancy as the emperor, yet in making the announcement of its conclusion, he had the audacity to state it had reduced his power and increased his responsibilities.

In Yuan's mind his failure to assert his central authority was due to the elimination of the monarchy, which bound the classes in accordance with the Confucian code and conduct. Thus he had concluded, albeit with self-serving interest, that only way to resolve the disorder and lack of loyalty to his authority was to restore the monarchy. Since he was the current leader, then he believed he should take over as the emperor. This view, however ridiculous, was held by many Chinese at the time since the Confucian code was so ingrained in their minds. Additionally, Yuan's family, especially his eldest son, Kèdìng, was obsessed with succeeding his father and firmly pushed him to become the emperor.

❖ ❖ ❖

When World War I broke out in 1914, Japan fought on the Allied side and seized German holdings in Shandong Province. In January 1915 the Japanese set before the Yuan Shikai's government the so-called Twenty-One Demands, aimed at securing Japanese economic controls in railway and mining operations in Shandong, Manchuria, and Fujian. The Japanese also pressed Yuan to appoint Japanese advisors to key positions in the Chinese government. These demands would have made China effectively a Japanese protectorate. Yuan rejected some of these demands but yielded to the Japanese insistence on keeping the Shandong territory already in its possession. He also recognized Tokyo's authority over southern Manchuria and eastern Inner Mongolia. His acceptance of the demands was extremely unpopular.

Since the dissolution of the parliament in November 1913, Yuan Shikai had been moving toward a return to the monarchy. The Japanese demands hastened this movement. The arguments for the monarchy were three: First, that a monarchy, and one of militaristic tendencies, was stronger than a republic. Germany and Japan were cited as examples. Second, that at the close of the war, a republican government would be perceived as weak since there was no clear succession after Yuan and the other nations would step in and take control of China, as Japan had done in Korea before its annexation. The final reason was the Confucian code would allow for a unified governing authority.

In February 1914, Liang Chiyao, the newly appointed justice minister, was invited to dinner by Yuan Keding, along with several other close advisers of Yuan Shikai. The group discussed various aspects of republicanism versus monarchism. It became apparent to Liang that Yuan Keding had expected to be the crown prince. Liang resigned the next day and moved to the Japanese concession city of Tianjin, out of the reach of Yuan. In his resignation letter to Yuan, he quoted part of an ancient classic.

Justice, incorruptibility, duty, and a sense of shame are
the principles of an administration, without which the
government shall not survive!

❖ ❖ ❖

Soon thereafter an anti-Yuan movement was secretly established
by Liang Qichao and Cai E, joined by Boqun, Dai Kan, and others gathered in Tianjin, where Cai E brought a house away from the constant
surveillance of Yuan's spies. Cai pretended he was living a hedonistic
life for all to see with the most sought-after courtesan at time. Since
Boqun was considered the most junior of this group, he was not strictly
monitored by Yuan and was thus able to write and to travel without
drawing Yuan's concern.

Boqun returned to Guiyang in August 1914, after the disastrous
Constitution Revision Conference, which had removed the last ves-
tige of the republic and given Yuan dictatorial powers. He advised
Dilun to accelerate the training and buildup of the Guizhou Army,
saying,

There is no doubt in my mind that Yuan will abandon
all republican consideration and make himself the next
emperor, and we must prepare to go to war.

Dilun replied,

There is no way to tell which side Uncle will be taking,
but knowing him as a willow that will sway by the wind,

I am certain he will stay neutral till the last moment to be on the safe side.

Boqun said,

He'll realize the buildup is necessary whichever way he decides to join up, and I will come up with a plan to finance the buildup.

Dilun concluded,

Assuming that we have the necessary funding and Uncle's blessing for the buildup, I do believe we can train and ready a new Guizhou army of twenty thousand troops within a year. Furthermore, in such a case, I believe I will be in a better position to assert our political view into the future of Guizhou.

When the Qing government decided that each province must have a modernized army, it mandated in 1904 that each province should establish a three-year elementary military school. After Dilun arrived in Guiyang in 1912, he was given the responsibility for training. He had convinced Liu Xianshi that it was necessary to expand the elementary military school program to include a two-year middle military school, as it was already done in other provinces in the north under Yuan's control. Dilun argued,

It is imperative that Guizhou has more than the elementary school to train future officers since the military has become the backbone of our political system. Yuan Shikai foresaw this requirement and did this as a feeder for the northern provinces to the Baoding Military Academy. The status of the military has been elevated. The old adage that *soldiers are not to be made from good iron* is long gone. We should stress the intellectual as well as the physical aspects of military training. Most of the graduates from the elementary and middle military schools are from gentry families, which shows the elevation of the military in the society. The military training and subsequent career path will substitute the former examination system in providing the necessary personnel for the government. Most importantly, young people today believe that a strong military is the only deterrent to continued foreign incursions. Given your past belief and experience with education in Xingyi, I trust that you will agree and approve this program and provide the funding for its implementation.

The Middle Military School was established 1913, and Dilun served as its headmaster and recruited almost all the graduates to serve in the Guizhou Army. Dilun also reorganized the army from the tradition pyramid structure to German system of a branch structure of infantry, cavalry, artillery, engineering, and supplies under a centralized command, which was also adapted by the Japanese Army from their German trainers, as well the Beiyang Army with its Japanese trainers. Dilun undertook this reorganization such that it would apply readily to a full division as soon such expansion was approved by Liu and funded accordingly.

At Boqun's suggestion, Liu Xianshi issued two million yuan of provincial bonds to fund and train a Guizhou Army of six brigades of some twenty thousand troops armed with a complement of modern weapon, including pistols, rifles, hand grenades, machine guns, light assault guns, and armored cars. At the time, Dilun was the commander of the Guizhou Army's first and only brigade with the rank of captain. More importantly, he had the overall responsibility for army recruitment and the training program as Liu's adjutant.

Dilun brought in additional staff consisting of mostly Japanese and Yunnan trained officers, including He Yingqin and Lu Tao. The most senior was Lu Tao, a Guangxi native, Yunnan Military Academy's Special Infantry Division graduate and a member of the RA since 1909. He served as a captain and the commander of the Yunnan Seventy-Third Brigade of the Yunnan Army that invaded Guizhou and was stationed in Guiyang under Tang Jiyao. Dilun appointed him as a captain and assistant commander of Dilun's First Brigade. In late 1914 Dilun organized an Officers Training School. Lu was appointed its commandant, and he proceeded to bring additional Yunnan officers into the school as instructors, thus vastly improving the military talent pool in Guizhou under Dilun. Dilun would personally conduct seminars with the officers, and he would stress Sunzi's *Art of War*, particularly chapter 3, "The Strategy to Win." It stated the five ways to victory:

1. To foresee whether one can win or cannot win.
2. To know the different principles of combat of small versus large forces.
3. To have the full support of the troops.
4. To counter an ill-prepared enemy with a well-prepared forces.
5. To have competent commanders and not to interfere with their decisions.

In addition, chapter 4, "Military Strength," indicated the wise in ancient warfare first ensured their own invulnerability and then sought the opportunity to defeat the enemy. Dilun always emphasized that to increase the probability of winning, one must first assure one's own defenses against being defeated, especially against a larger enemy forces, as in case of any revolution. Sunzi further stated in chapter 5, "Momentum," "Training, planning, knowledge of the enemy, the terrain, and surprise are the elements of victory against numerical superior forces." Thus the training of Dilun's army centered on many stimulation exercises, discipline drills, and procedures to win over the civilians' support in addition to the usual military practices.

Liu had given Dilun most of the power and responsibility of running the army even though Dilun had only been the commander of one out of now six brigades. Liu made sure Yuan Zuming was to be the commander of the Second Brigade under Dilun. Liu made sure Yuan understood his role, saying,

> As you know I have the utmost confidence in my nephew to achieve our objective for the army, and I am counting on you to devote yourself in helping him. It is prudent, however, that I have realistic feedback about his thinking so that I can do my best to support him. Thus, I need to hear from you independently and discreetly when it becomes necessary. Is it understood?

❖ ❖ ❖

Since the dissolution of parliament in 1914, the Chinese republic had been one in name only. The monarchical movement moved quickly to gain momentum under Yuan. Nevertheless, most of the people of the Yangtze Valley, the south, and the southwest seemed strongly against the monarchy. By June of 1915, it had become increasing apparent that a monarchy was all but a foregone conclusion. Yuan restored the peerage that existed under the Qing and began to award the generals and governors to ensure their allegiances. He granted most of his Beiyang generals noble ranks. Feng Guozhang and Duan Qirui both were granted the peerage of duke of the first rank. Both refused the rank. Duan had served as minister of war and premier since 1912 but was against the monarchy since he hoped to succeed Yuan as the president. Using the proverbial excuse of illness, Duan left the government in June of 1915 but remained in firm control of a large portion of the Beiyang Army. Feng was stationed at Nanjing after winning the second revolution. He also still controlled the Hubei Army, which was about the same size as the troops controlled by Duan. Liang Qichao persuaded Feng that monarchy was the wrong path. He initially did not believe Yuan would actually take such a step, and he asked Liang to join him on a visit to seek Yuan's clarification regarding his intention. Yuan assured them both that the rumors were groundless. He said,

> As president I already have all the power of an emperor. Thus the only reason for me to be the emperor would be succession. My eldest, Keding, has a chronic illness. The second, Kewen, wishes to lead an ascetic life, and the third is not suited for any serious duty. The rest are just too young. I would not make them clerks, let alone take on the stately responsibilities of an emperor. Besides, since time immemorial, royal offspring have been enthroned only to face disasters. and why would I want to impose such on them?

About this time, an American scholar and a constitution law professor at Columbia University, Dr. F. Goodnow, became a political adviser to the government. He wrote a paper in favor of a Chinese monarchy, as long as such is the choice of the people, a line of succession clearly defined by law and not by the emperor, and a government under a constitution approved by proper representation of the people. Goodnow's paper was published in China and abroad, which provided substantial legitimacy to the monarchy movement. The monarchy movement then published its own manifesto, citing Goodnow's conclusion as proof positive for a monarchy with Yuan as the emperor. Liang Qichao then wrote a rebuttal and published it in spite of a bribe of two hundred thousand yuan from Yuan Shikai for not to do so. Nevertheless, the monarchy movement continued to gather momentum through the fall of 1915. All of a sudden, people are showed up from all over China to Beijing, and messages wired by many military leaders, including Tang Chiyao of Yunnan, urged the government to implement the monarchy.

On August 30, 1915, the first secret telegram was dispatched from Beijing concerning the proposed change of government. It was a code telegram to the military and civil governors of the provinces, to be deciphered personally by them with the state council code. After certain initial steps were mentioned in detail, the document stated:

> The plan suggested is for each province to send in a separate petition for the change of government, the draft of which will be made in Beijing and wired to the respective provinces in due course...You will insert your own name as well as those of the gentry and merchants of the province who agree to the draft. These petitions are

to be presented one by one to the legislative council as soon as it is received. It is your responsibility to ensure the change in the form of the state is according to the will of the people.

The Monarchical Society, as the campaigner for Yuan, on September 27 dispatched a code telegram to the military and civil governors, asserting that all opposition to the monarchy movement be eradicated. The telegram concluded:

> In order to cloak the proceedings with an appearance of regularity, the representatives of the districts, though they are really appointed by the highest military and civil officials of the province, should still be nominally elected by the people of each district. As soon as the representatives of the districts have been appointed, their names should be communicated to the respective district magistrates, who are to be instructed to draw up the necessary documents in detail and to cause a formal election to be held. Such documents should, however, be properly antedated.

The final telegram was most telling, and it invoked Yuan Shikai's own hand.

> Please personally take charge to destroy all previous communications on this matter, for they should never be included in the permanent records. This is to avoid any future criticism by any opposition to

cause chaos and discord for the new dynasty at its infancy.

On October 28, 1915, a notice to Yuan was put forth by the representatives of Japan, England, and Russia, later supported by France and Italy as allies, toward the inadvisability of taking steps that would threaten the peace of China. The Yuan government replied that it was too late to retract, as the matter had already been decided by the Chinese people. Yuan sent the following state telegram to the provinces, which stated in essence:

A certain foreign power (Japan), under the pretext that the Chinese people are not of one mind in support of the monarchy, has lately persuaded England and Russia to take part in tendering advice to China. In truth, all foreign nations know perfectly well that there will be no trouble, and they are not obliged to follow the example of that power. If we accept the advice of other powers concerning our domestic affairs and postpone the enthronement, we shall then recognize their right to interfere. Hence, action should under no circumstances be deferred. When all the votes of the provinces unanimously recommending the enthronement shall have reached Peking, the government will, of course, ostensibly assume a wavering and compromising attitude, so as to give due regard to international relations. The people, on the other hand, should show their firm determination to proceed with the matter at all costs, to let the foreign powers know our people are of one mind. If we can only make them believe that the change of the republic into a monarchy will not in the least give rise to

trouble of any kind, the effects of the advice tendered
by Japan will have come to naught.

The so-called National Congress of Representatives was convened and
unanimously voted to adapt a monarchy as the governing system, with
Yuan to be crowned as the emperor. Some changes were made from the
Qing court practices, such as replacing the eunuchs with women selected
by criteria established by the emperor himself. The lavish budget for the
coronation totaled a whopping 30 million yuan on top of 1916's estimated
deficit of almost 90 million. This would be passed on to the Chinese people
as additional taxation to pay for bonds issued for the occasion.

The European powers were engaged in the aftermath of the First
World War, and they had no time to deal with this change of government in China; they stayed neutral and waited for the situation to play
out. Japan, however, only nominally engaged in the war and were successful in their negotiation with Yuan over their twenty-one demands.
Japan was content to wait it out the war. After the new administration
took over in late 1915, Japan became concerned about continued opposition and unrest in China that would affect the investments Japan had
made in the last five years. It then asked Britain, Russia, and the United
States to join its position of non-recognition. Although no action was
taken further, Japan began to encourage the opposition by providing
safe haven for its leaders, such as Sun Yatsen, and selling arms to them.

Finally, Liang Qichao and Cai E switched their position of supporting Yuan Shikai because of Yuan's sabotage of the national parliament and reverting back to the monarchy. Many provincial governors
who had declared their independence from the Qing court in 1912
found the idea of supporting another imperial court utterly ridiculous. Yuan also alienated some of his Beiyang generals by central-
izing tax collection from local authorities. In addition, public opinion
was overwhelmingly anti-Yuan. Liang Qichao was completely disillusioned about Yuan's intent to serve the republic, and he said to
Boqun and others,

My dear friends, I must apologize to you all for believing that my humble influence and sincere trust in Yuan will prevail in spite all the evidences to the contrary. I must ask you now to join me in resisting further erosion of the reforms for which so many of us have toiled for so long. We must be united against China being brought back to its colonized past!

It was agreed that an opposition to Yuan must be carefully organized since he had become all powerful, especially in the provinces the Beiyang Army controlled, which had become more expansive since Yuan had taken over the position of the president of the republic. Liang urged,

We must remain in our posts and show no opposition until we are ready to face down the Beiyang Army. Yuan is extremely cunning and skilled in the art of divide and conquer! Beware of all the titles and gifts for you will receive for abandoning of our cause.

Boqun remained in Beijing, along many other parliamentarians, and tried to recruit and to organize an anti-Yuan movement. He secretly wired Dilun:

I am now one of increasing number of our friends and compatriots who are now convinced that Yuan is no better than the Manchu! No doubt he has served them so long to believe the mandate of heaven is now passed to him. I just hope that we are able to prevent him from selling China out to the foreign powers in order to become the emperor. Dear brother, I do believe a war will be upon us, and now the enemy is the Beiyang Army, and it is a formidable opponent. You must do your utmost in getting your forces ready for upcoming battle with the Beiyang Army. Also we must be prepared to convince Uncle to come to our side in this crucial moment.

As these activities were being monitored by the anti-monarchical groups around the country, and most were now primed for action. On November 17, 1915, Liang Qichao and Cai E, now out of Yuan's reach in the Japanese concession of Tianjin, sent for seven confidants, including Boqun and Dai Kan, to meet there for a coordinated opposition plan. Cai was particularly interested in the position of Guizhou of joining Yunnan as the initiating group of province in the now named National Protection Movement and wanted to know the opinions of both Boqun and Dai Kan, who were Guizhou natives.

Dai said, "Frankly, I am doubtful that we can depend on Liu Xianshi since he is known to wait in any political situation such as this until the outcome is clarified. He will not take a chance with the overwhelming advantage of the Beiyang Army as shown."

Boqun said, "Although Brother Dai is right about Liu, I have spoken with Dilun, who assured me that the staffing and the training of the Guizhou Army has been completed, and he has a firm grip on the officers. Dilun is confident he can convince Liu Xianshi to join the movement."

Cai said, "I really hope you are right, for we need to have Guizhou to be in unison with Yunnan to bring in Guangxi and Guangdong so we will have the necessary critical mass for the movement to gain quick momentum. Thus, my young Boqun, unless you and your brother can bring Liu and Guizhou abroad within a month of Yunnan's declaration against Yuan, we will not succeed."

Boqun said, "Please be rest assured that Guizhou will join Yunnan in time as planned, for I have complete confidence in Dilun to accomplish what he has told me, and we will in turn convince Liu Xianshi to join the movement."

Later there was a discussion between the two old friends, Dai Kan and Boqun, about the motivation for Yuan's wish to become the emperor. Dai believed he was a self-serving egotist who wanted to establish a family dynasty. Boqun felt it was more complicated. Boqun said,

Boqun 1915

Yuan has consistently been a monarchist since he got involved in the reform movement in 1898. The 1912 military uprising had insufficient time to give rise for a social and political revolution among the people. Yuan was the only one who had enough credibility to assume the presidency, yet he found himself to be hamstrung by the constitution and the parliament. Even after he revised the constitution and closed the parliament, he still felt insecure from the GMD and the provincial military leaders as well as the foreign powers. In his mind, royalty to an emperor was more basic to the Chinese mind-set than royalty to a president, who is just a man. He hopes that by making himself the emperor, stability will replace chaos, centralization will diminish regionalism, and finally a unified China will decrease foreign influences.

In November 1915, Yuan Shikai declared himself the Hongxian (Grand Constitution) Emperor of the Empire of China. In anticipation of the opposition from the provinces, including Guizhou, where the

97

Beiyang Army had no control, Yuan consulted with Long Jianzhang, who was his man in Guiyang, to assess Liu Xianshi's intent.

In a meeting with Liu, Long said,

> Yuan needs your support to shore up his control over the southern provinces. We have seen how his Beiyang Army is the strongest in the country and how the second revolution was crashed. Besides, you always believed China is not ready for a republic. All your CPA friends here in Guiyang welcome this development.

Liu replied,

> Guizhou is a poor province, and what we need the most is funding for economic development. Yuan will have my support if we can depend upon Beijing to provide such funding, which is of critical importance to the well-being of this province and its leaders.

On December 21 Yuan awarded peerage to various heads of provinces. Liu Xianshi was granted the rank of viscount of the first degree and his cousin, Liu Xianqian, the rank of baron of the first degree. Others in the military, including Dilun, were promoted in rank and of course received various pay raises, land grants, and cash rewards. In addition, Beijing promised also to reimburse the 20 million yuan bond issued for the funding of the military training and equipment. Yuan had purposely withheld the funds until Liu's position on the pending monarchy had been clarified.

The Tianjin meeting concluded with Cai responsible for Yunnan, Liang for Guangxi, and Boqun for Guizhou for the initiation of the opposition movement. The schedule was for Yunnan to declare independence in late December and Guizhou would follow in late January and Guangxi in February. Liang Qichao drafted the various declarations of secession and independence. The one for Yunnan and Guizhou were given to Boqun to take to Kunming for the various parties' signatures and release at the agreed to dates. Boqun was sent to inform the leadership of Yunnan and Guizhou of the schedule and plan of the National Protection Movement. He arrived at Kunming, met with Tang Jiyao and the others on December 15, 1915, and reported the result of Tianjin meeting. Tang then briefed all the military and civilian officials who were supporting the movement, including those from Guangxi and Guizhou. Cai, with the help of his famous courtesan and Japanese counsel in Tianjin, was able to leave Tianjin without detection. He arrived in Kunming on the nineteenth and conducted a conference of representatives of each southern province. Boqun and Dai Kan participated in the conference that ended in a signature-by-blood oath ceremony to launch the movement.

On December 23, 1915, Cai sent Yuan an wire demanding the absolution of the empire and the execution of thirteen monarchist leaders. Cai gave Yuan twenty-four hours to respond, and Yuan choose to ignore the wire. Instead he wired Tang to confirm that Cai's wire was authentic and reminded him of his earlier support via telegram on December 13. Tang showed the wire to the others and ignored Yuan's inquiry. Since this had failed in dividing the opposition, Yuan decided that only military

Dai, Cai (center), 1916

99

response would be appropriate. Two days later Yunnan declared independence and in its declaration drafted by Liang signed by chairman of the military council of the movement, Tang Chiyao, and commanders of the First and Second Armies, Cai E and Li Liehchun, military governor of Guangxi, which stated in part:

> Since Yuan Shikai has betrayed the republic, he thereby lost all his claims to be the head of state. We hereby declared independence to pursue a noble course of protecting the constitution of the Republic of China at any costs and to eliminate the traitor. We wish then to reconvene the national assembly for the election of a new president; to rescind all laws that have not been approved by the national assembly; to establish the principles of a democratic government for both local and national unification under the con-stitution of the republic; and to reconstitute China as a federation of provinces with its governors elected by its citizens.

❖ ❖ ❖

Meanwhile, back in Guiyang considerable debate was underway between the CPA members of the provincial assembly as well as Liu Xianshi's cabinet of old friends and the military, led by Dilun and including his new officers and instructors recruited from Yunnan. The Guizhou Army had now completed recruitment and training of the six brigades, as planned; it became a powerful force in the politics of the province. Liu Xianshi ordered Liu Xianqian as the southwest regional commander to lead his now-enlarged brigade of five thousand troops to seal the border to Yunnan and Guangxi, thus assuring Yuan Shikai that he would not support the National Protection Movement and hoping he would receive the funds Yuan had promised.

Boqun arrived late night on January 10, 1916, to meet with Dilun before reporting to Liu Xianshi the next morning. After learning about Liu's reluctance to join the movement, Boqun outlined what was discussed and agreed to meet in Kunming.

> Cai and Dai both anticipated that Uncle would be hesitant, and we agreed on the following tactic, which we hope you will agree to as well. We hope Cai will have some initial success in Sichuan by the time Dai leads his troops into Guizhou for Sichuan. He will have a full Yunnan regiment of three brigades and a support battalion, which is far superior to Liu Xianqian's force at the borders. I will brief Uncle of this, and I believe he will be convinced that he cannot win against Dai's contingent. As you know, the fourth and fifth brigades of Guizhou Army will join Dai's forces for the Sichuan campaign, and you will lead the remaining three brigades into west Hunan but under the direction of Cai. Dai's forces will be at the border when I meet with Uncle tomorrow, and you should bring some of your key officers to show how strong they feel about the movement. I trust that this will convince Uncle to get off his fence.

The next morning after a breakfast meeting with Boqun, Liu called a meeting with his cabinet of his key advisers and the military officers, led by

Dilun. There was over an hour of discussion, mostly among the CPA members favoring the status quo, even after Boqun had read them the wires and letters of Liang Qichao sponsoring the movement, which should have ended the conversation since Liang was the founder of National CPA.

One of the young brigade commanders, Wu Chuan, finally stood up and stated,

> General Wang had called all officers of the army yesterday from all areas to meet in Guiyang, and they would have already met with their men in the previous day regarding the current events in Beijing. I feel that it is now my duty to share with this group what is the conclusion from all of our meetings in the field with the troops. We feel this is a great opportunity for us to serve the province and the nation. We would rather die on the battlefield than live in peace and shame with this traitor's monarchy.

Dilun noticed that Liu continued to vacillate, which was true to the man's nature, and he said,

> Please allow me to offer a solution. You should wire Yuan and advise him that you have sent me and the Guizhou Army to Yunnan to counter the movement. After I have departed with the troops toward Hunan against the Beiyang Army, you then shall wire Yuan again and advise him that I have mutinied against your order. If our movement is successful, you will take the credit, and if it fails the Wang family shall suffer the

consequences for generations to come and the Liu family will be blameless.

Liu was stunned, and before he had a chance to comment, Dilun took his Mouser pistol out of its holster and placed it on the table in front of him, and continued.

Yuan has now made himself emperor against his own vow to support the republic. This crime against the nation cannot be tolerated by any citizen. Yunnan has already taken the lead to protect our motherland with their troops. Those who decided not to follow are Yuan's lap dogs and shall be treated with this—*pointing to his pistol*—as their just reward!

The meeting ended without a definitive conclusion, but Liu gathered his two nephews and his cousin, Xianqian, for a private meeting for dinner that evening. Liu stated,

I generally agree with what you said, Dilun, and Cai's initial victory in Sichuan has also given me heart. I do believe that the right cause can win against all odds. We need, however, the funds Yuan has promised, and we must do all we can to secure it before we declare independence. I am placing my trust in you two nephews that we are taking the best course for the nation and the province. Please be patient, and I do trust that the funds will be here before Dai needs to cross the border.

The Wang brothers, upon hearing their uncle, both kowtowed before him and begged his forgiveness for having doubted him and behaving not in accordance with the filial duty they held toward him. Later when they recounted the day with their mother, she praised her sons' comportment but warned them to be vigilant for "smiling tiger will always have his hidden agenda."

Yuan Shikai did send the funds to Liu on January 26, and Guizhou declared its independence on the next day. Liu Xianshi as the military governor wired all provinces with its declaration that in part stated:

> Speaking for the citizens and soldiers, we declare independence from the Yuan Shikai government of Beijing, which used forgery and lies to the people to justify his own treason. We will join with our brothers from Yunnan and the other provinces to do battle for the protection of the nation and the restoration of the republic.

CHAPTER 6

1916-1918

NATIONAL PROTECTION WAR AND THE WARLORD ERA

Duan Qirui, 1915

As 1916 began, Yuan Shikai had lost the support of some of his key Beiyang generals, such as Duan Qirui and Feng Guozhang, who had been his closest allies. Both used ill health as reason for not being involved in any state matters in 1915 when they realized Yuan was planning to become the emperor. Duan was a graduate of the Baoding Military Academy at the top of his class and then studied military science in Germany for two years. After returning to China, he was able to gain the sponsorship of Yuan Shikai. He had military successes in the Boxer Rebellion, and in 1911 Duan commanded the Second Beiyang Army Corps against the Sun Yatsen's revolutionary army in the Battle of Yangxia and succeeded in taking back Hankow and Hanyang. After Yuan Shikai forced Emperor Puyi to abdicate, Duan was made military governor of both Hunan and Hubei Provinces and named to Yuan's cabinet as minister of war in 1912 and then premier in 1913.

Feng was also a Baoding graduate and longtime associate of Yuan. In October 1911, after the outbreak of the Wuchang Uprising, he was ordered by the Qing court to lead his Beiyang Army First

Corps to suppress the revolution in Wuhan. Feng held back until Yuan Shikai was restored to power and then joined with Duan in the suc-cessful Battle of Yangxia. When Yuan attempted to make himself the emperor, Feng broke with him and rejected the peer-age of first class duke. Feng was tipped off to a subsequent assassination attempt. He then moved out harm's way to Nanjing and joined the anti-Yuan opposition.

Feng Guozhang, 1915

Upon hearing the independence decla-ration of Yunnan, Guizhou, and Hunan, Yuan Shikai decided that he must quell the rebel-lion with overwhelming force before it spread to the other prov-inces. He organized an expedition force of the Beiyang Army of almost a hundred thousand men into three columns: the center of thirty thousand under Ma Jizeng to attack Guizhou from Hunan; the north of fifty thousand under Chang Chingyao to attack Yunnan through Sichuan; and the south of fifteen thousand under Long Kunlie to attack from Guangxi. These were battle-hardened, fresh troops under the overall command of Cao Kun, one of Yuan's most trusted Beiyang generals. Additionally, there were the local pro-vincial armies that Yuan was not certain of either their allegiance or fighting capabilities.

The National Protection Army consisted of three armies under the overall command of Tang Jiyao; the first was commanded by Cai E, the second by Li Liehchun, and the third by Tang Jiyao now the military governor of Yunnan. The plan drawn up by Cai E, who had himself led the first army, consisted of three Yunnan regiments, which had the responsibility to face Yuan's forces being deployed in Sichuan and Hunan. The second was under Li for Guangxi, Guangdong, Jiangxi, and Fujian Provinces. The First Army was then organized into three columns. The left, led by Cai himself, consisted of three Yunnan regi-ments of about fifteen thousand troops, which moved directly from

Kunming to capture Luzhou, a key city in southern Sichuan. The center was led by Dai Kan with a Yunnan regiment and was to go from Kunming through Guiyang, where they were to join with the Guizhou Army's Fifth and Sixth Brigades for a total of about five thousand men moving into eastern Sichuan with the objective of Chongqing. The right, led by Dilun with the First, Second, and Third Brigades of the Guizhou Army of three thousand men, was to go into western Hunan and then encircle Chongqing and meet up with Dai.

The interesting aspect of the organization did not escape the Wang brothers. Dilun questioned why Cai was not assuming the overall command instead of Tang, with his superior experience and political connections. Knowing that Dilun did not know Cai as well as himself, Boqun explained.

> You are right about Cai, but he is not a Yunnan native, and Tang is part of a powerful Yunnan clan. The Yunnan army is the backbone of the National Protection Movement, and the officers are mostly from Yunnan and closely associated with Tang. By deferring to Tang, Cai is setting an example to all that he is willing to stake his life on winning the battle himself and he trusts Tang to cover his back. He is the best general of this movement, with more experience than anybody else. He has a better chance to win against a numerically superior enemy. He knows all the top commanders in the Beiyang army and in the local Sichuan armies. Most importantly, Cai is a true patriot and has no ambition for power and glory. He wishes to do whatever he can for China to become a republic and a world power. In many ways he and Sun Yatsen are very similar, and I respect and honor them both for who they are and feel privileged to have worked with them.

On January 3, 1916, Cai E led his force into Sichuan with only about two months of supplies. The opposing local Sichuan Army consisted of two divisions and a mixed brigade under the command of Chen Huan, who had been a friend and classmate of Cai in Japan. Yuan had decided to send both Chang Chingyao and Cao Kun with three Beiyang divisions to shore up the local forces. The joint operation of the Beiyang and Sichuan forces would receive orders directly from Yuan in Beijing. Cao was stationed at Chongqing and Chen at Chengdu, which caused great confusion and morale issues. Taking advantage of such disorganization, Cai was able to make steady progress after entering the Sichuan border by mid-January. He captured and held a key city, Shufu, by January 31. Cai then secretly approached several officers in both the Sichuan and Beiyang armies who were his schoolmates or students or had served under his command for them to defect to his camp. He was successful and thus able to reinforce his forces with an entire regiment of the Sichuan Army and proceeded to capture the major city of Luzhou by February 6.

On January 28, 1916, Dai Kan led his troops across the border north of Xingyi, where he avoided any possible confrontation with Liu Xianqian and proceeded to Guiyang. He met Liu Xianshi briefly to thank him for his support and then had dinner with the Wang brothers and stayed overnight with them. Even though Dai continued to be a member of the Progressive Party led by Liang Qichao and Boqun had joined the now-outlawed GMD, they remained good friends. Dilun had great respect for Dai for his contribution as Guizhou's civil governor and because he was doing his best in battle for the movement. Neither man had any actual combat experience, but both were confident they would do well in the upcoming battle. Boqun expressed his regret for not joining them in combat. He told Dilun there was a lot he could learn from Dai, as he had through their association. Dai then expressed his appreciation for what Boqun had accomplished in his work in Shanghai, Beijing, and Tianjin, and he felt better about Liu Xianshi's managing the support activities in Guiyang with Boqun by his side. The next day Dai gathered up the Fifth and Sixth Brigades of the Guizhou Army and headed for Sichuan.

In January 1916, the Guizhou Army consisted of six brigades and a police battalion. Out of the six brigades, Dilun had direct control over five, and the sixth was under the command of Liu Xianshi's cousin, Liu Xianqian stationed at Xingyi. In the winter 1915, Dilun had been planning an expedition into either Sichuan or Hunan to counter the joint forces of the local armies loyal to Yuan Shikai and the Beiyang Army itself. He also anticipated that his army would face an enemy force up to ten times in numbers and almost unlimited supplies.

In accordance with Sun Zhu's principles, Dilun concluded that in spite its size, the enemy had several weaknesses he could exploit, as he expressed to his staff.

First, the enemy is made of two different forces under separate commands with different interests. The Beiyang Army is an expeditionary force with little knowledge of the terrain and the culture of the people. Their objective is to serve Yuan the emperor, trying to expand his kingdom, and the reward is mostly monetary. Whereas the local army's main concern is to protect their property and families. We must contact the local gentries and army officers on several routes of approach in both neighboring provinces to assess the extent of their loyalty to Yuan, whether they have doubts, or if they can be persuaded to join the movement. We will then select the attack routes according to the degree of potential cooperation.

Second, the Beiyang army will have to travel almost three times our distance to reach the possible contested region in both Sichuan and Hunan, and they are weighted down by heavy load of supplies. Thus we have the advantage of time. We have acquired horses of different types for transport and the lightest carriages to enable more capacity. I calculated that our troops and equipment can move at a speed advantage of twenty five percent over the enemy.

Finally, our enemy is arrogant and overconfident since they triumphed over the Sun Yatsen's revolution forces in 1912; whereas the Guizhou Army is untested and considered the weakest among all the National Protection armies since until a year ago it did not even exist. Also as in previous wars, the Beiyang generals deployed their troops to areas where the locals are malleable so they can relax and rest before engaging in battle. We can anticipate where they will be and possibly set up ambushes with local help.

Dilun first shared his route and terrain-planning information with Dai Kan for his route to Sichuan. He then selected the towns and routes in the Hunan border area where he would meet the enemy. He planned to avoid areas where the local army was strong and pro-Yuan and send his troops into those areas where the locals were friendly or could be brought off so he could position his forces in ambush for the Beiyang Army. Dilun configured and scheduled his force to arrive days before the arrival of the Beiyang army to rest and to pacify the local gentry and populace and move them out of harm's way. He then planned his attacks in several areas where he knew the terrain well enough to position his troops or artillery in favorable positions to surprise the enemy.

On February 3, 1916, Dilun's army faced the advanced group of the Beiyang army, led by Ma Jizeng, of some ten thousand men three times of Dilun's troops. Dilun had instructed each brigade commander to give food and money to the villagers around the battleground and recruit them to help in the ambush of the northern invaders. With the villagers' cooperation and the bravery of his men, Dilun won a resounding victory in his first battle on February 10.

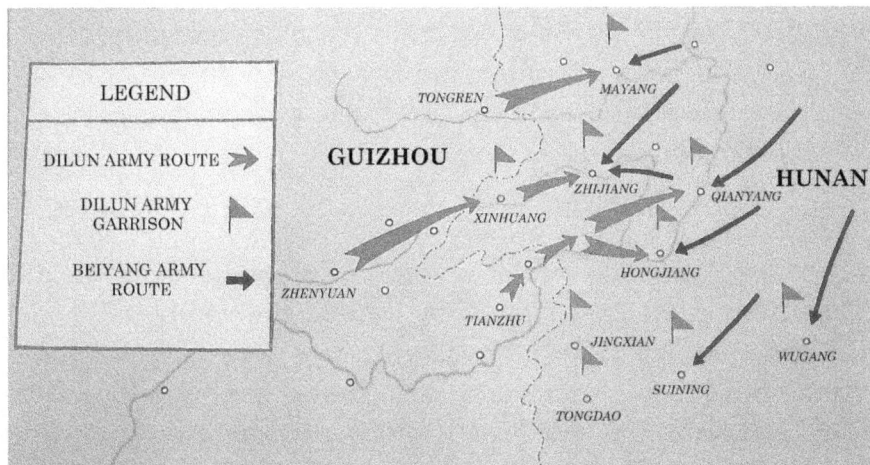

Dilun's Army's Routes and Garrisons

In the next three days, the enemy was defeated and Dilun took Songkan, a key city in Hunan. The victory was costly to the Guizhou Army, with hundreds of deaths plus others wounded, including one of the forward brigade's commanders, a close friend of Dilun's and the man who bravely spoke up for the movement during the Guiyang meeting with Liu Xianshi. By the sixteenth, Dilun had arrived and taken Mayang and Qianyang in western Hunan as the Beiyang army had retreated and it commander, Ma Jizeng, committed suicide by poison in fear of retribution by Yuan Shikai. Dilun gathered the troops and awarded medals and money to those who had shown exceptional bravery and then expressed his feeling to the troops.

> My dear and brave brothers, I could not be any prouder than I am at this moment of what you have accomplished against such overwhelming odds. Heaven blessed us to live and to win for the republic. You and I are fighting for our families, our clans, our province, and our nation. We must and will prevail, for our clause is right and just! Brothers, the battle is not over. We must continue to move forward until the traitor is dead and the republic is restored. I know you are with me and will do your very best to finish the job!

National Protection armies under Li, Cai, and Dai all had been equally successful. Cai's First Army battled the combined Sichuan and Beijing Armies of fifty thousand over a wide area and rapidly captured substantial towns and forced the enemy into a broad retreat. Dai Kan, with a similar strategy and the intelligence provided by Dilun, led his army steadily advanced toward Chongqing and gathered up additional defectors from the Sichuan army as well along the way. Li's Second Army had equal success on defending the Yunnan and Guangxi border. Cai announced by wire to all in the movement:

> Rare indeed to win,
> So few against so many.
> Thousands li at lightning speed,

Key city captures are at hand.
Defeat the enemy at his heart,
Enable courage and motivate bravery.
Opposition demoralized,
Success for the nation!

As the Beiyang Army retreated across the southwest and National Protection armies held the territories they had gained, momentum had turned in their favor. Even the ardent 1898 reform monarchist leader, Kang Youwei, sent Yuan these words:

You are a usurper of Manchu imperial dynasty who had caused His Majesty's death. You are traitor to the republic, to whom you have pledged your loyalty. Heaven's wrath and the people's discontent are omens to a disastrous end to your present folly. At the least, you should do the right thing and withdraw now from public life.

On March 22, 1916, Yuan Shikai was ill and finally realized he had overplayed his hand, particularly when the British ambassador notified him that all the foreign powers were against the monarchy given the widespread opposition and instability now existed in the country. Yuan then, as the president of the republic, declared the abolition of his Hongxian Empire, which lasted just eighty-three days. In his declaration, Yuan stated that he merely followed the people's will for the birth and the demise of the empire. He painted himself as a victim of circumstances and blamed himself for the present turmoil. Yuan emphasized it was his sacred duty as president to preserve peace and keep order in the nation. He hoped this action coupled with offering public offices to the opposition would allow him to stay as president. Although Yuan's declaration itself did not secure his position of president, it did allow many Yuan's supporters to shift their position to the republicans and thus begin a discussion on the future of Yuan and the successor government.

By April 1916, Liang Qichao and Cai E won out on ousting Yuan from the government. They convinced most of the military governors previously loyal to Yuan, such as Chen Huan of Sichuan, along with those in Hunan, Guangxi, and Guangdong, to join the movement. The final blow to Yuan was a letter asking him to step down from five of his most royal and powerful Beiyang generals, including Duan Qirui and Feng Guozhang. Yuan brought Duan back as premier on April 24, 1916, to run the government and thus stripped himself of all power as sign of his sincere wish to establish a true republic government; but by now even the provinces not part of the National Protection Movement were calling for his resignation. The issue of what to do with Yuan Shikai became moot when he died. Yuan had suffered from uremia and nervous exhaustion for some time, and he died a painful death on June 6, 1916. Yuan was given a state funeral and buried in his native Anyang, an ancient capital city of Henan Province.

When Yuan died, the Beiyang generals led by Duan and Feng pressed Vice President Li Yuanhong back into office as president. Duan himself was acceptable as premier by the southern provinces since he had opposed Yuan becoming the emperor. Feng Guozhang became vice president as part of the deal made by Duan with the Beiyang generals to secure his own position. On July 14, 1916, Tang Jiyao ordered a ceasefire for the National Protection Army and rescinded the declaration of independence. Dilun's return to Guiyang on July 30, 1916, with his men was met with a resounding welcome as heroes. President Li appointed Liu Xianshi as the military governor of Guizhou with the rank of lieutenant general. The provincial government under a CPA-controlled provincial assembly remained unchanged.

Liu then promoted Dilun as the commander of the Guizhou Army with the rank of brigadier general, and his officers received promotions and monetary rewards. After the celebration, Boqun congratulated Dilun but urged him to continue his vigilance, saying,

> Mother and I have both heard about complaints from the Liu family, particularly Liu Xianqian, that Uncle Xianshi has given you too much power and he is too tolerant of your political views. You must continue you role as the filial nephew, especially in public. You need time to consolidate your military support as well to gain further political acceptance. We must defer to Uncle Xianshi's overall authority for Guizhou. Any perception of disloyalty will bring disaster to our family and our clan.

Dilun grudgingly expressed his agreement. In fact, Liu Xianshi did make sure his cousin, Liu Xianqian, was appointed the commander of southwest border army and the rank of major general equal to his own but higher than Dilun's rank of brigadier. Liu's troops were not under the control of Dilun, even though in public and in private, Liu Xianshi showed the utmost respect and confidence of his nephew and vice versa. Despite their respective efforts to show unity, the gap between Liu and Wang families was noticeable in public.

❖ ❖ ❖

After Yuan Shikai's death, Sun Yatsen returned from Tokyo to his home in the French concession of Shanghai and began work on the reorganization of the GMD and a plan to restart his vision of the republic government for a unified China. He wrote two of the three treatises later incorporated into his *Principles of National Reconstruction*. The first part, *Social Reconstruction*, was completed in February 1917, and Sun had attributed the failure of democracy in China to its people's lack of knowledge and practice in implementation. The second, *Psychological Reconstruction*, argued that popular acceptance of his program had been obstructed by acceptance of the old adage, *"Knowledge is easy, action is difficult."* Sun proposed the transposition of this to read, *"Knowledge is difficult, action is easy."* Once the knowledge had been made available and understood, the people should have no difficulty putting it into practice. The third part, *Material Reconstruction*, constituted a master plan for the industrialization of China, which needed to be financed by investments from abroad since domestically little resources were available.

After the National Protection Movement, President Li Yuanhong appointed Cai E as governor-general and military governor of Sichuan and Dai Kan as the civil governor of Guizhou in July 1916, along with Liu Xianshi as the military governor. Cai E was already ill when the National Protection Movement started, and he left for Japan for medical treatment in September 1916. In August, Dai Kan had to take over from Cai as the provisionary civil governor of Sichuan stationed in Chongqing where his Guizhou Army was stationed. Luo Tijin, Cai's chief of staff, the acting commander of the Yunnan army, was appointed at the same time as the provisional military governor at Chengdu, where the Yunnan army was stationed.

Cai E died in Tokyo on November 8, 1916, at age thirty-three from throat cancer shortly after his arrival for medical treatment. He was buried in his native Changsha, Hunan, where the Yuelu Mountain meets the Xiang River. Cai was a true republican patriot and military hero. It was fortuitous for him to live through the success of the movement he started under very difficult circumstances. He had become a national hero in republican Chinese history for what he accomplished. When Boqun heard the news, he wept and recited a famous poem of Ming poet Su Dongpo repeatedly, knowing it was one of Cai's favorites as well.

> Deep at the bottom of the well no warmth has yet returned,
> The rain which sighs and feels so cold has dampened withered roots.
> What sort of man at such a time would come to visit the teacher?
> As this is not a time for flowers, I find I've come alone.

❖ ❖ ❖

In April 1917, Duan Qirui called a meeting in Beijing for all provincial military governors. Liu Xianshi decided not to attend but to send his younger brother, Liu Xianzhi, as political representative, who also was already in Beijing, and Dilun as the military representative. Liu Xianzhi was well known as a student of Liang Chiyao, with a lot of connections in the Beijing government, but had no military experience and duties. In contrast, Dilun was now militarily renowned from his success in the National Protection Movement but was virtually unknown and had never even been to Beijing. Since Duan decided to seat only one representative from each province, he elected to seat only Liu since he was the brother of Liu Xianshi and the older of the two. Dilun felt slighted and was extremely angry and disappointed that he was not chosen as the sole representative since he was certainly better qualified and better known in Guizhou.

Dilun stayed with Boqun, who was in Beijing as a member of the parliament. He tried to mitigate the circumstance and to console Dilun, saying,

The political situation is still extremely fluid, and I am not sure why this meeting is called. Duan is of the old-school generation, and direct family ties in this incidence are all important. I think that Uncle Xianshi may have misunderstood that only one representative is to be seated. In fact, no other province has sent more than one. I don't understand why he chose not to come himself knowing how vain he can be. I can only surmise that he wanted you here to support Uncle Xianzhi, for he is not experienced in military affairs. Other provincial representatives have all such a support team, though none of whom are seated at the meeting.

Dilun was not satisfied, and he decided not to remain at Beijing and instead to visit Sun Yatsen in Shanghai, who he had not met before, at the invitation of Li Liehchun, who had become a good friend to both the Wang brothers. Li thought Dilun was just the kind of young military talent the GMD needed to help in the effort to build its own military base. Sun was forced into exile in Japan after the unsuccessful second revolution. He was active in promoting and supporting the National Protection Movement and sensing the political vacuum and chaos in the country when he returned in late 1916. He was well aware of Dilun's accomplishments and wrote to both Liu Xianshi and Boqun to express his admiration for such a young relative of theirs and expressed his hope that Dilun would become a part of his effort to restore the republic. Boqun arranged for Dilun to travel by train to meet with Sun. Dilun developed an immediate affinity to Sun and like Boqun became a member of GMD. Dilun would later remark to Boqun,

Sun is everything you told me and more. Yes, I agree that he is an idealist, but he is keenly aware of his mistakes over the course of the revolution. His three principles of the people are what we need now to be the foundation of a republic. I really believe in the principle of democracy, which is based on our Chinese tradition. His character is as you described, and he will need a lot other patriots to support him for our shared dream of a republic to come true.

Sun Yatsen was equally impressed by Dilun's earnestness and his military accomplishments. He remarked to Dilun,

My dear young Dilun, the Wang family is indeed fortunate to have a pair of sons like you and Boqun. You complement each other in many respects. You realize, of course, that in the current chaotic state, the priority must be to secure financing and to gain military control. In most cases, I am able to raise the necessary funds, but I need many of you who have military backing to join in my effort. In spite of the difficulties that poses, I do believe we can succeed. To be more specific, I believe the Beijing government currently under the control of the Beiyang generals will not become the republic we have all aspired to, and thus armed conflicts may be still necessary and I will need the military support from southwestern region of Yunnan, Guizhou, and Sichuan. I know your history with Tang Chiyao and Liu Xianshi, but I consider you and Boqun to be essential for me to achieve our objectives.

Before Dilun's return to Guiyang, Boqun suggested a tourist visit to Hangzhou, an ancient city 110 miles southwest of Shanghai and one of seven ancient capital cities of China. It was most recently the capital of the Southern Song dynasty. It is well known for its beautiful natural scenery, architecture, man-made West Lake, and indigenous cuisine. A visitor in the thirteenth century, Marco Polo, after visiting the city wrote, "It is beyond dispute the finest and the noblest city in the world." Dilun was immediately enchanted and in his usual impromptu manner brought a piece of land with a relatively small house overlooking the lake. He also noted to Boqun that he wished to be buried there for all eternity.

❖ ❖ ❖

President Li Yuanhong took office on June 6, 1916. Liu Xianshi sent Boqun to Beijing to attend the 1913 parliament reconvened by President Li on August 1, 1916, after it had been disbanded by Yuan Shikai over two and a half years earlier. The original 1913 constitution was restored by the GMD majority in parliament. The Beiyang generals, however, held the real power in three factions or cliques. Premier Duan Qirui had de facto control of the government, and he was supported by the Anhui clique, which controlled the provinces of north Zhili, including Beijing, Johol, Chahar, Suiyuan, Shandong, Shanxi, Fukien, Zhejiang, and Anhui. Vice President Feng Guozhang had control of largest Beiyang faction, known as the Zhili clique, which controlled the provinces of Hupei, Jiangxi, Kiangsu, Honan, and south Zhili. The third was the Fengtian clique of Zhang Zuolin that controlled the three provinces of Manchuria: Heilongjiang, Jilin, and Liaoning. The major ministerial positions were assigned to men acceptable to the GMD. Liang Qichao was appointed as the minister of finance and served in the parliament as the head of the Progressive Party. Liang tried to convert both Duan and Feng to be true republicans in cooperation with Sun Yatsen to form a united government, with little success.

Zhang Zuolin was from a poor family in the Liaoning (formerly Fengtian) Province; he was thin and short, without any education.

In 1896 Zhang joined a well-known bandit gang, and by his twenties, he had formed a small personal army of his own. In 1900 the Boxer Rebellion broke out, and Zhang's gang joined the Qing Army. Thereafter, Zhang hired his men out as escorts for traveling merchants and as mercenaries of the Japanese Army in the Russo-Japanese war of 1904 till 1905. Toward the end of the Qing dynasty, Zhang was leading his men as a regiment of the Qing army, patrolling the borders of Manchuria and suppressing other bandit gangs. Yuan Shikai recognized Zhang's potential and helped him to gain increasing power and funding. After Yuan died, in June 1916 the Beijing government named Zhang both military and civil governor of Liaoning. Zhang spread his power base over the neighboring two provinces as well.

As year 1916 came to a close, the Beiyang army seemed to have maintained its unity through various negotiations and alliances. World War I had reached a crucial point by 1917. Duan Qirui saw an opportunity join the Allies against Germany to retrieve many of the indemnities and concessions China had been forced to accept from the Allies. Duan was support by Liang Qichao and the parliament, which voted to declare war again Germany on March 10, 1917. President Li felt it was a mistake since the central government had yet to establish a firm control over the many factions still in play. Vice President Feng Guozhang tried to mediate between Li and Duan, without much success. In May, a Beijing English newspaper disclosed Duan had negotiated a large loan from the Japanese, without approval by Parliament. Li dismissed Duan as premier on May 23. When Duan left for Tianjin, most of the Beiyang generals withdrew their support of the government. A power vacuum ensued since President Li was now without any military support. It is interesting to note that Liang Qichao as head of the Progressive Party had withdrawn his members from the parliament, leaving it without a quorum.

President Li then turned to an independent Beiyang general, Zhang Xun, no relation to Zhang Zuolin. Zhang was a diehard eccentric Qing royalist who never cut his cue and required that his troops keep their pigtails as well. He served as the head of the palace guards for

Dowager Empress Cixi during the Boxer Rebellion. After his mentor, Yuan Shikai, died, he reverted back to his obsession of Qing restoration. Zhang had the wholehearted support of the reform monarchist Kang Youwei, who resided in Beijing at the time, and Zhang Zuolin, the governor of Liaoning, who saw this event as his entry into Beijing power vacuum, declared support for Zhang Xun.

Zhang Xun and his army marched into Beijing, dissolved the parliament, declared the 1913 constitution as invalid, and arrested President Li. Zhang announced the restoration of Emperor Puyi and the Qing court on July 1, 1917. Outraged, the other Beiyang generals, led by Vice President Feng and retired Premier Duan, mobilized and joined their forces and ended the short-lived restoration attempt by July 17. Zhang took refuge in Dutch legation and retired. Feng took over as president, replacing Li, who was sick of the politics of the Beiyang generals and decided to retire. Duan was returned to power as premier, appointed by President Feng. Liang Qichao broke with his old mentor, Kang Youwei, who had to seek exile at the British Embassy for his part in the restoration.

The big winner of Zhang Xu's short-lived restoration was Zhang Zuolin, who remained neutral after he had agreed with Zhang Xu initially. Later, he actually supported Duan Qirui in suppressing Zhang Xun after it became clear Duan would win. Zhang was able to absorb the troops of nearby commanders who had joined the restoration. Zhang Zuolin also intervened and took control of China's northernmost province, Heilongjiang, after a rebellion there forced the local governor to flee. The governor of Jilin Province also had been linked the restoration. Zhang had his Jilin allies agitated in Beijing for the governor's dismissal, and Zhang took Jilin as well. By 1918 Zhang Zuolin had complete control of Manchuria save for small pockets held by the Japanese.

The elimination of Zhang Xu ushered in the Warlord Era. Feng Guozhang as president appointed his subordinates as military commanders in Kiangsi, Hupei, and Kiangsu Provinces to strengthen his Zhili clique. Beside Duan's Auhui and Zhang Zuolin's Fengtian cliques, there were other cliques of various types and sizes. Examples are the independent warlord of Shanxi, Yunnan, with great influence over Guizhou, or several warlords dividing control over a province, such as Sichuan, Guangdong, and Guangxi. The three Beiyang cliques were the largest and the most powerful. Each of the cliques had their own agenda of expansion, and collectively they became the major obstacle for the unification of the Republic of China.

After the Qing restoration was reversed, Duan Qirui refused to restore the 1913 constitution, which was endorsed by most of the southern provinces. Duan wished to continue with Yuan's 1914 constitution, which provided for a strong presidency with little civilian control. He had the support of the rest of the Beiyang generals. The southern provinces, primarily consisting of those in the National Protection Movement, wished to restore the original 1913 constitution and its provisional parliament with a GMD majority. In spite of several attempts by President Feng to mediate between the two sides, the north and south remained as divided as ever. In August 1917 Duan decided to consolidate his control by sending his Beiyang armies to both Hunan and Sichuan Provinces as a prelude to attack the southern provinces.

Being close to Hunan and realizing they would be next on Duan Qirui's list for conquest, the governors of Guangdong and Guangxi set up an independent government near Guangzhou in support of Sun Yatsen's call to protect the original 1913 constitution of the republic. Sun left Shanghai for Guangzhou on July 20, 1917, to lead the movement. He wired the original members of the parliament of 1913, including Boqun, to come to Guangzhou to establish a new republican government. On July 22, the Naval Minister Cheng Biguang decided to support Sun. Cheng was the son of a Chinese merchant in America, and his family returned to China when he was ten years old. He was a classmate of Li Yuanhong at the Fuzhou Naval Academy and was appointed by President Li as the minister of navy in 1917. Cheng had been a longtime supporter of Sun, and he led the navy's fleet as it sailed from Shanghai to Guangzhou on July 22 to join the newly formed republican government.

On August 14, 1917, China entered World War I on the side of the Allies after evidence of Germany's support for Zhang Xu's restoration was uncovered as well as intense lobbying by Duan. Duan sent about hundred and thirty thousand men in the poorly trained so-called Labor Troops to the Western Front, Mesopotamia, and German East Africa. Additional troops were sent into Russia to assist the allies. Duan negotiated a loan with Japan to fund military buildup for the entry into the war. His real purpose of the loan was to fund the Beiyang army to pacify the south and the southwest provinces. Financing was improbable from the European and the United States due to their wartime expenses. Duan secretly completed the first of the many loans with Japan on September 29, 1917. Japan was given the right to station troops in Shandong Province, then a German concession, as well as the right to build and run two new Shandong railroads. There would be a high price to pay when these negotiations came to light later on, but in the meantime Duan got the money for the Beiyang Army and the support of its generals.

❖ ❖ ❖

On August 25, 1917, Boqun traveled to Guangzhou and joined one hundred other members of the 1913 parliament to establish a military government under Sun as the generalissimo and two field marshals, each in charge of a region of the country. Sun hoped cooperation with two main southern warlords would give him the military backing needed for the unification of the country. Tang Jiyao was one of the two marshals in charge of the southwest, including Yunnan, Guizhou, and Sichuan. Liu Xianshi saw an opportunity to further his power base outside of Guizhou, accepted the position as Tang's deputy, and gained tremendous personal prestige throughout Guizhou and the southwest. Tang also named Liu Xianqian the roving commander-in-chief of the Guizhou army to strengthen the Liu clan's position in Guizhou. The other marshal was Lu Rongting in charge of Guangxi and Guangdong. Lu began his career as a Guangxi bandit whose gang was absorbed into the local Qing Army. He rose to the rank of general commanding a brigade and supported the 1911 revolution. Luo was appointed by Yuan Shikai as the military governor of Guangxi, but he joined the National Protection Movement in 1916 against Yuan's monarchy.

Sun Yatsen's Guangzhou military government in January 1918 had an impressive start on paper. The Constitution Protection Movement had signed up six southern provinces: Guangdong, Guangxi, Yunnan, Guizhou, Hunan, and Sichuan. Sun's three-man coalition, however, was very tenuous. Tang Jiyao, unlike Cai E, was not a true republican but rather a pragmatist who harbored the ambition to become the "king of the southwest." His interest in joining Sun was to protect his own independence from the Beiyang cliques, especially Duan's Anhui clique and to expand his power base into neighboring Guizhou and Sichuan. Lu Rongting's support was also conditional since he hoped this move would entice the Beijing government to appoint him as the man in charge of both Guangdong and Guangxi Provinces. Lu's control over Guangdong was somewhat dubious since there were several independent military units. The most important was one led by Chen Jiongming. In addition, Lu was counting on Sun to fund him for consolidating his control over Chen and others in Guangdong.

Chen Jiongming was from an old Hakka gentry family of Haifeng in eastern Guangdong. His early classic education earned him a Shangyuan degree, but he switched his study to law and became a lawyer. He followed the Reform Movement of Kang Youwei and Liang Qichao but joined the RA in 1909. Chen was closely associated with Huang Xing and Hu Hamin when they led the Guangzhou uprising in April 1911. In June 1913 President Yuan Shikai appointed him as governor of Guangdong Province, replacing Hu Hamin. Chen participated in the National Protection Movement in 1916 and established a power base in his native east Guangdong. Chen, along with Admiral Cheng Biguang, escorted Sun Yatsen to Guangzhou to set up

Chen Jiongming. 1917

the military government in July 1917. Chen also supported a number of revolutionary intellectuals, including the founder of the Chinese Communist Party, Chen DuXiu.

Sun's main purpose for the Guangzhou government was to unify the country against the Beiyang warlords. Both Tang Jiyao and Lu Rongting had different and self-serving objectives, and they kept stalling any move in Sun's direction. The navy was the only military force Sun could count on, but its collection of cruisers and gunboats with limited number of naval personnel was no substitute for troops on the ground. With Lu's agreement, Sun appointed Admiral Cheng Biguang as the governor of Guangdong. Unfortunately, Cheng was assassinated on January 28, 1918, at the Guangzhou train station. Sun Yatsen became even more militarily vulnerable. When Lu Rongting engineered a coup to remove Sun as the top man and replaced him with a junta, putting Lu in control, Sun Yatsen resigned and returned to Shanghai in February 1918.

CHAPTER 7

1917-1922

CONSTITUTIONAL PROTECTION AND BEIYANG WARLORD WARS

After Cai E's departure from Chengdu, Sichuan, in 1917, Dai Kan as civil governor in Chongqing had been under both political and military pressure from local Sichuan warlords. They were encouraged by Duan Qirui to end the occupation by the Yunnan and Guizhou armies. They also sensed a rift between the armies under Dai and Luo Tijin of Yunnan due to their respective self-interests. Dai and Luo both wished to stay on in Sichuan and become the sole strong man of the province since their respective native provinces were under well-established strong men in Tang Jiyao and Liu Xianshi. The local Sichuan warlord, Liu Cunhou, at the urging of Duan Qirui and with funding from Beijing started an effort to drive a wedge between Dai and Luo.

Duan instructed Liu to call a military conference in April 1917 on the subject of the withdrawal of the nonnative armies. Dai Kan suddenly switched his position in support the local warlords headed by Liu and thus exposed Luo's position to continue the occupation. Liu then led a coalition of Sichuan forces to attack Luo's stronghold of Chengdu. Both sides deployed heavy artilleries and land mines. The intense battle lasted seven days and nights, and Luo was defeated and retreated to Yunnan. The Beijing government then appointed Dai as military governor in addition to civil governor seated at the ancient capital of Chengdu. At the same time, Duan appointed Liu Cunhou as the commander of the Second Division of the Sichuan Army and provided funds to increase the size of his force to counter Dai's presence. After Luo withdrew with his forces, Dai and Liu began to contend for sole control of the province.

Their difference came to a head when Zhang Xu took over Beijing and restored Emperor Puyi. Zhang appointed Liu as the military governor of Sichuan replacing Dai Kan. In effect, this united all the Sichuan forces against Dai. At this point, Dai was left with two choices: attack Liu or retreat back to Guizhou. With less than seven thousand troops in the two Guizhou brigades against fifteen to twenty thousand mustered by Liu and his Sichuan allies, Dai realized he was at a disadvantage. Dai wired both Tang Jiyao and Liu Xianshi for help and both promised help, but none had arrived in time to join the conflict. By July 5, 1917, after losing fierce battles and thousands of his troops, the enemy surrounded Chengdu. Mediations by the British and French consulates were not successful. Dai, out of desperation, negotiated an agreement with Liu for safe passage back to Guizhou and handed over to him the three official Sichuan seals of authority: civil governor, military governor, and chief representative to Beijing. On July 15 Dai led his remaining troops out the south gate of the city and retreated toward Guizhou. The next day while Dai's force made camp in an ancient temple grounds just outside the city wall, Liu's troops surrounded them in a surprise attack with overwhelming numbers. After most of Dai's officers had been killed and it seemed to be impossible to escape, Dai committed suicide July 16, 1917, at age thirty-seven.

Most of Dai's Guizhou troops of some five thousand were captured or killed in action. Many homes were destroyed; civilian deaths totaled more than three thousand, with the injured exceeding six thousand. Both Boqun and Dilun were away from Guiyang at the time. Communication being what it was, news did not reach them until it was too late for either to be of any help. Upon hearing what had transpired, Boqun wept and proclaimed the great personal and national loss of another hero for the National Protection Movement, for the republicans, and for the nation. In his sorrow, Boqun cited Tang dynasty poet Du Fu:

> Who can say there is justice
> Under heaven? Yet in the end,
> You have met this trouble.
> When they are but forgotten dust,
> Your name for a thousand years, and then,
> Ten thousand more, will stand with men,
> Yet I grieve,
> That such will be small comfort to you,
> When you have already passed.

❖ ❖ ❖

After Liu Xianshi had been made Tang Jiao's deputy by Sun Yatsen's military government in Guangzhou, Liu with his CPA supporters in the government used their power and influence for substantial personal gains. One example was in the spring of 1917, the British consular in Hankow had contact Liu Xianshi regarding the ban of production and sales of opium and the impending inspection of the British ambassador as a loan condition agreed to by the Beijing government. Liu appointed a committee to look into the matter and then assured the ambassador that Guizhou would no long deal with the production and sales of opium. He ordered the temporary shutdown of all area opium production and then led the British through the inspection and even bragged,

> For the good of our nation, we in Guizhou have shut
> down all opium production and closed all borders for
> opium commerce. You can be assured that opium will
> be eradicated from our province now and forever.

In fact, however, this was a temporary show only since the opium tax was one of the economic pillars of Liu's program to maintain his government. He actually approved Dilun's proposal to expand the army in 1918 based on the opium tax revenue. As a result, opium addiction became commonplace for the poor and the rich alike in Guizhou. Another example of Liu's business dealings involved a very profitable local leather business, which was owned in part by both Tang Jiyao and Liu since 1912. They both profited handsomely from the purchases by both the Yunnan and Guizhou armies. Liu even collected a commission of the purchase of electric generators from the United States for the streetlights of Guiyang.

Since taking over the control of the province in 1912, Liu had reaped considerable financial gain from his expanded power base that he guarded with great zeal. Liu also generously rewarded his supporters, including the Wang brothers. The Wangs became rich as well even though Boqun and Dilun both had trepidations over the money but expressed thanks to their uncle, as it was their filial duty to do so. Their mother did make them felt better about themselves as she explained that they really do not have any choice in the matter.

> From beginning of history, power and money are joined together; this is how things are done through the centuries in our history. You both now have great influence over the future course of our clan, province, and nation. You should accept the money with genuine appreciation since you can do what you consider best with it. On the other hand, refusing it would create suspicion and further the doubt of the Liu clan about you two. I see that you have no choice but to do what I have suggested and be glad and grateful for it.

When Liu Xianshi was appointed as the assistant commander-in-chief of the Southwest Constitutional Protection Army, he grandly announced the reasons he had decided to join up with Tang were to seek revenge for Dai Kan and for the loss of the Dai's Guizhou Army. He further declared that he would seek financial reimbursement from Sichuan for the cost expended in the National Protection Movement. With such funding, the Guizhou Army was able to make up its losses and increase its size from six brigades to ten, reaching a total force of over twenty-five thousand men.

❖ ❖ ❖

After the establishment of the Guangzhou Military Government in July 1917, Sun Yatsen announced the Constitution Protection Movement to unify the nation. In fall of 1917, Duan Qirui mobilized the Beiyang Army as well as the local provincial armies of Sichuan and Hunan to attack the Constitution Protection armies in one fell swoop to counter the movement and Sun's Guangdong government. In November Dilun, under direct orders from Sun Yatsen, led the Guizhou army to join with the friendly part of the Sichuan army into Sichuan against Duan's army and its Sichuan supporters. He sent Yuan Zuming to lead the First Regiment with the First and Third Brigades in a pincer formation with Zhang Jiangjin of the Third Regiment with six brigades against the joint Beiyang and Sichuan armies of considerable superior strength. In twenty days of furious combat, the Guizhou army was able to take Chongqing. The Guizhou army had again proven to be well trained, disciplined, and battle-worthy. Elsewhere in Hunan, Guangxi, and Guangdong, the Constitution Protection armies beat back the Beiyang Army as well, and as a result Duan resigned as premier and President Feng Guozhang called an armistice with the south. Sun then appointed Dilun as commander-in-chief of the Guizhou Army with the rank of major general. Others were promoted as well; notable among them was Yuan Zuming's appointment as brigadier general.

While in Chongqing, Dilun received a wire from his wife that his five-year-old son, Chongxi, was ill but the doctors thought there was little danger. Since Chongxi had been sort of a sickly infant from birth, Dilun was not overly concerned, and he tried to put this out of his mind and continued to concentrate on the battle at hand. Three days later a wire arrived from his mother that Chongxi had died and his wife was inconsolable with grief. Upon reading this, Dilun felt as though he was stricken by lightning, but when he heard artillery fire all around, he had to be back in the battle. It was the hardest day of his young life.

When Dilun left Chongqing for Guiyang to visit his family and console his wife, he named Yuan Zuming as acting commander-in-chief in his absence to reward Yuan for his success in the capture of Chongqing. In his first meeting back to Guiyang with Liu Xianshi, Liu showed him a wire from several of the officers under Yuan's command suggesting the Guizhou Army be split into divisions and Yuan be promoted to the first division commander and deputy commander-in-chief. Liu further added that his brother, Liu Xianzhi, also endorsed such a proposal. Dilun rejected it on the grounds that it would not be efficient; given the size of army, the addition of another command level of would only cause confusion.

When Dilun returned to Chongqing, he convened a meeting of all the officers, including Yuan, and stated,

Dilun and wife 1917

The Guizhou Army is an efficient organization without the usual overburdening hierarchy. To change the command organization now will only cause inefficiencies that we can ill afford. Titles and prestige have no place in this army; only results are what count. Furthermore, if any officer has suggestions regarding our organization, I would appreciate hearing from you before I hear it from my uncle. Such is considered to be insubordination and will be dealt with accordingly!

Dilun then turned and faced Yuan and said,

I know you think I have this position because of my connection to the Liu family. Liu Xianshi is no fool, and I am in my position because what I have accomplished in getting our army ready to win the last two wars. General Yuan, you are a good combat officer, and that is why I put you in charge in my absence. To be ready for general command, you still need to develop more strategic sense, so I am transferring you to my staff as my chief strategy officer."

Knowing Yuan was Liu's man, Dilun wanted to keep him close without direct control over his troops. Yuan understood this, and for him this was the ultimate humiliation, and he vowed to make Dilun pay. In later discussions with Boqun, who was concerned about Yuan's reaction, he said,

I understand your decision. Yet I am concerned it will prompt some rash actions by an impulsive person. Were you angry over Uncle Liu's agreement with the proposal? Or were you concerned about Yuan's loyalty? By trusting Yuan with your command in your absence, you obviously believe he is trustworthy. I am afraid that you may have turned him from a man on the fence into your enemy. Now that the rice has been cooked, you will have to watch Yuan closely.

As 1918 ended, the Wang brothers were both still involved in the effort to unify the nation. Boqun spent most his time as the Guizhou representative to national assembly, first in Guangzhou and then in Shanghai following Sun Yatsen's retreat from Guangzhou. While Dilun served as the military governor of part of Sichuan with the Guizhou Army in Chongqing, Boqun in a letter to Dilun from Shanghai stated his regrets and frustrations of reaching that all-elusive goal of a unified republic.

> My dear brother Dilun, it has been six long years since we managed to throw out the Qing emperor and the Manchu government, and in spite of the lives given and sacrifices made, we still have no republic. Why has heaven not looked down on our effort and grant us our wish for a unified republic? Is not our cause just? Is Sun the man we should support? Are we being too optimistic in believing Sun will somehow manage to lead us to accomplish that objective? Are we Chinese so steep into the dynastic tradition we are incapable of adapting to the necessary changes? How are we to be sure that our continued effort will actually bear fruit? What are the signs that we are even making progress?

❖ ❖ ❖

After Sun Yatsen led the southern provinces to began the Constitutional Protection War of 1917, tensions between the Anhui and Zhili cliques developed. Duan Qirui's plan was to rid southern China of Sun Yatsen and his supporters to unify the country, but his 1917 campaign in Hunan and Sichuan was not going well. President Feng Guozhang favored compromise and negotiations, hoping to sway the south with financial and political support. Duan ignored Feng and continued to build up the Anhui clique–controlled army using the Japanese loan. In 1918, Feng appointed his protégé, Cao Kun, as the military governor of Zhili and his successor of the Zhili clique. Feng's proposal for a negotiated settlement with the south was endorsed by all the Zhili-controlled provinces. A new parliament convened in August 1918 with Liang Qichao as its leader, and it continued to support Duan's effort to raise funds from Japan. The parliament elected Xu Shichang as president to succeed an ailing Feng Guozhang at the end of his term. Feng retired and died a year later. Xu was Beiyang's elder statesman and Yuan Shikai's closest friend and adviser. He served as the last viceroy of Manchuria and the chief of the general staff as a civilian at the end of Qing dynasty. Xu had resigned as premier in protest to Yuan's imperial endeavors in late 1915.

Xu's election as president was instigated by Duan Qirui and his Anhui clique. Xu was chosen because he was a civilian with Beiyang credentials and was neutral to both its Zhili and Anhui cliques. Without military power of his own, Xu had to position Duan, Cao Kun, and Zhang Zuolin against each other to maintain his position. Xu reappointed Duan as premier after his resignation on November 20, 1917. He held a massive celebration in Beijing for China's victory in World War I on November 18, 1918. He negotiated a cease-fire with Sun Yatsen's rival Constitutional Protection government in Guangzhou. Xu granted greater freedom to students and intellectuals. This hopeful period lasted until news from the Paris peace conference showed how Duan Qirui promised German concession in Shandong to Japan in exchange for the loan. Large student protests of the May Fourth Movement led to Xu's cracking down with mass arrests.

In 1919 Duan Qirui, stymied in his effort to pacify the southern provinces, sent his right-hand man, Xu Shuzheng, to conquer Outer Mongolia when it declared independence. Xu came from a scholarly family in Jiangsu and was one of the youngest, at age thirteen, to pass the examination. Xu went to Japan in 1905, graduated from the Imperial Japanese Army Academy, and returned in 1910 to join the Beiyang Army. In 1918 he founded the Anfu Club as the political arm of the Anhui clique, which won a majority in parliament in the 1918 election. Duan's strategy for the Mongolia expedition was to isolate and eventually eliminate the northwest Fengtian clique of Zhang Zuolin. Xu led the Northwest Frontier Defense Army to invade newly independent Outer Mongolia. On November 17, 1919, Outer Mongolia withdrew its declaration of independence and became once again part of China. Now being threatened by the Anhui clique, Zhang Zuolin decided to side with Cao Kun and began courting Sun Yatsen and those warlords in south China who were being threatened by Duan Qirui as well.

At the end of World War I, Britain and the United States renewed their interest in China and advocated or a peaceful solution to the infighting of the various factions. They considered Duan Qirui to be the cause of the military actions and decided to back the united Zhili and Fengtian cliques. Cao and Zhang persuaded President Xu Shichang to recall Xu Shuzheng, the Anhui leader of the Mongolia expedition. Xu and Duan denounced the actions and prepared for war against the Zhili and Fengtian cliques.

In November of 1919, Wu Peifu, one of the Zhili clique's most capable leaders, met with representatives of Tang Jiyao and Lu Rongting at Hengyang, Hunan, where they signed a treaty to form the basis of an anti-Anhui alliance. Wu, a Shandong native, had a classic education before joining Baoding Military Academy. He was considered the best strategist of the Beiyang generals. Wu rose in Cao Kun's third Beiyang Army to its commander and become Cao's military arm. In April 1920, while visiting a memorial service at Baoding for soldiers who died in Hunan, Cao Kun added more warlords to the alliance, including the warlords of Hubei, Henan, Liaoning, Jilin, and Heilongjiang. Now the stage was set for both sides to prepare for war.

Wu Peifu, 1920

In early July 1920, the Anhui clique mustered five divisions and four brigades with Duan Qirui as its commander-in-chief. It deployed in two fronts, the western covering the regions around Zhuozhou, Hebei, while the east covering the areas around Beijing. Zhili and allied forces gathered a division and nine combined brigades with Wu Peifu as commander-in-chief. Meanwhile, Zhang Zuolin ordered a detachment of his troops to enter the Shanhai pass at the Great Wall to take the city of Shanhaiguan. Battle commenced on July 14, 1920. The Anhui army attacked the Zhili army on both fronts along the Beijing-Hankou and Beijing-Tianjin railways. Zhili troops were forced to abandon their positions and retreated. Two days later, with help from Japanese troops, the Anhui army also succeeded in gaining additional ground, forcing Zhili forces to form a second line of defense.

On July 17 Wu Peifu took personal charge of the Zhili army's western front . With a high-speed and daring maneuver, he outflanked the enemy and took the western Anhui headquarters. He captured the Anhui army's front-line commander-in-chief and many of his officers, including the First Division commander. After taking the town of Zhuozhou, Wu pursued the retreating enemy toward Beijing. The remainder of the Anhui army on the western front was annihilated. On the same day, the Fengtian army attacked the Anhui eastern front. Upon learning of the collapse of the western front, Anhui's eastern commander, Xu Shuzheng, fled Langfang, Hebei, to Beijing, leaving his troops to surrender to the combined Fengtian and Zhili armies. On July 19, 1920, Duan Qirui resigned from his post and fled to the Japanese legation in Tienjin. On July 23 the combined Fengtian and Zhili forces entered Nanyuan to take Beijing. Little more than a week of fighting led to the unexpected defeat of the Anhui clique and the permanent breakup of the Beiyang Army. Wu Peifu was nationally credited as the strategist behind the Zhili clique's victory, while the Fengtian clique provided token support and participated in the formation of a joint government.

The big winner of the Anhui-Zhili war was Zhang Zuolin who, for relatively minor military contributions, took over former Anhui territory in Inner Mongolia with its armies and munitions. Zhang also was able to station his thirty thousand troops under his most trust commander in the Beijing area that provided considerable influence in the Beijing government in the hands of Zhili clique. Wu Peifu, on the hand, pulled out his troops from Hunan and left a vacuum that was filled by one of Sun Yatsen's close associates. Hunan's independence was short lived when Cao Kun sent Wu back to pacify both Hunan's and Sichuan's incursions into Hebei. As of late 1921, the Zhili clique–controlled provinces contained the two north-south railways and the two principal east-west routes, the Longhai railway and the Yangtze downstream from the three gorges. Its principal rival was the Fengtian clique of Zhang Zuolin with its newly gained military forces and territories.

Zhang Zuolin, 1920

The uneasy coalition between the Fengtian and Zhili cliques started to fray soon after they defeated the Anhui clique in 1921. While the Zhili clique had the backing of the British and Americans, the Fengtian were backed by Japan. On December 25, 1921, the two sides came to an impasse over Fengtian-backed cabinet decision not to fund the military budget promised to the Zhili army. In January 1922, Zhang Zuolin threatened to resolve the conflict by force. By April Zhili armies deployed around one hundred troops, while the Fengtian army deployed some hundred twenty thousand troops.

After the war broke on April 29, 1922, the Zhili army on the eastern front was driven back. Western Zhili forces did not make any progress under the heavy shelling of Fengtian army. On April 30, 1922, Wu Peifu personally went to the front to direct heavy shelling of the Fengtian front, while his main force outflanked the Fengtian rear. As Zhili troops launched their surprise attack on May 4, 1922, the Sixteenth Division of the Fengtian army, previously under Feng Guozhang, defected to Wu Peifu. The Fengtian army was forced into retreat, and their defense collapsed on the western front.

The subsequent Fengtian counteroffensive was short lived. Wu Peifu changed tactics by faking a retreat and luring the advancing Fengtian army into an ambush. As the unsuspecting Fengtian troops advanced, the army overstretched itself. Seizing the opportunity, Zhili troops flanked the enemy and seized victory once again. This time, the victory was complete; the remaining Fengtian troops of the western front were completely annihilated, with the Zhili army turning its attention eastward.

The Fengtian army on the eastern front was initially successful, with the Zhili forces holding on in a desperate rearguard action. As news of their defeat in the west reached the Fengtian army, it hesitated and caused its flank to be dangerously exposed. In danger of being cut off, Zhang Zuolin ordered a general retreat to avoid total annihilation. Having achieved complete victory in the west, Wu Peifu redeployed his crack troops and personally directed the attack on the Zhang retreating army. By this time it was obvious the Fengtian clique was soundly defeated, and on May 5, 1922, the Zhili army entered Tianjin. Fengtian forces suffered over twenty thousand killed, ten thousand desertions, and forty thousand surrendered to the Zhili army, which had relatively insignificant number of casualties.

The British consul mediated a ceasefire whereby Zhang Zuolin would withdraw all Fengtian troops from the region inside Shanhaiguan and Zhili forces would cease hostile action. On June 18, 1922, representatives from both sides signed the peace treaty aboard a British warship. Shanhaiguan subsequently became the border between the two cliques, ending the First Zhili–Fengtian War with a resounding Zhili victory. The Fengtian clique retreated to Manchuria, while the Zhili armies led by Wu Peifu took control of the Beijing government.

❖ ❖ ❖

In the fall of 1920, Boqun received a wire from Sun Yatsen indicating that Chen Jiongming had provided military support for him to form a military government in Guangzhou after the conflict ended between Lu Rongting and Chen Jiongming. As the progressive governor of Guangdong, Chen banned opium and gambling, promoted education, built roads, improved health care, and in general provided social changes for the people in the province. Sun asked Boqun to join him in Guangzhou as member of the military government's parliament and its minister of communication. Boqun gladly accepted for a national role in the field of his interest: communications. In November Boqun left Shanghai to meet Sun and followed him to Guangzhou in December.

In the two years since Boqun had first established a working relationship with Sun Yatsen, he had gotten to know some key persons in his inner circle as well as his new and young second wife, Soong Chingling, twenty-six years Sun's junior, who married Sun on October 25, 1915, against her rich and influential parents' strong objections. She was a graduate of Wesleyan College in Macon, Georgia, and like her siblings, she spoke fluent English for most of her life. Sun's three most senior associates were Hu Hanmin, Wang Jingwei, and Liao Zongkai. All three were supporters of Sun before he organized the RA in 1905 and all three are from Guangdong Province. Both Hu and Liao served at different times as the governor of Guangdong during the first two Sun-led governments. Wang, a good speaker, like Sun and Liao, was fluent in English and became a hero after his

**Sun and Soong
Qingling 1920**

attempted but unsuccessful assassination of the Manchu prince regent. He was responsible for some of Sun's speeches and doctrines and accompanied Sun in many overseas fundraising trips. Hu and

Wang helped Sun to develop the principles for the reorganization of the GMD. Liao Zongkai was the closest to Sun and his most faithful follower.

Liao was born in San Francisco where his father, a Hakka from Guangzhou, served as the manager of the British-financed Hong Kong

Liao Zongkai, 1920

and Shanghai Bank. Liao's uncle was a high Qing official engaged in industrialization and reform in the late 1900s. He returned to Guangdong with his mother at age sixteen in 1894 and lived in Guangzhou. Liao married He Xiangning, the daughter of a wealthy Hong Kong tea merchant. The couple married in 1897 and moved to Tokyo to pursue further education and their shared revolutionary interests. He's dowry and jewelry financed their trip and subsequent living expenses. Liao enrolled at the Waseda University, one of the most prestigious universities in Japan. They met Sun Yatsen in 1903 and both became founding members of the RA in 1905. For security purposes, the Liao residence in Tokyo became a meeting place as well as a guesthouse for such RA members as Sun, Hu Hanmin, and Wang Jingwei. Liao became Sun's chief financial adviser and fundraiser for the overseas Chinese.

After the Xinhai revolution of 1911, Hu Hanmin became the governor of Guangdong and Liao in charge of financial affairs. Although never a communist, Liao fervidly believed in social changes through organization of the masses. He was favorably impressed by the Soviets in Russia, but as Sun Yatsen, he did not believe in class struggle as defined by Lenin. Since 1919, the Soviet Comitern had tried to exert its influence on political situation in China by extending organizational

Hu Hanmin, 1920

support to the nascent Chinese Social Communist Party, offering diplomatic recognition to the Beijing government, and providing political
and financial assistance to Sun Yatsen. After two years of effort by various Soviet representatives, the Comintern decided to work with Sun
to form a joint front for the GMD and the Chinese communists. Liao
Zhongkai was in charge of the negotiation of the terms of a joint manifesto with Comintern representative Adolf A. Joffe in Tokyo, which led
to eventual admission of the communists into the GMD and financial
and military support from Russia.

Boqun became friends with all three of Sun Yatsen's senior associates. He knew Liao Zhongkai from his Chuo University days. Liao
enrolled there in 1907 to study political economy, as Boqun did, and
graduated in 1908. Liao befriended young Boqun and included him as
a guest at the Liao household frequently, where Boqun became friendly
with both Wang Jingwei and Hu Hanmin. Boqun worked part time as a
junior editor at the RA paper, *Minbo*, where Hu Hamin was one of the
senior editors. Hu had impressed Boqun with his obvious intellect and
quick grasp the essence of any discussion. Hu passed the provincial
examination and became a Juren at a young age of twenty-one; he
studied law in Tokyo since 1902. Even though Hu's nature was cool and
standoffish, he was courteous and patient in his discourses with Boqun.
Boqun had enjoyed and learned from lively discussions among Liao, his
wife, He Xiangning, and Hu Hanmin. Boqun considered all three to be
original political thinkers. Boqun did not know Wang Jingwei as well
as Liao and Hu but certainly spent many hours in group meetings with
Wang and appreciated his passion and charisma. Wang was the most
effective and articulate speaker among all the revolutionaries.

In Boqun's time in Shanghai working with Sun Yatsen, he met
another person of future importance. Jiang Jieshi was Sun's military
adviser, who began his military education at the Baoding Military
Academy in 1906 and then left for the Japanese Imperial Army
Academy, as did He Yingqin, who started there later. Then in 1911,
he followed his mentor and closest friend, Chen Qimei, to Shanghai

after he had served in the Imperial Japanese Army from 1909 to 1911. Chen was another close associate of Sun and a founder of the RA in Japan, where he underwent military training. He befriended Jiang in Tokyo, and in 1908 Chen brought Jiang into the RA. Upon his return to China, Jiang joined the Chen's group of revolutionaries in Shanghai and participated in 1912 uprising there. Chen has extensive connections in Shanghai with the business community and the underworld of secret societies, such as the infamous Green Gang. After the success of the revolution in 1912, Chen was made the military governor of the Shanghai region, and Jiang became commander of a brigade of the local revolution army funded by the merchants. During the Yuan Shikai period, Chen and Jiang both followed Sun's exile to Japan. They returned in 1915 to lead several uprisings in Shanghai without success. Chen was assassinated 1916, and Jiang inherited his Shanghai connections. In the fall of 1920 when Sun formed his government in Guangzhou, he named Jiang as his military adviser and in charge of field operations under the overall command of Chen Jiongming. The two did not get along well, and Jiang resigned after only a couple of months and returned to Shanghai.

In 1920 Jiang, at age thirty-three, was a restless and ambitious young man subject to impulsive moods and erratic behavior. Others thought him to be self-centered and suspicious of others. Although Jiang considered himself to live by his strong Confucian beliefs, his behaviors often showed just the opposite. After Chen Qimei's assassination, Jiang lived a self-professed life of debauchery in Shanghai. He abandoned his wife and son. He had many concubines, frequented brothels, and chased a thirteen-year old girl until she married him at age fifteen in 1921. When Boqun first met Jiang in Shanghai, he was in a meeting with

Jiang Jieshi, 1920

Sun and others; Jiang, with his rather average height, small face, and close-cropped hair, would stand out by his ramrod straight posture with his long, thin hands on his thighs when he sat. Although his posture reminded Boqun of He Yingqin, Jiang was more impressive and charismatic in his demeanor. He greeted everyone with quiet efficiency, eschewing warmth and friendliness, yet at the same time appeared to be man of considerable authority and keen awareness to his environments. In spite of all the scandalous talk about Jiang, Boqun left with the impression that Jiang would make a significant contribution to the republican camp.

Dilun had met him as well and formed a different opinion,

> Jiang reminded me of all Beiyang warlords in their ever-present self-centered interests. He is no doubt well trained in a military sense as He Yingqin, but he will never be content of taking orders from a political leader and carry them out without question, as Yingqin will. I agree with Chen Jiongming about his dependability. Comparing the two men, I would be much comfortable have Chen with me or even take command from him than Jiang. I believe Chen shares the same objective as us on the development of the republic by the steps outlined by Sun Yatsen, whereas Jiang considers Sun to be just the stepping stone for his own agenda.

CHAPTER 8

1918-1920

LIU-WANG CONFLICT AND THE MINJU INCIDENT

In the six-year period of 1912 till 1918, the Guizhou Province had gained considerable prominence in military and political stature under Liu Xianshi's military governorship. There was, however, an ever-enlarging rift developing between the Liu and the Wang families, based on their respective political and ideological views. Liu Xianshi, his brother, Xianzhi, and his cousin, Xianqian, all were a generation older than the Wang brothers. Liu Xianshi as the head of the clan clearly believed in the status quo of the civilian elites as they have enjoyed over the centuries as the nation went through the changes in the central Beijing government. Liu's rise in power and position was due to his family's position in land ownership and a self-maintained militia as well as his carefully cultivated connection with the elites in the more influential Yunnan Province. Once Liu Xianshi had gain control of the province, he tried to maintain his position and was extremely cautious in picking through the military and political landscape at the time. The Wang brothers, younger idealists, had a different vision of changes and more identified with Sun Yatsen's Three People Principles. Although the Wang brothers both have risen in their respective careers through the traditional family connection to the Liu clan, they fervently believed in a republican government as the salvation of China as an independent nation. It was the desire for revolutionary change that drove their political and military objectives. Boqun believed they could work and convince their uncles Liu of their direction, but Dilun thought a direct confrontation might be the only way. This difference of opinion did not divide them but in fact strengthened them since they became the checks and balances of each other with some of their mother's advice thrown in.

The training of the military became the opening salvo of the Liu-Wang conflict. Dilun hoped to utilize the Qing-established Guizhou Military Academy as the base for his officers and men. While Dilun was away in combat, Boqun would use his many revolutionary connections and travels to Beijing, Shanghai, and Guangzhou to recruit men who were graduates of the Japanese Imperial Army Academy, the Yunnan Military Academy, or the Baoding Military Academy to serve in the Guizhou Army or the academy. He Yingqin, his brother-in-law since 1917, was an example of such a man. He returned to Japan in December 1913 to complete his training and served in the Fifty-Ninth Regiment of the Japanese Army. Such was standard for Japanese military academy

He Yingqin 1910

cadets, designed to put the officer candidate in close contact with enlisted men like those he would command one day.

The training and discipline of the Japanese Army were rigorous, but He enjoyed and excelled in such an environment. He worked hard and earned a promotion after six months. Instruction and training in the Japanese military focused on the practical skills required of ordinary soldiers and squad leaders, with the aim of producing troops who mastered basic skills and exposed to all the things a soldier or lower-ranking officer might encounter in combat. It also emphasized the development of moral character, known as the Bushido spirit, which stresses absolute obedience, honor, courage, and loyalty to superiors. Chinese cadets lived and trained exactly as their Japanese counterparts did, experiencing the same indoctrination in the way of the warrior. He had acquired a solid educational and practical foundation for his military career. After graduating from the Imperial Army Academy and completing his army assignment, He Yingqin returned to China with the equivalent training of a second lieutenant in the Japanese Army, a total of nine years of elementary and advanced military training behind him. At the time, such credentials almost guaranteed work opportunities, as Chinese graduates of Japanese military academies formed an elite group within the Chinese military, enjoying greater prestige than graduates of Chinese military academies.

In 1916 He Yingqin had three different offers of employment waiting for him in China. He could return to serve in the Shanghai Army as he had in 1912, he could go to Yunnan and serve under Tang Jiyao, or he could return to Guizhou. Along with a few other Guizhou cadets, He Yingqin decided to return to his home province, and in the autumn of 1916, he began his career as a Guizhou Army officer. In early March 1917, he married Boqun's youngest sister, Wang Wenxiang, in Xingyi, which was another grand affair for the county. This was not your ordinary arranged marriage, for it lasted till death of Wang at age eighty-one and was apparently a happy one. He then served as the commander of the Guizhou Army's Fourth Regiment with the rank of colonel and as the chief instructor and the cadet battalion commander at the Guizhou Military Academy.

Seeing military strength as the path to political power, Dilun planned to reform the Guizhou Military Academy with He Yingqin's help, since Dilun himself had little formal military training. Dilun hoped He would be able also to emphasize Sun Yatsen's principles and the republican form of government. It was Dilun's aim to become militarily independent from Yunnan since he realized Tang Jiyao was not a true republican and he had ambition to become Sun Yatsen's successor in China. Liu Xianshi, however, concerned about Wang's increasing military power, did not wish him to serve as the commandant of the academy. As usual in such perplexing issues, Liu consulted Boqun.

Boqun mitigated his concerns with the following suggestion.

> I agree with you, dear uncle. Dilun may not be the best man for the job because of his lack of formal military education in spite of his battle-proven successes in Hunan and Sichuan. That man would be He Yingqin, who has the respect of Dilun and the other officers, and he would not only be able to establish the appropriate curriculum but also serve as a role model for the cadets. If you agree, I would convince Dilun and him accordingly.

Liu promptly endorsed the idea since he also like the fact that He was now part of the Liu-Wang family and obviously vetted by his elder all-knowing sister.

In July 1917, He Yingqin began his duties as commandant of the Guizhou Military Academy. Though without extensive battle experience, his personal character, training, and meticulous attention to detail served him well as the commandant, and in short order he instilled discipline and rigor in the academy. Using the instructional techniques he learned in Japan, He developed a curriculum that emphasized physical fitness, tactics, terrain, and weapons and communications training. Most of the instructors came from the Baoding Military Academy, which also operated on the Japanese military educational curriculum. The academy welcomed students who had completed high school and met the physical requirements, providing them with basic military training over the course of one year. In order to build the corps of cadets and to retain local talent, He offered immediate acceptance and financial assistance to the academy for any Guizhou student who tested into the better-known Yunnan and Wuchang Military Academies.

As in Liu Xianshi's nature to always hedge his bet, he decided to reform the military academy in Xingyi as well, at the urging of Liu Xianqian. The Xingyi School was established and called the Military Operations Academy, under the command of Liu Xianqian, in August 1917. It did not take long for Liu Xianshi to realize that the Guizhou Academy was head and heels above the academy in Xingyi in all respects. Indeed, He Yingqin set a fine role model for both officers and cadets alike in his rigid disciplines and personal behavior standards. The Guizhou Academy skimmed off the cream of top of qualified Guizhou student pool and even attracted students from the neighboring provinces. The Xingyi School was then left with the rejects. The Guiyang Academy produced a group of young military officers who would not only strengthen Guizhou's position against Yunnan and other potential enemies but would also form a base of support for the Wang brothers in future political and military moves for the republic.

❖ ❖ ❖

When Yuan Shikai died in 1916, the traditional Chinese order seemed have died with him. Among the intellectuals, the writers, the artists, and some others of the cultured elites began to call for a replacement, which would be more profound than the changes of the previous generations in new institutions and new political forms. This New Culture Movement saw China as a nation among a world of nations, not as culturally unique and not at the center of world as previous generations believed. A large number of Western doctrines became fashionable, particularly those that reinforced the cultural criticism and nation-building objectives of the movement. In this same period, the Beijing government was preoccupied with suppressing provincial revolts and political instabilities and thus did little to counter the increasing influence of the foreign powers. The annexation of Korea, which was a Chinese protectorate, by Japan in 1910, the Russian revolution of 1917, and the Treaty of Versailles all served to create a sense of nationalism among the emerging middle class and culture leaders in China, particularly the university teachers and students. Leaders of the New Culture Movement believed that traditional Confucian values were responsible for the political weakness of the country and called for a rejection of such traditional values and the selective adoption of Western ideas of science and democracy.

Student activism in Guizhou grew as the influence of the New Culture Movement spread from Beijing, Shanghai, and other major cities to the more remote areas of China. Periodicals and newspapers such as *New Youth* and *Weekly Critics* published news, editorials, and essays that inspired young, educated Chinese to consider new ideas and practices. In 1917, Guizhou newspapers had started to reprint articles on world news as well on democracy, the Bolshevik Revolution, culture reform, and different practices of republic governments around the world. Following the lead of the National New Culture Movement, the like-minded teachers and students of Guiyang educational institutions started similar discussions of the same issues, such as nationalism, materialism, and socialism. As communication improved and public information became national and widespread, local demand began for educational reform to add Western thoughts and literature, foreign languages, science, and mathematics into the standard curriculum.

Initially in Guizhou, the student movement was relatively small in numbers, and it showed little organization. They concentrated on new educational ideas and curriculum, and they protested against the ineptitude of the Beijing government and the Japanese encroachment rather than any local political reform. When the students did turn to political protest, they generally targeted the Beijing government. Although one might indeed describe Liu Xianshi as a warlord, his rule might not appear overly oppressive when compared to other provincial militarists. He did not maintain a particularly large army or exact exorbitant sums from the relatively poor people of Guizhou. His use of Guizhou military forces usually came in conjunction with the larger forces from Yunnan, and the fighting typically took place outside Guizhou.

In this same period, Dilun was stationed in Chongqing after the successful campaign of the Constitution Protection War against the Beiyang Army in late 1917. While Boqun followed Sun Yatsen to Beijing, Shanghai, and Guangzhou, he had experienced the political dynamics and changes that the New Culture Movement had brought about. Whenever Boqun came home to Guiyang, he would report to Liu Xianshi and held more private discussions with Dilun on his periodic home leaves and most of the time with their mother as well. The conclusion the Wang brothers reached about the situation was summarized by Boqun in mid-1918.

The student movement is becoming a potent political force on the national level. It is the harbinger of the finally awaking Chinese people. I have met some of the leaders in Beijing, Shanghai, and Guangzhou; they are seemingly dedicated to the current course of political change to bring about Sun Yatsen's republic. All over China the students are getting organized, and no doubt they will be a force to effect positive changes. What the students need is leadership and organization to deliver the changes. I see a great window of opportunity before us in Guiyang in spite of the small number of students since whatever takes place in Guiyang will spread to the entire province. I believe that if you, Dilun, get involved behind the scene to organize the students and channel them into specific political objectives, it will be the pivot for the republic's cause. More importantly, Uncle Liu will not object to such efforts since it will not be directed against him personally, and wherever changes it brings, he will think he can shape them the way he wants. This, of course, is not true, but by the time he realizes it, the tide will no longer be able to be turned, especially if you are not involved personally.

Subsequently Dilun and He Yingqin discussed creating a new youth organization, modeled after the progressive student organizations then sprouting up elsewhere in China, such as in Beijing in June 1918, when the Young China Students' Association was established. The Young Guizhou Association (YGA) was formed in September 1918, which called on the young people of Guizhou to join together to modernize the province. The Wang brothers and their supporters believed that if properly developed, this organization could be an effective tool for advocating their republican programs, strengthening their own political base, and convincing Liu Xianshi of the necessary reforms.

With the creation of the YGA, a power struggle began to spread from the military academies into the larger realm of teachers, students, and eventually the military and political leaders in Guizhou. Thus He recruited representatives from other schools and organizations. Advocating the New Culture principles of patriotism and humanitarianism, the YGA urged its members,

> To sacrifice yourselves for the country, to unite with the masses to protect the country, to advance learning and knowledge, and to exercise and develop their bodies.

At YGA meetings, He Yingqin described China as a sick old man who needed to be revived and reinvigorated through the actions of young people. This transformation required a program of reforms to make Guizhou militarily strong and politically progressive. The YGA consistently pushed a revolutionary agenda that contrasted with Liu Xianshi's cautious and conservative approach to govern. YGA was an instant success through its events, wall posters, and support of local newspapers and culture journals. By the end of 1918, YGA membership reached over two thousand.

Liu Xianshi became increasingly concerned about the unexpected political momentum gained by YGA. Even though Dilun had kept a low profile, Liu suspected that his nephew had to be involved in YGA and He Yingqin was acting as his straw man. In typical Liu fashion, he decided to organize his own student organization, the Republic of China Patriotic Students' Association (PSA), to counter the YGA. As with the Xingyi Military Academy versus the Guizhou Military Academy, PSA proved no match for the better organized and experienced YGA. In March of 1919, the YGA began publishing a newspaper in Guiyang, the *Guizhou Youth Daily*, and its articles dealt with typical New Culture issues, such as opium suppression, women's rights, and opposition to Japanese expansion. The paper advocated political and social changes as solution for these issues. Boqun had advised Dilun to not overtly criticize Liu Xianshi's policies and programs but instead make the Beijing government the reform target. Liu couldn't help but felt threatened since many of speeches of the YGA spoke about replacing conservative older people with progressive younger people, and many of reform requests of the Beijing government applied to the similar organization and policies of the Guizhou government as well.

After the Allies defeated Germany in World War I, it was agreed in the Versailles Treaty of April 1919 to give the previous German rights in the Chinese Shandong Province to Japan, ignoring Chinese requests for the abolition of all extraterritorial privileges of foreign powers in China; cancellation of all items under the twenty-one demands of the Japanese; and the repatriation of Shandong, which Japan had taken over from Germany. In the peace conference held in Paris, only President Wilson advocated self-determination for all nations, but he also failed to back up his rhetoric with action. This caused massive demonstrations in Beijing attended by over three thousand students. They stated that the Allies had betrayed China and the Chinese government was spineless in its ineptitude to secure China's rightful interests. The demonstration spread throughout the China with the same vigor and turnout as in Beijing.

In early June, workers and businessmen alike in Shanghai went on strike in support of the students. The center of the protest moved from Beijing to Shanghai. In addition to students, a wide array of different

groups also publicly displayed disagreement with the Beijing government. The lower class was also very angry at the current state of affairs,
such as mistreatment of workers and perpetual poverty of peasants.
Chancellors of China's advanced education institutions called for the
release of students held in prisons. The media, citizen societies, cham-
bers of commerce, and other civil organizations offered their support
for these students as well. In Shanghai, these protests culminated in
strikes by merchants and workers that affected the entire Chinese
economy. As a result, the Beijing government released the arrested
demonstrators, dismissed the negotiators of the Paris conference, and
refused to sign the Versailles Treaty. This latest protest, known as the
May Fourth Movement, seemed to have been successful, but the government was powerless to dislodge Japan from the control of Korea
and Shandong. It did, however, demonstrate that the student movement could serve important political aims within the nation.

News about these events eventually reached Guiyang; its newspaper began to publish detailed stories on the Versailles Conference and
on the activities of students in other cities. Local newspapers reported
on the activities of Guizhou students in Beijing, which sparked student activities in Guiyang and elsewhere in the province. Sensing an
opportunity to advance its objectives, the YGA increased their political activities. In late May 1919, the leaders of the YGA in Guiyang met
with representatives from eighty-one provincial counties to prepare
and to create a new representative body called the Guizhou National
People's Assembly. Wall posters throughout Guiyang described the
assembly and its purpose, calling on the people of Guizhou to fight
for the return of Shandong Province, the abolition of the twenty-one
demands, and an end to Japanese expansion. More than one thousand province-wide representatives attended the assembly's opening
session conducted by He Yingqin in Guiyang in June 1919.

Liu Xianshi's concerns were exacerbated by the inability of his
PSA to take the lead of the students from the YGA. In fact some the
most capable PSA members actually switched to the YGA. Liu next

tried to call on his allies among the educators to control the students. He established an editorial board of his supporters to control the publishing of newspapers and student journals. When none of these activities deterred the YGA in any substantial way, Liu finally take the most hostile measure by resorting to restriction and prohibition by the police. The students were initially intimidated by the police, but He Yingqin then sent military cadets to protect the students, and together their number forced the police to back off. The chief of police had to state that the confrontation was due a misunderstanding and the demonstration was indeed a patriotic activity and allowed to continue.

Although YGA's success had become an addition to the political base of the Wang brothers, the Guizhou Army and Military Academy remained the most important element of their influence. As commander-in-chief, Dilun had substantial authority over the army, but Liu Xianshi and his officials controlled the provincial financial resources. Thus the Liu and Wang factions now had to extend their confrontation to financing and economic programs. In early 1919, the two factions debated a plan for a foreign loan to build a railroad across Guizhou, and the controversy propelled their confrontation into a new and more violent stage.

❖ ❖ ❖

Since his student days in Tokyo, Boqun had been convinced that the railroad was at the heart of progress and modernization for China. He had many discussions with Sun Yatsen, who was also a strong supporter of the railroad. In fact, when Sun resigned his provisional presidency in favor of Yuan Shikai, he asked for the job of building a network of railroads throughout China as his alternative contribution to modernize the country. Sun returned from his Japanese exile soon after Yuan Shikai's death in 1916 and set up his operation for the reinstatement of the republic in Shanghai.

Boqun (c) with Guizhou Provincial Assembly Members

In mid-1918 when Boqun met Sun in Shanghai, he was introduced to an overseas Chinese man named Zhao Shijin who had helped Sun in raising funds from overseas Chinese for railroad construction in China. Boqun realized the railroad might be the stone that could kill two birds; he approached Zhao with a plan to raise money to build a new railroad from Chongqing, Sichuan, to Liuzhou, Guangxi, through Guiyang. Zhao agreed to assist in raising five million US dollars for the project. Upon return to Guiyang, Boqun presented the project to Liu Xianshi.

> This is a unique opportunity for Guizhou. You have agreed in our many previous discussions about the railroad being the backbone of modern transportation, which would allow Guizhou to tap the full potential of its coal, silver, and other natural resources. With modern technologies and the railroad, Guizhou will finally move from one of

the poorest provinces up to top half of better-off provinces, and here are my financial calculations. Second, we will have also enough funds for the army to expand and modernize so we can keep up and become independent from our neighbors. Finally, Zhao is absolutely trustworthy because of his experience with Sun Yatsen.

Liu agreed to proceed with the project, and in March 1919 Boqun signed a preliminary agreement with Zhao that required the authorization of the Guizhou provincial assembly within three months. When the provincial assembly began to discuss the loan, Liu Xianshi initially supported the plan. Others suggested taking the loan but using the money for different projects that might benefit Guizhou more, such as developing silver mines or constructing roads. Dilun made a strong case to set aside $1 million of the loan for the refitting and expansion of Guizhou army.

Several officials of Liu's provincial government dissented, most notably Zhang Xielu, the director of public finance, and Cheng Tingce, the director of political affairs, both long-time and ardent supporters of Liu Xianshi. Zhang and Cheng opposed the proposal publicly that such a large loan would burden the province with too much debt. They disapproved of borrowing foreign money even though it would come from overseas Chinese, who had financed the various Sun Yatsen–led revolution uprisings. They also realized organizing and managing such a large project might be too much for them, and if they failed in the project in any way, they would be held responsible, while the Wang brothers would reap the rewards of any success. Zhang Xielu therefore demanded that the assembly restrict the loan amount to a maximum of $2 million and not allow any part of it to be applied to other purposes than for the railroad. Zhang explained his opposition to both the loan and the railroad project in a report of several hundred pages to the assembly. In private, Zhang joined by Cheng and other political allies of Liu in warning Liu that strengthening the army meant vesting more power to Dilun, which would be like adding oil to a blazing fire for the

Liu faction. They persuaded Liu to withdraw his support, and the project was scuttled.

❖ ❖ ❖

Since Dilun returned to Guiyang from Sichuan after his success in winning the National Protection War against Yuan Shikai's Beiyang Army in mid-1916, two personal tragedies had befallen him. In 1917 he lost his five-year-old, Chongxing, to pneumonia, which caused him great grief, especially because he was away in battles for almost half the boy's short life. It brought unbearable pain to his wife and mother as well. His wife was particularly despondent, and she took up opium to help her live through the pain, which was not considered taboo at the time. Dilun, out of loneliness and grief, decided to take a concubine, which again was not scandalous at the time. On April 4, 1919, Dilun's wife died of an overdose of opium at age thirty. She was a favorite niece of Liu Xianshi and much loved by Dilun's mother. There were numerous rumors that she committed suicide due to Dilun's taking on a concubine. It was impossible to establish what was responsible for her tragic and untimely death, but Dilun felt remorse and was despondent for some time. Liu Xianshi and the rest of the Liu clan, however, felt that Dilun did actually cause his wife's death, and this added to the political struggles that began to fray the close connection between the two families.

The controversy over the loan and railroad project finally brought the power struggle between the Liu clan and the Wang clan to a head. Boqun had lost a lot time, effort, and creditability, which led the Wang brothers to review their strategy of modernizing the province. Dilun proposed the direct approach of challenging Liu for his position.

Boqun thought this would cause bloodshed and the breakup of the two clans. Instead, he proposed,

The only chance we can be successful to implement some reform in the Guizhou government is with Uncle's cooperation. Tang Chiyao will likely to stand by him and send the Yunnan Army against us if we act militarily against him. Besides, we would lose the respect of the citizens and our supporters if we moved against him and against our filial duties to both families. There are uncertainties among his supporters, and we should try to convince some of them to see our position and help us to isolate him and hopefully change his direction of governance. If that fails then I would move against the key people around him who are set against us, such as Cheng and Zhang. I would never touch Uncle, to whom we both owe a lot, and also for Mother's sake, we must try our best to allow him to save face and suffer no harm.

Dilun didn't think Boqun's proposal was realistic, but he wanted to follow his advice and make sure no stone was left unturned. Dilun then ask several of his royal officers, including He Yingqin, to form a committee to advocate the division of civil and military administration as the Beijing government originally established under Yuan Shikai. Boqun and Dilun then approached Ren Kecheng, a respected CPA leader and a former teacher of Dilun, to serve as the chairman of the committee. In a private discussion with Liu Xianshi, Ren tested the idea of separating the administration and found that Liu was vehemently against it. He sensed immediately that Dilun was behind the whole idea and rejected it out of hand. Liu then asked Boqun what he knew about this proposal and in essence tried to determine whether he could persuade Dilun to back off. Boqun responded,

Of course I know Dilun is frustrated by the demise of the railroad project, as I am. I truly feel that Zhang Xielu and Chen Tingce are wrong in their assessments and we missed a great opportunity. Worse yet, we will not be able to attract any funds for reform or development so long as the CPA controls the assembly since they want to avoid any change that may undermine their position or status. We are indeed in debt to you for our respective careers, and you are putting us in positions perhaps to take your place when you are ready, but the world is changing fast and we must move with the tide now. Dear uncle, we are just trying to clarify the situation we face so you can go down in history as a patriot. Dilun is a man of action. He is just trying to show you how most of the people in Guizhou feel, which is not reflected in a report of hundreds of page but voices that dare to speak up.

While Liu Xianshi pondered his next move, the YGA organized a campaign against Zhang Xielu, denouncing him as a criminal for his financial administration, which had caused the province-wide poor economic development and inflation, which in turn made life difficult for many citizens. Demonstrators also claimed that Zhang's opposition to the loan and railroad project proved that he had no interest in modernizing Guizhou or helping its people. Hundreds of soldiers and cadets joined student protestors outside Zhang's office, and his home was ransacked as well. On November 26, 1919, while Boqun was in Shanghai, Dilun invited Liu Xianshi and several members of his faction, including Cheng Tingce, to a banquet to discuss provincial affairs. On his way home, Cheng was wounded by an assassin, who escaped. Cheng was justifiably shaken, and he accused Dilun of masterminding the incident.

Following the attack on Cheng Tingce, Dilun increased the pressure against Zhang Xielu. Once again he worked through the YGA. He Yingqin was joined by two of Dilun's trusted lieutenants, Gu Zhenglun and Sun Jianfeng, who organized students and cadets for a massive public demonstration against Zhang on December 3, 1919. They planned to increase the number of participants by handing out surplus army uniforms to local gang members and beggars. They would demand that Zhang stand trial for his crimes. In setting the stage for the event, the YGA paper announced on December 1 the impending demonstration and published several articles attacking Zhang for his crime and calling for his trial in court. Zhang realized Liu Xianshi would not risk putting himself in the target of the demonstrators. Thus he was in an impossible predicament since Liu would not defend him. To avoid the humiliation of mock trial, Zhang committed suicide by poison on December 2.

At this point, Liu Xianshi realized that, filial duties or not, Dilun would not settle for anything other than control of the provincial government to achieve his reforms. Backed into a corner, Liu decided he must act now to stop Dilun since even his life might be in danger. He sought out his elder sister and Dilun's mother for advice, and she replied:

> My dear brother, you have told me many times that you have been grooming my sons to take over the governance of Guizhou. You know that they are young, capable, and progressive. Guizhou now needs to be modernized so we can help our people to improve their lives. Frankly, you are not the man for job since you do not really believe in changes. Why don't you just gracefully bow out and let my sons take over? I can assure you they will protect you and the Liu clan's safety and wealth. Why not go and enjoy your life to pursue your intellectual and spiritual sides that you have always told me you wanted instead the hassles of politics and governance?

Liu was stricken dumb by his elder sister and told her she had lost her mind and worse she had lost her concern for her own clan. He then decided that his salvation was to remove Wang as commander-in-chief of the army. Thus, Liu embarked on a course that resulted in the so-called Minjiu (ninth republican year) Incident. As he had done several times previously, Liu asked Tang Chiyao of Yunnan for his help in removing Dilun from his command. Tang disliked Dilun's independence from his "supreme" command as the southwest leader and threatened his hidden agenda to become a contender for national leadership and successor to Sun Yatsen. Tang wired his agreement to help Liu to regain his control over the Guizhou army, for he considered Dilun to be not fit as a commander-in-chief since Tang had long held that Dilun's lack of formal military training disqualified him for military leadership. Then Tang, as the supreme commander of three southwest provinces, wired Liu that he would send one of his Yunnan generals to Guizhou to take over control from Dilun. Liu was hesitant to turn over the control of the Guizhou Army to Tang, which was not his original intent, but he realized he had no other choice at the time.

The wire from Tang was read by one of Dilun's supporters, who informed him of what had transpired. Dilun, still in Chongqing, Sichuan, became extremely angry that his uncle would actually turn over the army to Tang. Dilun then secretly contacted the Yunnan army commander in Sichuan, who happened to be Dilun's close friend, suggesting that both the Yunnan and Guizhou Armies were no longer needed in Sichuan and should return to their respective provinces. His friend agreed and received Tang's permission to start withdrawal. Dilun then exchanged wires with Boqun and brought him up to date on the recent course of events, and Boqun agreed that their uncle had left them with little choice but to remove him from power. He warned Dilun to do all he could to distance himself from the event and make sure no harm would come to Liu Xianshi.

In October of 1920, Dilun held a meeting with all Guizhou army officers, told them about the wire from Tang, and said,

> The state of our home province is a mess. Liu Xianshi has become a puppet of the CPA-controlled assembly and his conservative cabinet. In 1919 provincial income was over five million yuans, twenty percent growth over

the last year, yet our total army budget has stayed at only two million during our expedition in Sichuan in the last two years. We have scarified many lives of officers and men, and we are overextended in all the ranks. My request for an increase of twenty percent for this year has been disapproved by the assembly. Now I have heard Liu is about to cede the control of the Guizhou Army to Tang Chiyao and you are to be put under a Yunnan's general appointed by Tang, who is en route to Guiyang as we speak. Liu is now Tang's puppet, and Liu will give our army to serve Tang's own agenda instead that of Sun Yatsen. We cannot accept this and will have to take control of Guizhou ourselves. Are you all with me?

All the officers, including Yuan Zuming, gave Dilun a thunderous and resounding yes. Dilun then named Lu Tao as the acting commander-in-chief to lead the army back to Guizhou. He then asked Yuan Zuming to accompany him to Shanghai, where he would consult with doctors about his combat fatigue, as one usually did in situations where one wished to avoid direct responsibility. Dilun obviously did not want to be in Guiyang when his plan to dislodge his uncle was implemented, and he wanted Yuan Zuming to be with him so he could keep his eyes on him and keep him away from the troops who might be loyal to him. Dilun wired Liu and advised him:

As you no doubt know, the Yunnan army has started their withdrawal back to Yunnan. Our army has been away from home for more than two years. Most of the men need and deserve to return for a leave with their families and to rest up for the next crisis. Our army also needs weapons refitting and supplies. Thus I will direct

Lu Tao to lead the army back to Guizhou forward base
of Zunyi while I take my three months of medical leave
in Shanghai. The army will at your disposal till my return.

In secret, Dilun then discussed the takeover plan with his chief of
staff, Gu Zhenglu, and Sun Jianfeng, who, in conjunction with He
Yingqin, would implement the plan. His verbal instructions were that in
order to raise no suspicions, Gu should remain in Zunyi while Sun
would go to Guiyang and meet immediately with He Yingqin to round
up the key supporters of Liu Xianshi so Liu would be isolated and
forced to resign both of his positions of civil and military governor.
Dilun stressed that no harm must come to his uncle. It was rumored
but not proven that Dilun actually drew up a list of who was to be killed
and detained among the supporters, or he
actually left the choices up to the men he
sent to implement the plan. After this, Dilun
and his companions boarded a ship in
Chongqing harbor, embarking for Shanghai.

In October 1920, all Guizhou forces left
Sichuan and returned to Guizhou via Zunyi,
north of the capital. On November 10 Sun
arrived in Guiyang, where he met with He
Yingqin and went over the list of those targeted for assassination. He argued to keep the
list short, while Sun argued for more names so
they might destroy Liu's entire faction. After
consulting two other trusted politicians, they

**Dilun (l) and
Lu Tao, 1920**

agreed that excess bloodshed could turn the citizens and students of
Guiyang against them, and therefore they settled on four men, all key
supporters of Liu Xianshi: the leader of his political organization, his chief
secretary, and his heads financial affairs and of military affairs.

After these assassinations, Liu Xianshi would be forced to resign and to surrender the seal of both offices. Liu knew no specifics of this plot, but rumors reached him through his spies. He sent orders to Liu Xianqian in Xingyi to return to the capital with his military force. He also got in touch with Yuan Zuming, telling him to agitate against Wang from inside and perhaps seek to turn the troops against Dilun. Late on the night of the tenth, random shots rang out in various parts of Guiyang, signaling that the coup had begun. He's police brigade was put into action for the coup; He remained in the background while Sun led four squads each targeting the four Liu supporters to be killed. Two of the four were killed, and their heads were displayed on stakes at the main square as criminals. The other two managed to escape, but most of their male relatives were killed when the soldiers couldn't locate them.

While his close supporters lost their heads or fled the city, Liu Xianshi spent a sleepless night in his compound, surrounded by his twenty or so personal guards. Over the next few days, Liu found out what had happened to his supporters. He realized that his own life could be in danger; Liu resigned his positions as both civil and military governor and turned over the seals to Sun. Liu decided to leave Guiyang and return to his home in Xingyi, but clearly he was not in a position to fight his way back with the limited troops he had, and he feared for his life if the coup leaders come after him.

At first Sun wanted to detain him until Dilun returned. Liu threatened suicide, without avail. He then turned to his elder sister, the mother of the Wang brothers, for help. She persuaded He Yingqin to allow Liu to leave for Xingyi. On November 18 she personally escorted her brother from Guiyang to Anshun. At Anshun Liu Xianshi met up with his cousin, Liu Xianqian, and his troops. They continued together to Xingyi, while Mother Wang returned to the capital. Evidently Liu's fears for his safety had some foundation. The escort leader later reported that Sun Jianfeng had ordered him to accompany Liu Xianshi to Anshun and had urged him to set up an ambush to kill Liu along the way. He did not do that since Dilun's mother had warned him that the Wang brothers would not want anything to happen to Liu, particularly while she was with him.

After Liu had left the city, rumors circulated that Tang had ordered his Yunnan forces to join with Liu Xianqian's troops to retake Guiyang and restore Liu Xianshi to power. He Yingqin quickly moved to implement the second part of the plan, which called for Ren Kecheng to serve as acting provincial governor until Dilun's return. Though critical of Liu Xianshi, Ren wanted no part of the coup and refused the position. Dilun then ordered Lu Tao to advance his arrival in Guiyang with the army. In late November 1920, Lu Tao took over as the acting governor awaiting the return of Dilun, who assumed the position of military governor of Guizhou in addition to his position of the commander-in-chief of the army. At this point Boqun was also absent from Guiyang to attend Sun Yatsen's new military government in Guangzhou.

CHAPTER 9

1921-1924

SOVIET ASSISTANCE AND THE DEATH OF HEROES

In January 1921, Sun Yatsen reconvened the GMD parliament in Guangzhou to plan for the unification with the Beijing government. After confirmation of the successful coup in Guiyang, Dilun and Boqun met Sun Yatsen in Guangzhou. Dilun reported to Sun that Guizhou was now part of the GMD republic and ready to serve his government in the unification process. Sun was extremely pleased since he always had been concerned about Tang Jiao's motives, and having a true believer like Dilun in the southwest would greatly enhance the republic's cause. Sun appointed Dilun as member of the Standing Military Committee of the GMD and asked Dilun to meet the other members of the committee, including Chen Jiongming and Jiang Jieshi. Sun also gave him a list of various European and American munitions suppliers for the Guizhou Army's needs.

When Dilun returned to Shanghai with Boqun in January 1921, he stayed in the French concession residence of Boqun. The brothers spent much time together talking about their plan for Guizhou. Boqun express his wish to remain with Sun in Guangzhou for the formation of a new government, and Sun had already asked him to serve as the first minister of communication. Boqun felt that he could make a real contribution since the foreigners controlled the network of communication from the post office to the railway, road building, and air travel. Dilun, of course, wanted his brother to be running the provincial government and himself to serve on the national military level as well as being the military strong man of Guizhou. Boqun stated,

> Dilun, you must return to Guizhou and secure your control of the military, for that is all important now for China and for Guizhou. You have to be the counterweight to the ambitious Tang, who, like Yuan Shikai, is aspiring to be the emperor. If after your return you need me to come and help in any way then I will do so since I think securing Guizhou for the republic takes priority over any national service when we don't yet have a unified nation.

Dilun promised he would return as soon as he could complete the purchase of arms needed by the army that he estimated would require another thirty days or so for the bidding and selection processes among numbers of foreign vendors. Dilun decided that in his rarely available free time, he should enjoy the bright light and beautiful women of Shanghai, and thus he rented two rooms in an English hotel in the British concession as his base of operation. He also made sure Yuan Zuming stayed at a hotel nearby with several of his other associates so he could keep track of him. Yuan spent most of time wining and womanizing in the hotel, but one day he asked Dilun's permission to go to Beijing to interview several foreign weapons suppliers from whom might be able to get a better deal than those in

Dilun, 1920

Shanghai. Dilun granted his permission for Yuan to go to Beijing. Once in Beijing, Yuan was surprised that the weapons supplier turned out be Liu Xianzhi, Liu Xianshi's younger brother and his representative to the Beijing government. Liu stated,

> General Yuan, my older brother has always had the highest regard for your ability to lead, and he also has understood the humiliation you have suffered under Wang Dilun's command. Since the Minjiu Incident, our two families are now enemies. The Wang family's power rests entirely in the hands of Wang Dilun. We would like to have your assistance to eliminate him and restore Liu Xianshi's position in the province, and in return, you will replace Wang as the commander-in-chief of the army. Although I am now speaking to you on my own volition without my older brother's knowledge, I am certain that if we can eliminate Wang, you will be the one he would choose to replace Wang due to your long-standing relationship."

Since Yuan already had the idea of assassinating Dilun, this opportunity just fell into his lap, and he accepted without hesitation and wanted to know the plan Liu had in mind. Liu then told him that a professional assassin in Shanghai, Zhang Keming, had already been engaged, and Yuan needed to give Zhang Dilun's daily routine and schedules in Shanghai so Zhang would have the best opportunity for success. Actually, Yuan had another secret meeting in Beijing with Jin Yunpeng, the premier and minister of war of the Beijing government, who had just replaced Duan Qirui. Jin told him that Beijing wished to remove Wang Dilun's control of the Guizhou Army and replace him with Yuan. Yuan readily agreed, and Jin promised him the position of general of the army and commander-in-chief of the Guizhou Pacification Army. In addition, Jin promised a 20 million yuan funding for the province. Thus, a short trip to Beijing netted Yuan all he had wished for and dreamed of.

Yuan returned to Shanghai, set up the assassin, Zhang, in the hotel opposite to Dilun's residence, and gave him as much as Yuan knew about Dilun's activities. Zhang observed Dilun for over a week without success since Dilun had been forewarned about possible assassinations, and he did not follow a set pattern or time schedule. Most the time he would sneak out of the hotel and take a rickshaw instead of using his car, and he scheduled most business meetings in his hotel. On March 16, 1921, Dilun had concluded his business and gathered some of his associates in the hotel for a celebration, with Yuan in attendance as well. While the rowdy party was in progress, Dilun took a phone call from Boqun asking him to come to Boqun's residence to meet with Li Liehchun and the military governor of Zhejiang Province, both of whom were important to the GMD and Sun Yatsen's republic. Dilun agreed, and Boqun told him his car would be sent for Dilun in fifteen minutes. Yuan overheard all this, and he made an excuse for the bathroom and instead made a call to Zhang and informed him to get ready. As Dilun opened the car door, Zhang fired his rifle; the first one hit Dilun in his right arm. Instead of getting into the car, Dilun turned and looked at Zhang, as though to see who dared to commit this dastardly deed. Zhang's next two shots were on target, and Dilun died instantly at age thirty-three.

Boqun was notified by one of Dilun subordinates by phone as the car sped Dilun away to the hospital. Boqun asked immediately whether Yuan was present. Moreover, was he involved in the assassination? Boqun then left with his two guests to go to the hospital and found out that his beloved brother had died before arrival. All three men knew Dilun well, and all of them cried uncontrollably despite their respective well-practiced self-composure. Boqun, being Dilun's elder brother, felt extreme sadness and substantial guilt for not having counseled his younger brother well enough to avoid this tragedy. He had to muster all his strength to deal with the political aftermath and his family, particularly his mother back in Guiyang. He decided to keep the news of Dilun's death to a minimum of people but to announce Dilun had been wounded and was expected to make a full recovery in a short time. He arranged to store Dilun's remains in an undisclosed location and placed a double in a heavily guarded hospital room. He called Lu Tao and He Yingqin to make a carefully drafted statement to the rest of the concerned people. He secured the funds Dilun had brought with him for munitions. He called Sun Yatsen and told him about the assassination. Sun was as stricken and saddened as were the other two GMD members with Boqun; he gave his condolences and promised not to disclose the news until Boqun was ready to do so. The list went on and on until dawn of the next day. Before Boqun dropped off to sleep, he wrote in his diary:

> The bright sun of our lives has been sniffed out,
> Half of my body has thus lost, my mind has thus numbed.
> How will I deal with our world in my present state?
> How can do I do our duties without my other half?
> Show me that you still will be by my side,
> As surely as the moon will rise in the night.
> I will endeavor to push on for our cause,
> Till our dreams become real and history turns about.

On August 10, 1921, Dilun's remains were finally moved by train from his temporary burial place in Shanghai to his resting place in his new home in Hangzhou after a state funeral in Shanghai. Boqun never told his mother of Dilun's death, and it was possible since she seldom saw Dilun after he was made the principal military leader in

Guizhou. Sun Yatsen and most GMD officials attended the funeral. Sun then issued a proclamation in memorial for the occasion.

> Commander-in-Chief of the Guizhou Army, Wang Dilun, served with honor and bravery for establishing the republic. He made extraordinary and valiant contributions in battles for the protection of the nation and its constitution in Sichuan and Hunan against overwhelming odds. He worked with the president of the republic in Shanghai and Guangzhou to formulate the platforms of the republic's future unified national armed forces. As a lieutenant general, he served his country and made the ultimate sacrifice in the assassin's hands. Wang Dilun is by this order promoted to general of the Republican Army with all the respect and privileges therein. Signed by Sun Yatsen, generalissimo of the Republic of China.

❖ ❖ ❖

Since Liu Xianshi's had resigned and Lu Tao had assumed the caretaker's position awaiting the return of Dilun, Guiyang was in a power vacuum. Lu turned out to be a poor administrator and politician, and others in Guiyang began to jockey for power, which caused chaos all over again. Certain army brigades, especially those previously commanded by Yuan Zuming, began to call for his return. He Yinggin was appointed as chief of staff of the Guizhou army, and he did his best to hold a power base for the Wang family without much success given his junior status among all the contenders. After Dilun's death became common knowledge in late 1921, Sun Yatsen, at Boqun's request, appointed Lu Tao as the civil governor, but that did not seem to improve the situation. Boqun sensed that the political situation was extremely fluid, and he was concerned about his family's security there. Thus in April 1921, he initiated a quiet move of his extended family, including his mother, sisters, in-laws, and He Yingqin, to Shanghai to be housed in several houses he had purchased on the same street block in Shanghai. Boqun wired He to this effect and asked for his help in the move. At the same time, He had an offer from one his classmate, Wang Boling, from his Japan days, now serving in the Yunnan Army, and he felt that it would be better for his career than a move to Shanghai without a position. Thus, he wired Boqun:

> I appreciated you offer to set my family up in Shanghai, but I am a soldier and I wanted to be involved in military action. I realize that our family has had its differences with Yunnan under Tang Jiyao, but at least he has professed to support Sun Yatsen for the republic. I think the Yunnan position will be best for me in my career. It will provide more combat experiences, and I can be more useful in combat than in Shanghai. I have also discussed this with your sister, and she seemed to agree with me, subject to your approval, elder brother.

Boqun respond with his approval but suggested he still send his wife to Shanghai to keep her from harm's way until he had settled in and still come to Shanghai if he changed his mind for any reason. He Yingqin's assignment in Kunming was as a senior instructor at the famous Yunnan Military Academy, which was a stepping-stone to a combat army officer position. In December 1921, as he entered a teahouse in downtown Kunming and started on the stairs to go to the second floor, two men shot him in the leg and chest. He was rushed to a French hospital and operated on to remove the bullets. The bullets were safely removed, and He was left with a slight limp.

173

He then asked the surgeon to announce that the bullet in his chest was not removable and he might die within a short time to forestall further attempts on his life. Subsequent investigation connected the assassins to Yuan Zuming and the Liu family. When He was well enough to travel, he decided to go to Shanghai after all and stayed with his wife for recovery and to trust Boqun with what should be his next move.

In August 1922 the Beijing government, as previously promised, appointed Yuan Zuming as civil governor for Guizhou, and Yuan returned from Sichuan and took his office in Guiyang. Yuan, upon arrival, took control of the bank and authorized a bond issue of 10 million yuan partially to fund his own needs of building a new home and to give awards to his friends and clan. Almost at the same time, Sun appointed Boqun as the civil governor of Guizhou to replace Luo Tao. Boqun was unable to return to Guiyang since Yuan Zuming had taken over Guizhou. It was fortuitous that Boqun managed to move all his family in Guiyang to Shanghai to ensure their safety before Yuan arrived. Tang Jiyao was upset by Yuan Zuming's defection to the Beijing government and that Guizhou was lost from his sphere of power. As commander in chief of the Yunnan, Guizhou, and Sichuan Armies, he sent Liu Xianshi back to Guiyang with a division of the Yunnan Army under the command of Tang's cousin, Tang Jiyu. Outnumbered, out-gunned, and unsure of the loyalty of the Guizhou army, Yuan withdrew with his army from Guizhou into Xiushan, Sichuan, where no one had a firm hold of the province and Yuan thought he could gain dominance.

The Beijing government had its own political and military conflict among the various Beiyang warlords. Wu Peifu, who had his hands full in the north, promoted Yuan to general of the army, with specific responsibility of border patrol of Sichuan and Guizhou. In addition, Yuan was appointed as the commander-in-chief of the coalition army of the provinces of Sichuan, Guizhou, Shaanxi, Gansu, and Hubei, all provinces Wu had little control over, and he hoped Yuan might be able to provide some assistance. Yuan was extremely pleased with such grand titles and nominal control of the army's Thirty-Fourth Division, with over one hundred thousand troops spread out over the five provinces. Even with Beijing's support, Yuan was unable to pacify the entire Sichuan Province, and he wound up in Chongqing with control over the surrounding counties.

❖ ❖ ❖

In April of 1921, Sun Yatsen was the generalissimo once again when the provisional parliament met in Guangzhou, and he started to plan for the northern expedition to unify the nation. Chen Jiongming, however, was reluctant to follow Sun in his drive to war with the Beiyang warlords, which would require just about all his province's available funding. Chen had a plan of his own that limited military spending to only 30 percent, whereas social improvements in education and health care would take 50 percent. Chen also proposed a federation of southern provinces where he could make social changes, improve living standards, and leave the northern provinces to fight among themselves. Jiang Jieshi proposed to dismiss Chen and install himself as commander of Chen's army with an extravagant military plan of US$30 million funding to entice the Jiangxi and Sichuan warlords to join the expedition, which even Sun thought was questionable, and Boqun called it highly improbable. Jiang left in a huff for Shanghai to marry his second wife and to visit his sick mother.

Sun decided to launch his northern expedition from Guilin, Guangxi, on the border with Hunan, where there still was the National Protection Army second division made up of Yunnan and Guizhou troops led by Li Liejun, who was Sun's ardent supporter over the years and one of the Wang brothers' best friends. Li was appointed by Sun as commander of the First Route Northern Expedition Army. In July, Sun also order Lu Tao in Guiyang and his Guizhou Army to join the expedition in Gulin. En route, Lu's Guizhou army was weakened by an epidemic of malaria and attacks by bandits and opposing Guangxi troops. Lu Tao, sick and wounded, had to go back to Guiyang. Some of his staff officers remained with Li's army, and others decided to call on Yuan Zuming to come back to Guizhou to take charge of the province. Sun had to abort his campaign when his northern warlord ally, Zhang Zuolin, was defeated by Wu Peifu in the Zhili–Fengtian war of 1921 and was in no position to assist Sun.

In the meantime, Chen Jiongming grew increasingly wary of Sun militant activities using his provinces as a base and decided that Sun needed to leave. When Sun returned to Guangzhou with only fifty personal guards from his aborted northern expedition, he announced that he had advanced weapons that could destroy sixty battalions in three hours to scare off any idea of Chen's possible opposition of his return. Chen was undeterred, and on June 16, 1922, he decided to bombard Sun's compound and to drive him and his staff from the city. Sun, his wife, and others left on Sun's gunboat via the Pearl River for Whampoa Island, where his naval unit of six gunboats met them and sailed to a British concession island and away from the reach of Chen's bombardment. Upon hearing the news, Jiang Jieshi and his new wife left Shanghai for Hong Kong and joined Sun's group on the gunboat a few days later. After the British had interceded for an armistice, Chen agreed to let Sun and his party, including Boqun, leave in early August on a Russian cruise ship for Shanghai.

Sun Yatsen's experiences with the various warlords had proven that their sense of self-preservation prevented them from being true republicans. Sun was now convinced that to unify the nation, the GMD would need its own army that must be recruited and trained quickly to achieve its goal of the northern expedition. Sun then doubled his effort to seek financial and military assistance from the major powers of the world, including the United States, Great Britain, and France, all of whom refused any meaningful support due to their own economy recovery from the Great War. On the other hand, Soviet Russia had been interested in China since late 1919.

The Russian Soviets had promised Sun arms and financial aid of two million gold rubles that would allow him to build such an army and to forfeit all Russian extraterritorial rights on the condition that the Chinese Communist Party members would be admitted into GMD. In January of 1923, Sun sent Liao Zongkai to Tokyo to meet with the Russian ambassador to China and Comintern representative, Adolph Joffe, to negotiate an agreement for cooperation that was signed by Sun Yatsen on January 26, 1923.

The communist movement in China was one of the result of May 4 movement of 1919; it was an integration of various study groups of intellectuals and radical thinkers with an interest in Marxism and socialism. At the same time, Soviet Russia began to develop an interest in China. Lenin laid down a policy framework at the Comintern second congress in 1920 that revolutionary success in China, as in other colonial countries, necessitated forging a temporary alliance with the bourgeois while maintaining the independence of the proletarian. It was clear to Lenin and Trotsky that for the initial time the better-positioned bourgeois would control of the revolutionary movement. Soviet representatives in China held discussions with the various left-leaning groups throughout 1920 on establishing a Chinese Communist Party (CCP).

Most of the people involved in this initial stage were writers, professors, and students, who all shared the desire to replace Confucianism with new social and political practices to bring China into the modern world. Interest in labor and workers' movements also emerged as a political and social force after the May 4 movement. The first CCP organization was established in Shanghai in August 1920. Initially the CCP's focus was on the working class and hostility toward the bourgeoisie. Maring, the Comintern representative at the time, had a negative assessment of the nascent CCP as compared to the better-organized GMD in Guangzhou. Maring suggested to the CCP leadership that its members should join the GMD to form a bloc on the ground that it was not a bourgeois organization but one formed from the intelligentsia, patriots within and outside China, the military, and the labor. At the CCP's second congress of 1922, it agreed to join the GMD on a temporary basis, in spite of its doubt of Sun Yatsen strategy of military unification. On February 1923, Wu Peifu brutally crushed the CCP and instigated the Zhengzhou railway workers' strike, which killed forty workers and wounded some two hundred. This incident confirmed to the CCP leadership that its organization lacked the muscle to go it alone.

Sun Yatsen had in fact recognized the importance of labor and workers in the revolutionary movement. He abolished the anti-labor laws Yuan Shikai had promulgated during his administration. In January 1921 Sun created a department to manage labor affairs. The GMD, through its minister of finance, Liao Zongkai, extended financial assistance to the seamen's strike in Hong Kong during early 1920. Sun's labor policy was limited since his focus continued to be military unification and he considered labor "a mere support force." After Sun had finalized his agreement with the Soviets, he spent considerable time reviewing his position regarding mass mobilization for the revolution in discussion with his closest associates; Liao Zongkai was the most supportive of his position.

Sun with He (l), Jiang (c), Wang

Sun decided to send Jiang Jieshi to Moscow to study the Soviets' political and military systems and to secure the Soviets' promises. Jiang was excited about the trip, for he believed with this experience he would be the authority on the Soviet military, which would allow him to assume the military leadership role of the GMD. On September 2, 1923, Jiang arrived in Moscow via the

Trans-Siberian Express Railway, where he met Leon Trotsky, who promised that the Soviets would provide the aid it had committed if GMD would accept CCP members into its ranks.

In November, the Comitern approved the promised aid conditioned on Sun's agreement to give up his northern expedition and spend the money on winning over the populace and building up a GMD army. The Soviets considered that without the mass support and a well-trained army, the expedition would not be successful. Jiang was surprised by the added condition, and he left the next day for Guangzhou. The experience left him with a lifelong mistrust of all communists. When Jiang returned to Guangzhou, Sun was already working with the Soviets on the political front. Jiang convinced Sun to stick to his original idea of building the GMD army with the Soviets' money but only delay the northern expedition until such a force could be readied. Since Sun agreed that a GMD army would need some time to be organized, he decided to delay the northern expedition as requested by the Soviets. Sun then appointed Jiang as the head of the preparatory committee for the Whampoa Military Academy for training officers of a new army.

In early 1923, while Jiang was still in Moscow, Boqun had introduced He Yingqin to Sun Yatsen, who offered He a position to serve as an adviser on his military staff. He then was reunited with Jiang Jieshi, who he had met during their Japan training days and serving together subsequently in the Shanghai army. Knowing something about He's experience and accomplishments in Guizhou, Jiang recommended to Sun to assign He to the preparatory committee. After the first meeting on February 21, Jiang disagreed with some funding choices and Soviet advisers' role; he left in disgust for Shanghai. Liao Zongkai and a committee of seven, including He Yingqin, had to do all the planning, recruitment, staffing, and site selection. Liao assigned He to the recruitment and selection function. Jiang eventually returned a month later after both Sun and Liao had assured him that the funding would be forthcoming and he would be the final authority on Soviet advisers' advice.

On October 6, 1923, at Sun Yatsen's request, the Soviet Comitern sent its member, Mikhail Borodin, to Guangzhou, as requested by Sun, as an adviser on political affairs and party organization. Borodin, a Russian Jew, worked for Lenin, was exiled to the United States, graduated from Valparaiso University in Indiana, and became a teacher of immigrant children in Chicago. He return to Russia in 1917 after Lenin was successful in the Bolshevik revolution and took on a number of successful assignments in the United States, Europe, and Mexico. He was also highly regarded in his trade. Borodin greatly influenced Sun in the subsequent GMD reorganization, including the admission of members of the CCP. Borodin made great progress by working directly with Sun Yatsen and Liao Zhongkai to expand the cooperation of the CCP and GMD with the promise of additional financial funding. Liao in particular was eager to learn more from Borodin about the revolutionary tactics of mass mobilization. Out of these discussions, Sun Yatsen formulated his three policies of great alliances: alliance with the Soviet Union, alliance with the CCP, and support of the workers and peasants.

In May of 1924, Jiang Jieshi appointed He Yingqin as the chief of instruction of the Whampoa Academy, responsible for the training of twenty plus other military academy graduates, who would then become the instructors for 150 students of the first class of the academy. This placed He just below Jiang as he has been with Dilun, as a right-hand man, a position He fitted into naturally. In spite of the political storm and the Soviet adviser's presence around him, He Yingqin doggedly worked at a rigorous training program aimed at completing a course in six months that would have taken two years at Baoding Military Academy. The resultant training at Whampoa was a seven-day week, Monday through Saturday morning in classroom and field drills in the afternoon and political lectures on Sunday. Unlike the Japanese military training program, it was unique in that cadets were prepared to go into combat immediately after training completion without actual service time for further experience. This demand put tremendous pressure on He and the other instructors.

The training followed the Japanese concepts and techniques of stressing aggressive action, discipline, self-sacrifice, and above all teamwork. Teamwork showed what came to be known as the "Whampoa spirit," which emphasized overcoming sizes or material disadvantages. Jiang would be involved almost on a daily basis relating his own military experience in Japan living the Spartan lifestyle of a highly disciplined soldier and stressing personal attitudes and behavior, subordination to the party, and care for the civilians. Jiang would repeatedly point out that sacrifice of one's life is the key to achieve victory; unity in purpose, superior strategy, and coordinated action will overcome advantage in troop size. Jiang gave lectures sometimes for hours on end, and many time repetitive, but He Yingqin would stand at attention and listen to every word since he believed in the same attributes, even though they had different personalities. Jiang was emotion driven and charismatic and He was serious, thoughtful, and rather bland. Nevertheless, they formed a strong bond through their shared values and personal habits.

❖ ❖ ❖

In January of 1924, the first national congress of the GMD approved a new constitution and a Central Executive Committee with ministries in charge of propaganda, workers and peasants, youth, women, investigation, communication, foreign affairs, and military affairs. Sun then restated his Three People's Principles to emphasize anti-imperialism as the basis of the party. The most controversial development was the election of ten CCP members to the Central Executive Committee, including Mao Zedong. Mao, the son of a wealthy farmer in Hunan, adopted an anti-imperialist outlook in early life, particularly influenced by the events of the revolution of 1911 and May Fourth Movement of 1919. Mao converted to Marxism-Leninism while working at Beijing University and became a founding member of the CCP.

The congress reorganized the GMD headquarters with communists selected as members of GMD Central Committee Organization Department and the Peasant and Worker Department. Subsequently, most of the country, with CCP and GMD leftists as the backbone, restructured the established GMD headquarters at all levels. Liao Zongkai was appointed as chairman of both the Bureau of Workers and the Bureau of Peasants Thereupon the GMD established by the bourgeoisie became a united front for democratic revolution and consisted of workers, peasants, and the bourgeois, much to the delight and satisfaction of the Soviet Comitern, especially Borodin, who could not stop complimenting Sun Yatsen on his accomplishment.

Liao Zongkai had become Sun Yatsen's point man on the labor movement. His speeches and writing in 1924 and 1925 reflected strong Soviet influence; his emphasis was mass education and mobilization as a basis for national unification. Liao was considered the leader of the GMD left, but his emphasis was anti-imperialism and anti-warlords. He described warlords as "domestic reactionary forces" and natural allies of the Western powers and Japan. In his quest for labor support, Liao had to depend on his new CCP friends and his longtime GMD associates, such as Hu Hanmin. In the summer of 1924, Liao was the governor of Guangdong, chief GMD representative of the Whampoa Military Academy, director of the Central Bank of China, chair of the Bureau of the Workers, and member of both the Central Executive Committee and the Political Council. His wife, He Xiangning, headed the Women's Bureau.

In this charged political environment, the CCP began to observe in April 1924 the factional struggle within the GMD; the leftists were advocates of revolution, and the rightists tended to compromise with warlords and imperialists. Wang Jingwei noted,

> Those comrades who are anti-imperialist turn to the left! Those who are content to live under the unequal

treaties, who want China to remain forever a semi-colony, and who support the perpetuation of the world-wide influence of imperialism, turn to the right!

In May of 1924, Liao convened the Guangdong Conference of Labor to unify and centralize the various worker organizations, and this was opposed by both the merchants and powerful labor unions. In the ensuing confrontation, Liao had polarized the labor movement in southern China and made many enemies in the GMD right. Liao had also caused significant concern from his good friend, Hu Hamin.

❖ ❖ ❖

On February 26, 1923, Liu Xianshi was finally reinstated in Guiyang as the both the civil and military governor, and Liu Xianqian, who played a significant part in the restoration process, controlled Anshun and western Guizhou in addition to Xingyi. The rest of Guizhou now fell under the direct control of the Yunnan Army under Tang Jiyu. As he approached ripe old age of sixty, Liu became less interested in power struggles in the province and the corruptions of his cronies in Guiyang. Liu became increasingly despondent and was only a puppet to those around him. Early in 1924, he resigned his posts, to be succeeded by Tang Jiyu, and moved to Kunming for medical treatment and died there on January 7, 1927, at age fifty-eight. He kept up his correspondence with Boqun, who he considered dearer to him than his own sons. In his last letter to Boqun, Liu was full of regrets and laments:

My dearest and wise nephew, it seems be an eternity since we last met. As I am now facing the end of my days, I wish you to know that I much regretted that my pride prevented me from turning the control of our beloved

Guizhou to you and your brother as I indeed intended to do. In retrospect, we would have had a stronger and more independent province, and its citizens would have benefited from your progressive reforms. Instead, I have subjugated Guizhou to Yunnan and left its citizens worse off than when we took over. History will not be kind to me and my clan. I truly regretted also that Dilun's life was short-lived and my brother acted without my knowledge; I hope the Wang family, especially my dear sister and you, will be able to forgive the Liu family and me. Finally, I want to thank you, Boqun, for your wise counsel and your devoted filial piety toward me over the years.

Boqun shed tears in reading his uncle's words, and he believed Liu Xianshi did not know his brother's plan of Dilun's assassination. Boqun also lamented about how different things might have turned out if the Liu and Wang families could have worked together instead against each other as his father wished.

❖ ❖ ❖

Cao Kun, with the military support of Wu Peifu, bribed the Zhili-controlled Beijing parliament to elect him president on October 10, 1923. The Beijing government was recognized as the legitimate government of the Republic of China, with a constitutional façade, aura of legitimacy, diplomatic recognition, and access to the customs and tax revenues and the potential for foreign loans. In September 1924 the second Zhili-Fengtian war broke out. Since his defeat in 1921, Zhang Zuolin had been preparing for a second war on both the military and the political front. Zhang formed a triple alliance with Sun Yatsen and Lu Yongxiang, the lone Anhui clique military governor of Zhejiang, Zhili, and Jiangsu. Zhang also had secret contact with

Feng Yuxiang, son of a Qing army officer, who joined the army at age eleven. He was converted to Methodism and sought to convert all his troops as well.

Feng distinguished himself from other warlords by governing his domains with a mixture of paternalistic socialism and military discipline. He forbade prostitution, gambling, and opium use. In 1914, Feng commended a Qing army brigade joined by others pursed and killed the infamous bandit White Wolf. Feng was sent to Sichuan to serve under Chen Huan in 1915 against Cai E in the National Protection War. Cai tried to recruit Feng to join him, but the war ended when they were still negotiating. Feng then returned to the north, and by August 1921, he was promoted to a division commander based in Shaanxi. He was sent by Wu Peifu to guard Beijing in 1923. Feng was inspired by Sun Yatsen and secretly plotted to overthrow Wu Peifu and Cao Kun, who controlled the Beiyang government.

When the Second Zhili-Fengtian War began in 1924, Wu Peifu had Zhang Zuolin on the run again when Feng switched sides and seized the capital in the Beijing Coup on October 23, 1924. This turnabout prompted the Shandong warlord to join the Fengtian and led to a decisive defeat of the Zhili forces. Wu retreated to his power base in Hebei and Henan. Feng imprisoned the Zhili leader and president, Cao Kun, brought back Duan Qirui as provisional president, evicted the last Emperor Puyi from the Forbidden City, and invited Sun Yatsen to Beijing to resurrect the republican government and reunify the country.

On November 10, 1924, Sun Yatsen departed from Hong Kong by his gunboat and was escorted by a Soviet frigate for Tianjin at the joint invitation of the Feng Yuxiang, Duan Qirui, and Zhang Zuolin for the purpose of the unification of China. Sun made an unofficial stop in Kobe, Japan, to solicit support for the abolition of the unequal treaty concessions ceded to Japan. He received a warm public welcome with extensive press coverage of his speeches and interviews but a cool reception by the Japanese government, which did not even grant him permission to visit Tokyo. On the other hand,

Duan's new ambassador in Tokyo was warmly received at almost the same time. For its own agenda of expansion into China, Japan was clearly betting on the northern warlords to win out against Sun's republicanism.

Sun became ill upon arrival in Tianjin on December 4 and was taken to Beijing for treatment. He was operated on, and doctors discovered that he had cancer that had spread to his liver and it was incurable. He died on March 12, 1925, in a friend's house with his wife, son, and several close followers and friends, including Borodin, the only foreigner, Wang Jingwei, and Liao Zongkai's wife, He Xiangning. Hu Hanmin, Liao Zongkai, and Jiang Jieshi all had to stay in Guangzhou to ensure no uprising would result from Sun's death. On February 24 Sun had left his last instructions and will to a group that consisted of his son, his wife, Soong Chingling, her younger brother, Soong Tseven, also known as TV, her brother-in-law, Kung Hsianghsi, Liao Zongkai's wife, He Xiangning, and Wang Jingwei. Sun's will became a sacred document and was read to open subsequent GMD congresses.

CHAPTER 10

1925-1927
EASTERN AND NORTHERN
EXPEDITIONS, PURGE OF CCP

Before Sun Yatsen left for Beijing, he had not appointed an official successor, but he did appoint Hu Hanmin as acting generalissimo in charge of the government. Hu had been one of Sun's most senior associates, and he supported admitting the CCP into the GMD. Hu, however, did not trust the Soviets, and he disagreed with Borodin on many critical issues, such as land distribution. When Sun formed the Revolutionary Committee, Hu was not named as a member as suggested by Borodin. Though Hu Hamin and Liao Zhongkai were the best of good friends in their RA days in Tokyo, they became estranged in 1924 over the voting right of the peasants in the mayoral election in Guangzhou. Hu had emerged as the spokesman for the GMD rightists and as the acting generalissimo; he would be considered the most likely successor to Sun Yatsen. Liao became concerned that Hu would lead the GMD to overturn Sun's three policies of great alliances, which would mean change in the revolutionary direction as envisioned by Sun.

Wang Jingwei 1925

Out of concern to keep the revolution on course, Liao Zongkai convened the Shantou Conference on the east coast of Guangzhou on May 25, 1925, to counter Hu's succession. Liao had the support of Borodin and the CCP. Hu recognized the strength of his opposition, and not wishing to contradict Sun Yatsen's heritage, he suggested a committee leadership. Liao and his supporters were agreeable and made Wang Jingwei the chair for the Executive Central Committee. Wang had the support of Borodin since he had shown receptiveness toward communism and perhaps Borodin considered him more flexible than Hu.

In June of 1925, the Guangdong government proclaimed itself as the Nationalist government, led by an Executive Committee of sixteen, with Wang Jingwei as the chairman. Liao Zhongkai retained his position as the minister of finance, and Hu Hanmin became the minister of foreign affairs, which essentially consisted of a relationship with Soviet Russia. The GMD rightists were enraged that Hu Hanmin was not the new GMD leader, and they charged that Wang Jingwei and Liao Zhongkai had plotted with Borodin against their own GMD members. Jiang Jieshi sat on the eight-man military council under Wang Jinwei. Boqun remained as the minister of communications and a member of the committee, as was Jiang Jieshi as the head of the National Revolution Army (NRA). The NRA nominally consisted of seven armies, with the Whampoa Army as the First Army under direct control of Jiang. The others were provincial armies of Hunan, Guangdong, Guangxi, Yunnan, Fujian, Guizhou, and combinations of parts of these provinces. While all leaders of these armies proclaimed support to the Nationalist government, they varied in size, training, and readiness. They, like the northern warlord armies, were divided by their regional differences and only loyal to their respective commanders.

The May 4 movement had started a modern labor movement in China that was most active in Shanghai and Guangzhou. The successful Hong Kong seamen strike in January 1922 ended in victory for the workers. This action spurred the growth of labor movement all over

China, and it was used by both GMD and CCP as their own propaganda for anti-imperialists and anti-capitalists. The movements thus expanded at breakneck speed, and many strikes followed through the next years. Several major strikes, particularly one in May 1925 against Japanese-owned plants in Shanghai, extended to the students and office workers as well, which involved hundred fifty thousand persons and lasted for over a year. The strikes then became political since many of the owners are foreigners, warlords, and GMD members. CCP seized this opportunity to organize the workers and strikes, and its membership soared to thirty thousand by May 1925. These events resulted in hundreds dead and injured and spread out throughout industrialized cities, including Nanjing, Guangzhou, and Hong Kong. The June 23 incident at the sand-banked Shamin Island resulted in many killed and injured. Liao Zongkai assumed a leading role in the anti-British strikes and boycott of foreign goods in Guangzhou and Hong Kong. He characterized these events as imperialistic oppression of the Chinese people and urged the strikers to work for the abolition of the unequal treaties.

Ironically, for Liao Zongkai, the mass mobilizations in 1925 had created more chaos and financial drain on the GMD treasury than moving the revolution forward, at least in the short term. Liao was assassinated at age forty-eight, just before arriving at a GMD Executive Committee meeting on August 30, 1925, in Guangzhou, when five gunmen riddled him with bullets as he stepped out of his limousine. During the period of mourning, He Xiangning called on GMD comrades to emulate her husband's example in the revolutionary struggle. A committee, including Jiang Jieshi, formed to investigate Liao's murder determined that a cousin of Hu Hanmin was responsible, who had fled. Hu Hanmin left for Moscow for "reeducation."

Boqun was extremely saddened by the turn of events since Sun Yatsen's death. Liao Zongkai was not only a friend, but he had been also a mentor to Boqun in Tokyo. He had read Liao's translation of Henry George's *Progress and Poverty* and spent many hours discussing it and others, such as the works of W.D.P. Bless. Boqun learned about the difference between socialism and communism and understood that socialism was not a class movement. He discussed his thoughts about Liao with his mother and He Yingqin.

Liao was neither a rightist nor leftist and certainly far from a communist. He was a nationalist, and his ideological difference from the rightists was insignificant indeed. I personally have observed how close he was to Hu Hanmin, and their differences were strictly in the tactics, not the objectives of the revolution. I have to say that Hu's acquiescence to the Shamin compromise validated that he is also a true nationalist in putting away his disagreement with Liao and not making it a personal matter. Like Sun Yatsen, Liao was also somewhat naïve to expect mass mobilization could be accomplished in such a short time to deliver its ultimate revolutionary potential. Sun himself pointed out that a tutorage of the mass is necessary before it is ready to contribute. I am discouraged that we have lost such important leaders before our dream republic can establish its sure footing. I realize now that such a dream maybe several lifetimes in the future, and it would be foolhardy to think it can be realized in shorter period.

❖ ❖ ❖

In February of 1925, when Sun Yatsen had left Guangzhou, Chen Jiongming, sensing a possible opportunity to attack Guangzhou, with an army of about fifty thousand spread across east Guangdong. At this time in Guangzhou, the chief Soviet military adviser was Galen. He was from a peasant family but rose through the ranks in the Red army to become its commander-in-chief. Trotsky considered him to be a theatrical figure and politically unaware, but he was viewed by the Soviet military leaders as an immense military talent and possessed the gift of foresight. Galen was placed under Borodin, but he had the respect and confidence of Jiang, who knew him from Jiang's Moscow mission. Thus Galen was able to work with Jiang independently from Borodin. Upon hearing about Chen's intent, Galen recommended preemptive action by the NRA. Jiang agreed, and he asked He Yingqin to assemble a training regiment composed of soldiers recruited from nearby provinces, company commander from officers of local military units, and Whampoa instructors and cadets serving as battalion and regiment commanders.

In October the First Training Regiment was activated, with He in command, and the second was activated in December under the command of Wang Boling, another Japanese-trained officer and friend of and Jiang and He. These two regiments, led by Jiang Jieshi, would do most of the fighting in eastern Guangdong. This first field test for the Whampoa officers became known as the "Eastern Expedition." The two regiments were joined by part of the Guangdong Army loyal to Sun, engaged the Chen Army, and won two key victories at Danshui in February and Mianhu in March. Lacking in supplies, communication equipment, and intelligence about the enemy caused confusion to Wang's regiment, which actually engaged the friendly Guangdong forces.

When the three units finally coordinated their attack, with He's regiment in the lead, they breached the Danshui city wall and allowed both training regiments to enter the city. The enemy, however, with reinforcements of some two thousand men, mounted a sudden attack and drove Wang and his men out of the city. He's troops managed to repulse the attack and preserved the victory. The capture of Danshui netted the training regiments much-needed weapons and ammunition. The regiments lost ten men, and forty were wounded. Both the Soviet adviser and Jiang were impressed with the victory and small casualty numbers.

Wang Boling's shortcomings were highlighted by He Yingqin's accomplishments, and Jiang replaced Wang with one of He's battalion commanders. Jiang then ordered He's regiment on March 9, 1925, to take Mianhu, a small but strategic town in Guangdong. Local intelligence estimated the Chen forces numbered ten to thirteen thousand and He's own estimate put it at five to ten thousand, which was still five to ten times the size of He's force of about twelve hundred. Completely outnumbered and outgunned, all three battalions were in deep trouble but held out until the arrival of the Second Regiment and Sun's Guangdong Army. The First Regiment forces fought valiantly as Jiang had urged their officers to do at Whampoa. At the end of the battle, they had exhausted their artillery ammunition and suffered up to 20 percent casualties in each of its battalions. Obviously Jiang had misjudged the numerical superiority of the Chen's army and placed He and his regiment at risk unnecessarily.

This first outing of the Whampoa trained army was all-important for it had broken Chen's army, and Chen fled to Hong Kong and died in 1933. It also confirmed the fighting competence of the revolutionary army and ensured the survival of the GMD party. The revolutionary army had captured much-needed munitions, including hundreds of machine guns and canons and over ten million cartridges and shells. More importantly, many of the Chen's officers and troops had surrendered and absorbed into the revolutionary ranks. At the conclusion Jiang gave He's regiment one thousand yuan on behalf of the GMD Central Executive Committee, and Galen presented his sword to He as a token of his personal admiration.

Later Jiang named He as the overall leader of all Whampoa-trained revolutionary forces. He then rose rapidly through the ranks. In 1925 He was named division commander, and several months later, he took command of the First Army. The Soviets had recommended adding political commissars to the army, and Zhou Enlai was the head of that function at the Whampoa and later became the same for the revolutionary army. Zhou was from a scholar-official family of Zhejiang, was educated at the best modern school, and went to Japan in 1917. He became fluent in Japanese and studied the revolutionary Soviets of Russia and Japan. He returned in 1919, began to participate in the various student movements, and spent six months in jail. He then went to Paris for further studies upon his release in 1920. Zhou spent the next four years in Europe organizing a CCP overseas group and raising funds for the party. After the GMD and CCP formed a united front, Zhou returned to China and joined the Whampoa as the director of the Political Department of the Academy at

Zhou Enlai, 1925

the recommendation of Liao Zongkai to succeed him. Using propaganda techniques as Dilun did in the National Protection War, Zhou's commissars were able to persuade the peasants to support the army by promising them land tax reforms and the army's assurance for their security and land ownership. Jiang paid tributes to both the Soviets and the political workers under Zhou by saying, "The GMD and the CCP are cooperating, and we have the support of the whole country. As we mourn the passing of Dr. Sun, we fortunately still have our Soviet friends here to guide us."

Although the left and right factions had lost their leaders, the two sides continued to struggle for control. To determine the future course of the GMD, Wang Jingwei called for a second party congress to convene in January 1926. Its proceedings surprisingly showed the predominance of the left over the right factions. In particular, the congress voted to continue the all-important issue of

Mao Zedong 1936

continued cooperation with the Soviet and collaboration with the CCP, as Sun had promulgated in the first congress. The congress also confirmed the leadership position of Wang Jingwei, and CCP members took one-fifth of the seats on the expanded thirty-six Central Executive Committee members and one-third of the seats on the committee's standing committee, which had the overall governing authority. The CCP had also made gains in the government organization by replacing GMD members as department heads. One of the notables was Mao Zedong, who took over as deputy to Wang Jinwei as head of the Propaganda Department. Boqun agreed with Sun's Three Great Alliance Policies but was alarmed and concerned about the margin of victory of the CCP and their proposed changes for rapid social development. Borodin was extremely pleased that CCP was able to make substantial gains over the GMD. He left for Beijing soon after the congress ended to meet with the northern government about unification.

❖ ❖ ❖

In 1925 Sichuan was in the hands of several warlords, including Yuan Zuming, who was supported by the Beijing government but had the least influence since he was a native of Guizhou with a relatively small army of mainly men from Guizhou. Liu Xiang was the most influential of the Sichuan warlords, and he drove Yuan out of his Chongqing stronghold in 1925. Yuan had to move to Chengde in northern Hunan, with the permission of its military governor, Tang Shengzhi, a graduate of the Baoding Military Academy in 1914. He participated in the National Protection War and Constitutional Protection Movement. He joined the GMD in the Northern Expedition and was given command of the Eighth Army of the NRA. Tang became the military and civil governor of Hunan in March 1926. Tang, with Jiang Jieshi's approval, had decided to recruit Yuan and his troops to join up with the Northern Expedition.

In November 1926, Jiang Jieshi asked Yuan Zuming to attend a NRA military commanders' conference in Nanchang. Yuan at the time was negotiating another deal with Wu Peifu, thinking himself the man of the hour, trying to play both Wu and Jiang to see who would come up with the best deal for his ragtag army. Yuan made excuses for not attending the Nanchang conference. Jiang asked Boqun his opinion about Yuan, and Boqun advised him that Yuan had always been an opportunist without any sense of loyalty. Jiang then ordered Tang to get rid of Yuan and absorb his troops into the Eighth Army. Tang gave the assignment to Zhou Lanfeng, his commander in Chengde, who had already established a friendly relationship with Yuan. Zhou invited Yuan and his senior staff to a New Year's Eve banquet at the town hall at the east gate of the city wall, where the chamber of commerce held its lavish annual banquet.

On the night of the banquet, Yuan brought along his chief of staff and several other officers of his army. Zhou welcomed Yuan with a round of toasts to Yuan's fame and battle successes in Guizhou, Sichuan, Hunan, and Hubei Provinces. Yuan in return complimented Tang in his successes and gave him his best wishes for his future with Jiang Jieshi. The men sat down to a scrumptious banquet of the famous spicy Hunan cuisine, such as General Tso's chicken, braised duck, smoked pork with dried long green beans, spare ribs steamed in bamboo, mashed shrimp in lotus pod, steamed fish head in chili sauce, orange beef, and a typical Changsha hot pot. There were plenty of Guizhou mao-tai and Hunan liquors on hand to go with the food. Knowing Yuan was extremely vain, Zhou continued to toast him with compliments:

> General Yuan, all of us in the southwest region have heard that your army is invincible and victorious in many battles over the years. It has been said that the mere mention of your name is enough to stop a baby from crying out of fear. We toast you for your next successful endeavor in the Northern Expedition, which will ensure your place in military history.

After Yuan had thanked Zhou, he brought up that he had asked the provincial government for the funds promised him to join with the Northern Expedition, and he was told that had to be approved by Tang as the governor. Zhou assured him that Tang had already approved a month of expenses of Yuan's army. Yuan was visibly relieved and went back to his eating and drinking with renewed vigor. Several hours of merrymaking went on, and Zhou excused himself for the bathroom downstairs. After half an hour, Yuan asked his adjutant to check on Zhou to see if he was already. When the adjutant reached the first floor, which was full of soldiers, before he could call out or draw his pistol, he was shot dead. Yuan and his companion

Yuan Zuming, 1924

heard the shots and jumped out the window to the garden below. They were chased by Zhou's soldiers. Both were wounded but not seriously and were taken into custody.

Yuan's officers and troops stationed at the other side of town were doing their own New Year's celebration and went to bed thinking that their commander was doing the same. The next morning Zhou's army surrounded the camp, and a loudspeaker made the announcement, "Yuan Zuming has been arrested on the charge that he secretly colluded with Wu Peifu to undermine the Northern Expedition. He and his officers will be tried by a military tribunal. We urge you men to surrender, and you will be treated fairly."

Yuan's men opened fire and engaged Zhou's troops in a fierce firefight. Yuan's men were seasoned soldiers, and even outnumbered they put up strong resistance. Zhou did not want to have heavy casualties on either side. He telephoned Tang Shengzhi to apprise him of the standoff and asked for his instructions. The original plan was for Tang to deliver Yuan to Jiang Jieshi's headquarters in Nanchang, but given the circumstances, he instructed Zhou to execute Yuan and his companion and place their heads for Yuan's men to see, hoping that when they realized Yuan had died, they would lay down their arms. Zhou followed through on the plan. Yuan was shot with his chief of staff, and their heads were mounted on bamboo poles and displayed in the public square for all to see. Yuan's officers and troops surrendered, sensing there was no more reason for them to fight on.

Jiang Jieshi asked He Yingqin to call Boqun to let him know about Yuan's death. Boqun, with tears in his eyes, sighed with relief upon hearing of the news. He said to He Yingqin,

> I have always resisted the urge of revenge against Yuan. I have been mindful of what the sage taught us that before embarking on a journey of revenge, one needs to dig two graves. I have grieved for Dilun's murder as well that of Dai Kan for personal and historical reasons, but killing Yuan would not have changed my grief. His death does provide some closure for me. I can now better concentrate on things to which I still can make a definitive contribution.

Since Sun's death in 1925, Boqun had several occasions to have a family discussion with He Yingqin and his wife and Boqun youngest sister, Wang Wenxiang, about GMD and Jiang Jieshi's emergence as the leading GMD figure. At the last discussion in late 1927 in Shanghai, He and his wife seemed to be happy about Jiang being the man who would be Sun Yatsen's successor. He said,

> Jiang's greatest fear is the Soviets and their proximity to the CCP, since they kept his firstborn son there as hostage,when the boy was sent there to be educated,

to make sure Jiang toed their line. He believed they had encouraged the CCP to foster a Bolshevik-style classic struggle here, and thus the CCP became his enemy number one. What he has achieved since Sun's death was nothing but miraculous with practically no military base to speak of. We believe he was the only one who could have united the country by the means available to him. For now, we still have the warlords controlling over half the country, the CCP agitating class struggle, and the Japanese flexing their imperial muscle. He is probably to best man we have to deal with all of that.

Boqun understood that He Yingqin admired what Jiang had achieved, but Boqun was doubtful Jiang was the man who would accomplish Sun Yatsen's vision. Boqun realized Jiang had accepted any warlord who would join forces with him as he marched north, and thus he may have nominally added another army and province to the GMD but had little control to effect any social or political changes. Although Boqun agreed that the CCP might have different political views and could cause potential social unrest, he disagreed with Jiang's emphasis on fighting them rather than Japan's encroachment into Manchuria. On the other hand, Boqun realized that no one, including Hu Hanmin and Wang Chingwei, was capable to assume Jiang's position. Boqun thus concluded that maybe it was time for him to make a career change to seek for other means of contribution to his beloved China away from forthcoming inevitable politic struggles.

In January of 1926, Tang Jiyao sensed the power struggle between the right and left of GMD and proclaimed himself the commander-in-chief of the Yunnan, Guangzhou, and Sichuan Armies. In September of 1924, Sun Yatsen named Tang as his deputy with the command of the Nation-Building Army, which consisted of the three southwest provinces' armies. Thus Tang considered himself the rightful successor to Sun.

Tang sent thirty thousand troops south into Guangxi and on February 23 took Nanning without much of a fight. From the north, Tang Jiyu led forty thousand troops from Guizhou through Hunan, attacked Liuzhou, Guangxi. The Guangxi Army defeated Tang's forces, which had to withdraw back to Yunnan. Tang then withdrew his forces from Nanning as well. On December 26, 1926, Tang established a federalism party called People Government Party with its stance similar that of Chen Jiongming and began to agitate against the GMD. In February of 1927, Tang's officers, led by Long Yun, become concerned about Tang's expansive ambitions and removed him from his position. Tang died a few months later, and Long replaced him as Yunnan's warlord.

❖ ❖ ❖

After Liao Zhongkai's assassination, tensions began to build between the CCP and the GMD right. On March 20, 1926, Jiang Jieshi declared martial law claiming a CCP plot to kidnap him. Jiang arrested fifty-some Soviet advisers and CCP leaders and closed trade unions. He convened a meeting of the Central Executive Committee in May to address the imbalance of CCP to GMD members in the committees relative to their respective total membership. He then negotiated with Borodin on the advisers' release for significant changes in GMD/CCP organization. These included restricting CCP activities within the GMD, abandoning its separate functions in the GMD, and its members no longer may serve as function heads of the GMD organization. Wang Jingwei was away on sick leave on March 20, and he did not respond, announced his retirement, and left for France via Hong Kong soon thereafter. Jiang followed through in May when the committee appointed Jiang as chairman to replace Wang.

After all that had been accomplished, Jiang apologized to the Soviet advisers and the CCP members for the arrests, claiming it was a misunderstanding. He then dismissed certain GMD members involved in the arrests as a demonstration of his continued commitment to

CCP and GMD collaboration and to the Soviet cooperation. Against Trotsky's opposition, the Soviet Comitern, based on the recommendation of Borodin, accepted the apology by Jiang and decided to continue supporting him. In one masterstroke, Jiang eliminated his opposition and elevated himself, and most importantly, he retained the continued financial and military support from the Soviets for the upcoming Northern Expedition. Jiang's move signaled the beginning of two significant changes to Sun Yatsen's vision of the inclusion and collaboration with the CCP and the civilian control of the military.

❖ ❖ ❖

In June, 1926 Jiang was named Commander-in-Chief of the Northern Expedition with virtual dictatorial power. On July 6, Jiang and his Soviet adviser, Galen, had decided first to march northward to Hunan which was easily taken by month end. Jiang's army, was now named National Revolution Army (NRA), took Wuhan by October 10. Borodin and Jiang disagreed on the next step. Borodin suggested continuing northward along the Beijing – Hankow railway to join the GMD-friendly warlord, Feng Yuxiang and his army in central China to attack Zhang Zuolin for the control of the Beijing government. Jiang decided instead to attack Sun Chuanfang, who controlled the five provinces of the lower Yangtze delta with the strategically and financially important cities of Shanghai and Nanjing. Initially the progress was slow due to the additional troops sent by Zhang to shore up Sun's positions, but by March 1927, Sun had been pushed out the region and Jiang secured the two great cities. It was a historical accomplishment by He Yingqin, who led the NRA first army. He and his follow Whampoa officers fought valiantly and effectively against superior enemy numbers. Many lesser warlords along the way joined up with NRA which had contributed to the fast progress. Also the spontaneous uprisings of the local populace instigated by the advance CCP political operatives, lead by Zhou Enlai, contributed to NRA's success with minimal casualties. After pacifying the Guangdong,

Zhijiang, Hunan, Hupei, and Fujian provinces, Jiang halted the expedition to deal with the unrest around the country including territory under the GMD.

❖ ❖ ❖

The second half of 1926 to the next spring was a period of accelerated growth of the labor movement. Union membership had tripled from about a hundred thousand in just three months. Strikes had increased at the same level as well both in Wuhan and Shanghai. CCP members were recruiting or organizing union workers in various trades. By the beginning of 1927, unions were formed for more than a million workers. The peasants were also getting organized. In Hunan and Hupei Provinces, about half a million peasants were organized in 1925, and eighteen months later, there were more than four million. Such increases in numbers and in demonstrations alarmed landowners, merchants, politicians, and military officers. They most likely were the targets of the demonstrations and strikes, yet they were also supporters of the GMD.

Meanwhile, in Moscow Stalin and Trotsky debated as how to respond to the situation of mass protests and the power struggles among the various factions of the GMD. Stalin argued for an opportunistic strategy at the expense of communist ideology. He believed the GMD middle and upper classes were better equipped and organized to defeat the Western imperialists and to unify China. Trotsky, however, wished for the CCP to follow a proletarian revolution course against the GMD. Ignoring Trotsky's position, Stalin authorized the continued support and funding of Jiang's Northern Expedition.

In a secret speech to the Comitern, Stalin stated,

> We must continue to support the GMD and the current leader, Jiang Jieshi, since it has the support of

the middle and upper class that are the only domestic funding source for the revolution. Jiang now has the military resources to accomplish the unification and to rid China of the Western imperialists. We need him to get this done so we can be free from such threats. We must support Jiang and his military like a lemon to be squeezed for all its usefulness and discarded after it has served its purpose.

The CCP members serving in the GMD government were in a difficult position. To support such mass movements, they would no doubt rupture the coalition with GMD. To maintain the coalition, they would have to restrain the movements they promoted and encouraged. In the end the CCP decided to decry the excesses of the movements and advised caution.

While the Northern Expedition took a breath to gather its supplies and rest its troops for the march northward to Beijing, the GMD Central Executive Committee chaired by Jiang had decided to move from Guangzhou to Wuhan since it was more central for the nation. The Wuhan government was staffed mostly with CCP and GMD leftist members. Also at the time Wuhan labor and workers formed the powerful three hundred thousand–member Hebei General Union and took over the British concessions in Hankou. When Jiang realized this, he changed his mind and moved the location for the government to Nanchang, the capital city of Kiangsi Province, and to staff the government with more of the GMD right faction. Thus began the open rift between the factions within the GMD, with Jiang on the right with the NRA in Nanchang, and Wang Jingwei, who returned from France and took charge of the GMD Wuhan government.

In March of 1927, CCP union workers led by Zhou Enlai launched an armed uprising in Shanghai, defeating the remnant of Zhang Zuolin's occupation army, which had occupied parts of the city and drove them into a retreat from the city. The victorious union workers occupied and governed urban Shanghai except for the international concession. Then the CCP attacked and looted foreign settlements and organized daily mass student protests and labor strikes demanding the return of Shanghai international settlements to Chinese control. They proceeded to the British, American, and Japanese concessions and consulates to search for suspected enemies hiding inside but left peacefully after none were found. The CCP's action alarmed the GMD right faction

Immediately afterward in Nanjing, NRA soldiers and local Chinese residents started large-scale rioting against foreign interests, burning houses and attacking the British, American, and Japanese consulates; the American vice president of Nanjing University was killed, and the Japanese consul just missed being assassinated. Apparently the Sixth Army of the NRA, with its large contingent of communist soldiers, systematically looted the homes and businesses of the foreign residents. Soldiers killed one American, two British, a Frenchman, an Italian, and a Japanese. By the end of March 24, Nanjing was burning and littered with bomb craters and casualties from the battle. During this mayhem, one foreigner observed that it was the Boxer Rebellion all over again.

By March 26, 1927, the NRA restored order in Nanjing and successfully restrained soldiers from further hostile actions against foreign nationals while requesting the Red Cross to mediate a ceasefire, with foreign naval vessels sent to protect their citizens. By the end of the next day, all hostilities ended. About forty people, including several foreigners, were killed. Afterward the GMD government issued a statement blaming the deserters from Zhang Zuolin's army for starting the attacks on the foreign consulates in Shanghai and accused the communist soldiers within the NRA of committing atrocities in Nanjing, which were wrongly assigned to the GMD.

On April 2, 1927, the GMD Executive Committee in Wuhan under Wang Jingwei determined that CCP's actions were antirevolutionary and undermined the national interests of China. It voted unanimously to purge the communists from GMD. On April 5, 1927, Wang Jingwei arrived in Shanghai and met with CCP leaders, and they issued a joint declaration reaffirming the principle of cooperation between GMD and CCP, despite urgent pleas from Jiang and other GMD elders to eliminate the CCP. When Wang left Shanghai for Wuhan the next day, Jiang arrived to meet with leaders of Shanghai's infamous Green Gang and asked them to form a union of merchants and other interested groups to oppose the CCP-sponsored Shanghai labor unions. On April 9 Jiang declared martial law in Shanghai and issued the Party Protection and National Salvation Proclamation, denouncing the Wuhan government's policy of cooperation with the CCP. On April 11 Chiang issued a secret order to all provinces under the control of his forces to purge CCP members from the GMD.

Before dawn on April 12, 1927, Green Gang members joined by other Shanghai's secret societies and criminal elements began to attack district offices controlled by the union workers. Under an emergency decree, Jiang ordered the Twenty-Sixth Army to disarm the workers' militias. That process resulted in more than three hundred people killed and wounded. The union workers organized a mass meeting denouncing Jiang on April 13, and thousands of workers and students went to the headquarters of the NRA to protest. Soldiers opened fire, killing over one hundred and wounding many more. Jiang dissolved the provisional government of Shanghai, labor unions, and all other organizations under CCP control and reorganized a network of unions with allegiance to the GMD and under the control of Jiang's gang leaders. Over a thousand communists were arrested, some three hundred were executed, and more than five thousand were missing. These events became known as the Shanghai Massacre.

The Wuhan government, now under Wang Jingwei, promptly declared Jiang as a counter-revolutionary and stripped him of his offices. Jiang responded by setting up his own GMD government in Nanjing. The GMD left and CCP in Wuhan were unable to deal with the increasing demands of the peasant movement and the chaos caused by the demonstration and strikes. On May 21 the only warlord backing the Wuhan government, Tang Shengzhi, the military and civil governor of Hunan Province and supporter of the GMD since 1916, decided to send in his troops to restore order in Hunan and Hubei, where mass protests and demonstrations had been going on for months. His troops secured Wuhan and ended the labor and peasant movements in those provinces.

Jiang's army then marched to Wuhan but was unable to take the city due to CCP General Ye Ting and his Fourth Army blocking its path. In Beijing Zhang Zuolin's troops killed hundreds CCP members, while in Changsha the NRA machine-gunned nine leading communists and hundreds of peasant militiamen. That May, the NRA killed tens of thousands of CCP members and their sympathizers. The CCP lost approximately fifteen thousand of its twenty-five thousand members. The CCP, nevertheless, at Stalin's urging continued to support the Wuhan government, a position Mao Zedong endorsed.

The CCP then founded the Workers and Peasants' Red Army of China, better known as the Red Army, to battle Jiang. A battalion led by Zhu De, a graduate of the Yunnan Military Academy, served under Cai E in the National Protection Movement, attacked the city of Nanchang on August 1, 1927, which was initially successful. They were, however, forced into retreat after five days, marching south to Shantou and from there were driven into the wilderness of Fujian. Mao Zedong became the commander-in-chief of the Red Army and led four regiments against Changsha, Hunan, hoping to spark peasant uprisings across his native province. His plan was to attack the GMD-held city from three directions on September 9, but the Fourth Regiment was bribed and deserted to the GMD cause and attacked the Third Regiment. Mao's army made it to Changsha but could not take it. By September 15 he accepted defeat, with thousands of survivors marching east to the Jinggang Mountains of Jiangxi.

Mao set up base in Jinggangshan City, an area in the Jinggang Mountains. Mao united five villages as a self-governing state, supporting the confiscation of land from rich landlords, who were "reeducated" and sometimes executed. He ensured that no massacres took place in the region, pursuing a more lenient approach than that advocated by the CCP Central Committee, stating, "Even the lame, the deaf, and the blind could all come in useful for the revolutionary struggle." He boosted the Red Army force to two thousand by incorporating two groups of bandits. He laid down rules for his soldiers: prompt obedience to orders, all confiscations belong to the party, and nothing must be taken from peasants.

While Jiang halted his Northern Expedition to deal with the rising mass demonstrations and political struggles among the GMD right and left and the CCP, Sun Chuanfang sensed an opportunity to counterattack the NRA and to regain Nanjing and other lost territory. Sun joined forces with Cao Kun and sought support from Zhang Zuolin. He gathered an army of a hundred plus thousand men for an all-out attack against the NRA positioned along the lower Yangtze River. The opposing NRA forces consisted of three armies: the first in Jiangsu north of Nanjing, the second at the west of the first in Xuzhou, and the third on the west of Xuzhou to prevent any incursions from Wuhan. Although the NRA had about the same number of men, Jiang had decided to concentrate the majority on the north side of the Yangtze to defend Xuzhou. Jiang had never explained when he favored this strategy. When Sun learned of this, he launched a surprise attack at NRA's weak link which forced the NRA's Second Army to withdraw. Jiang sacked the commander of the Second Army and took personal charge to counterattack, which resulted in a devastating defeat. This caused Jiang to resign on August 6 as the head of the Nanjing government, and he retired to Shanghai.

Li Zongren, a student of Cai E, commander-in-chief of the Guangxi army, military governor of Guangxi, and a supporter of Sun Yatsen from his RA days, then took over Jiang's position. In 1925 he led his army to Hunan, where he defeated Wu Peifu allied with Sun Chuanfang, in two successive battles and captured the provincial capital. After Li replaced

Jiang, he withdrew the entire NRA army back to the Yangtze, with the objective of defending Nanjing. By late August Sun's army counterattacked and took Longtan, defeating the First Army led by He Yingqin. The NRA regrouped, and with reinforcements from the Second Army, it was able to beat back the enemy and recapture the city. By August 30, 1927, Sun's army lost two-thirds of its troops and had to retreat across the Yangtze. Li then set out to negotiate with Wang Jingwei to purge the CCP and exile the Soviet advisers from Wuhan and reunited the GMD.

Jiang's resignation, as usual, was a ruse to determine who were his enemies and a plot to eliminate them. He Yingqin, though Jiang's faithful follower, had begun to doubt Jiang as the right leader for the republic instead of just the leader of the military under civilian control as envisioned by Sun Yatsen. In the meeting of the Military and Political Council in August 1927, when Jiang submitted his resignation, Wang Jingwei, backed by Li Zongren and other military leaders, had accepted it. Jiang had expected He Yingqin to protest the decision, and he remained silent. Later when Jiang recalled this event, he lamented that had He Yingqin provided him with some support, he would have had a reason not to resign. By the end of year, Jiang was back on top, and he dismissed He Yingqin from his command of the First Army and took over the position himself. He retired to Hangzhou, but eventually Jiang realized He was valuable to him; he buried the hatchet, visited He in Hangzhou, and persuaded him to return as chief of staff of the NRA and to direct all the military training for the NRA. This was a huge task, for it had the job of integration and the retraining of other warlords' armies into the NRA. Later He would resume the command of the First Army in some of the NRA's key battles.

Finally, in late April 1927, Stalin sent his instruction in a telegram to Borodin, who showed it to Wang Jingwei.

The land should be distributed to the peasants, except for that owned by the military. Get rid of unreliable military leadership and replace it with a new revolutionary army of twenty thousand CCP members and fifty thousand peasants and workers. Put representatives of workers and peasants on the GMD Executive Central Committee. Lastly and most importantly, for now continue the cooperation with GMD, the left as well as right, till the Northern Expedition has succeeded and the nation is united.

Stalin did not elaborate on how to accomplish his suggestions, and both Borodin and Wang Jingwei were shocked by Stalin's lack of understanding of the situation they faced. Left to their own devices, the Wuhan government led by Wang and backed by Tang Shengzhi's army mounted their own Northern Expedition against Zhang Zuolin while Jiang was bogged down by civil unrest, mass protests, and purges of the GMD left and the CCP. Wang asked Feng Yuxiang by letter to join with the Wuhan army at Chenghow, Honan, which is the junction of the two main railways. Wang and Tang believed they could defeat Jiang and absorb his army into the Wuhan army. Jiang's troops fought a fierce battle against the Wuhan army in most of May 1927. Feng, sensing an opportunity for himself, left his own base of Xian to arrive at Chenghow just before the Wuhan Army had arrived. Feng now held the critical junction for the two railways. Both Jiang and Wang met with him separately, and Jiang somehow won out. Wang's lack of strength and self-confidence made him dubious as a leader in Feng's eyes. Feng wired the Wuhan government and suggested that Soviet advisers, including Borodin, should go home; CCP members of the Executive Committee and in government ministerial positions were to be purged; and rest of the Wuhan government led by Wang Jingwei should join Jiang's Nanjing government.

Again, Feng played a pivotal role, as he did in the Beijing coup of 1924. After a few months of negotiations among the politicians and the military, Wang resigned and left for Europe. Sun Yatsen's widow, Soong Chinling, left for Moscow, arranged by Borodin. Tang Shengzhi joined Jiang's government as the military and civil governor of Hunan Province, and his army was named as the Eighth Army, with him continuing as its commander. Jiang convened the fourth GMD congress to confirm his position of the commander-in-chief of all military forces, chairman of GMD's Executive Central Committee, and chairman of the Military Affairs Commission. Jiang's action caused several unsuccessful CCP uprisings, most notably in Nanchang, which was led by Zhou Enlai, where eight thousand GMD members died and many more were wounded.

❖ ❖ ❖

Tragedy struck again for the Wang family. Boqun's only child, Senfu, died of pneumonia on July 11, 1927, at age eighteen. He was a studious young man with the likeness and manner of his father, and

Wang Senfu, 1927

the whole family took his death extremely hard. Senfu was buried in Shanghai. His mother was so despondent that Boqun had to send her back to Xingyi to be with her own family. She became progressively weaker and died on October 22, 1927, and was buried in Xingyi.

Boqun was deeply affected by both deaths. He went into a period of deep depression until the end of 1927 and thought about his revolutionary involvement over the last twenty years and how many sacrifices the Wang had made for the sake of the republic and how little time he had to spend with his family. Boqun and Dilun were always skeptical of Sun Yatsen's idealism and the practicality of his political theory, but they believed in his sincerity about developing a Chinese republic by his Three People Principles. Sun further envisioned a process of steps to bring about the unification of the country, the education of the populace, and finally a democratically elected government. Sun's vision was military pacification followed by social changes, education, and self-government from province by province. Sun never really understood how long the process would take and what structure it must have.

Boqun was extremely encouraged by the Eastern Expedition and the first part of the Northern Expedition when the various factions of GMD, including CCP, were united and operated as a team. Battles were won not only for the territories taken but for the hearts and minds of the people as well. Boqun personally knew CCP leaders like Mao Zedong and Zhou Enlai and respected their patriotism and intellect. He also knew Wang Jingwei, Hu Hanmin, and Liao Zongkai and considered all three true believers in Sun's visions. Out of the three, he thought no one could have replaced Sun as the leader. Hu and Liao were on the opposite end of the left-to-right spectrum, and Wang was weak in character and certainly not a leader by nature. Boqun, being a realist, had realized that to accomplish what Sun had envisioned, his successor would have to have a military background and his own military base. He thought about Dilun and his potential to become Sun's successor, and he thought about Cai E, who definitely would have been more seasoned and qualified. Of the current military leaders, Boqun had respect for Yan Xishan of Shanxi, Feng Yuxiang, and Li Zongren, who were all his friends, but Jiang Jieshi seemed to have the stars aligned for him, and it looked like he would be the one.

Soong and Jiang, 1927

On December 1, 1927, Jiang married for the third time. His bride was Soong Meiling, the youngest of the famous three Soong sisters, including Sun Yatsen's widow, Soong Chinling, who opposed the marriage, as did their parents. The parents finally agreed after Jiang showed his divorce decree and promised to convert to Christianity. Jiang told his future parents-in-law that he could not convert immediately, because religion needed to be gradually absorbed, not swallowed like a pill. Soong Meiling graduated from Wellesley College on June 19, 1917, with a major in English literature and minor in philosophy. Because of being educated in English all her life, she spoke excellent English, with a pronounced Georgian accent. The couple was married in Shanghai in a grand ceremony. The marriage lasted forty-eight years. The couple never had any children.

CHAPTER 11

1928-1932

NORTHERN EXPEDITION, GREAT PLAINS WAR, JAPANESE ENCROACHMENT

On January 4, 1928, the GMD established a new government in at Nanjing. Jiang Jieshi became the chief executive of the government. Jiang, after a year of dealing with conflicts within his party and delays and defeats by his northern warlord enemies, finally restarted the Northern Expedition on April 2, 1928. He and his minister of finance and brother-in-law, TV Soong, raised US$16 million from the Shanghai banks and industrial companies to fund the expedition. The NRA defeated the remnants of the combined Sun and Zhang armies and reached the Yellow River by mid-April 1928. An independent warlord, Yan Xishan, joined the Northern Expedition. Yan was the military governor of Shanxi, a graduate of the Imperial Japanese Army Academy in 1909, a longtime RA member, and supporter of Sun Yatsen. As Guizhou, Shanxi was one of the poorest provinces in China. Yan believed in modernization to improve Shanxi's economy and infrastructure so he could prevent Shanxi from being absorbed by rival warlords. He maintained neutrality among the violent national politics in the Warlord Era and devoted himself almost exclusively to modernizing Shanxi and developing its resources. Yan's reforms earned him the reputation as the "model governor."

Yan was inspired from his experiences in Japan and his contact with foreign medical personnel who came in 1918 to help suppress an epidemic that was ravaging his province. Yan was impressed with the zeal, talents, and modern outlook of these foreigners and subsequently compared foreigners favorably to his own apathetic officials. Although he was militarily weaker than many of neighboring Beiyang warlords, he often held the balance of power among them. He joined the Northern Expedition to resist the domination by Zhang Zuolin, the powerful Manchurian warlord who had held the post of the president of the Republic in Beijing since June 1927, when he succeeded Duan Quirui. With the help of Feng Yuxiang and Yan, Jiang Jieshi now could muster as large force as the northern warlords forces of Zhang Zuolin.

On May 1, 1928, the NRA and Feng's troops converged on Jinan, Shandong. Zhang's forces were easily defeated, and he and his troops retreated to Beijing. Jiang arrived in Jinan the next day, and he tried not to engage the Japanese forces that took over the German concessions after the Great War, but confrontation broke out and both sides suffered hundreds of deaths. While Jiang was dealing this crisis, Zhang's air force bombarded his position, and he narrowly escaped death. Jiang left the Japanese in the hands of the Nanjing government to negotiate a settlement through the League of Nations while Japanese troops killed thousands of Chinese civilians. Anti-Japanese demonstrations took place in most major cities, and a national movement developed against Japan. Somehow, through his propaganda, Jiang became a hero for being there even though he had counseled appeasement with the Japanese.

Meanwhile Feng and Yan were making progress on their own against Zhang Zuolin in the north. Their forces had moved over the plains and then toward Beijing from the south and the west in a pincer formation. Jiang left Jinan since he did not want Feng to take Beijing and agreed with Feng to let Yan, who was military the weaker of the two, to have that honor. Now facing a superior force, Zhang Zuolin decided to leave Beijing for his stronghold of Manchuria on June 4 by train. For his resistance of Japanese encroachment into Manchuria, Japanese agents planted bombs on his train. The ensuing explosions killed Zhang when the train left Beijing station. His son, Zhang Xueliang, succeeded him and decided to join with Jiang's GMD to avenge his father and drive the Japanese out of Manchuria.

As Zhang's troop withdrew from Beijing, Yan moved his troops in and secured the city for the GMD. Thus, the Northern Expedition was successfully concluded. Finally, China was united from the south to the north. It had taken sixteen years since the revolution of 1912 to get that far. After the Northern Expedition was concluded and Beijing was secured, Jiang Jieshi returned to Nanjing to a hero's welcome. He and Soong Meiling then traveled together first to Wuhan, where they received another huge welcome. They continued to Beijing and visited Sun Yatsen's temporary resting place in the West Hills. They wined and dined with Zhang Xueliang and his wife as

Zhang Xueliang, 1928

well most of the northern warlords, who now had become members of the GMD. The trip also provided Jiang with a chance to court the foreign representatives, and Meiling, with her charming persona and English language, was a tremendous help to her husband. By July of 1928, Jiang had reached agreements with the United States and Great Britain to settle the damages caused by the Nanjing and Shanghai Incidents. Jiang agreed to apologize, and pay significant compensation to both countries without disclosing the exact sum to save face for the Chinese and he blamed the CCP for all of the troubles. Although the GMD suffered a financial loss because of this settlement, the GMD government did receive international recognition and established a formal diplomatic relationship with two of the world's great powers for the first time since China had become a republic.

❖ ❖ ❖

On October 10, 1928, seventeen years after Sun Yatsen declared China a republic, the Republic of China was established at its capital, Nanjing. Jiang Jieshi became the president, and the government adapted the constitutional provision of a five-power system of government proposed by Sun Yatsen in 1906 to implement democracy in China. It provided for a central government composed of five yuans or branches, of government. As in the United States, there were to be legislative, executive, and judicial yuan. The other two were the traditional Chinese government branches throughout its history: the examination yuan, which was to administer the selection of government officials, and the control yuan, which was to ensure the honesty and efficiency of the government. Sun hoped these divisions would help safeguard and promulgate his Three People Principles.

At the GMD congress of March 1929, the left continued to urge its original goals of democracy, mass movements, and anti-imperialism. Jiang and his supporters showed their newly gained muscles by allowing only four of the thirty-eight party branches to select their representatives directly. The Central Executive Committee ruled that it would conduct political tutelage and initiate popular voting by1935. The anticommunist repression continued and killed thousands from crackdowns for mass movements. In spite of the continued unrest, a first functional republican government was established in Nanjing. Jiang took the senior political post of the chairman of the State Council and of the executive yuan. Hu Hanmin was the chair of the legislative yuan, and Jiang's new wife, Soong Meiling, was a member of the Management Committee of the Central Executive Committee. The friendly Beiyang warlords were appointed to various key positions: Zhang Xueliang joined the State Council, Feng Yuxiang was the war minister, and Yan Xishan was the interior minister and the deputy commander-in-chief all the NRA, which would now be referred to as the GMD army.

After the conclusion of the congress, Jiang held a military conference of all the principal military leaders who continued to control their own forces at the time. Jiang stated his intent to reduce the total army size by half, to centralize military command, and to nationalize all provincial government structures, including taxing authority. This caused the former warlords to have second thoughts about his leadership. First to strike was Li Zongren, who marched the Guangxi Army into Wuhan. Jiang responded with bribery wherever necessary to drive back Li to Guangxi. This was followed by Feng's resignation as the war minister, signaling his discontent, and again Jiang bribed a couple of his subordinates to nip the uprising in the bud. This provided a period of relative peace for Jiang to consolidate his gains, and he declared himself the true successor to Sun Yatsen.

In May 1929, as Sun had wished, his remains were brought from Beijing to Nanjing for burial. Sun's widow, Soong Qingling, had come back for the occasion from her exile to Moscow after the fall of the Wuhan government of Wang Jingwei. She had to share the spotlight with the man she considered a traitor to Sun's revolution. It had to be a poignant moment for her as her sister Meiling had married Jiang and become a prominent member of his government. Her older brother, TV, was now Jiang's minister of finance after serving in the same role for the Wuhan government; and her other brother-in-law, H. H. Kung, was the master of ceremonies of the event and serving Jiang's government as well. Sun was buried in a huge white marble mausoleum in the foothills of the Purple and Gold Mountain on June 1, 1929. After the ceremony Qingling left immediately for

Shanghai to the house she shared with Sun. She issued a statement that in essence stated:

Soong Qingling, 1929

My heart is full of sadness not only for the loss of the founding father of the republic and my dear husband and teacher but for the nation that is born of his eternal devotion to his dying days. Our beloved nation is now led by a false disciple who preaches his principles but acts in the opposite direction. In spite of the outward respect afford to the founding father, this son's actions have betrayed all the father hoped for. Now the revolution has been undermined, and I urge all to examine their consciences and take the path to put it back on the right track.

Anyone who made such a pronouncement would have been put away if not shot immediately, but Qingling, being whom she was, was allowed to live quietly in her Shanghai French concession house that she had shared with Sun Yatsen. Yet those weak and strong heard her voice. and those who still had the gumption would follow her call.

❖ ❖ ❖

After Sun Yatsen's internment, Feng Yuxiang of the northwest clashed with Jiang. In November Li Zongren issued an anti-Jiang declaration, along with Wang Jingwei, who returned from Europe to set up a rival GMD government in Beijing. In December Tang Shengzhi of

Hunan announced his support of the anti-Jiang coalition. The GMD government in Nanjing expelled Wang Jingwei from the party in March 1930. In February 1930, Yan Xishan demanded Jiang's resignation, which Jiang refused. The coalition set up its own GMD government in Beijing. Yan became the commander-in-chief of the coalition army while Feng, Li, and Zhang Xueliang were his seconds in command. In April, all of them were sworn into their positions except Zhang, who was not committed to either side at the time.

The confrontation erupted in mid May 1930. Battles in the north were generally in Henan and Shandong, and battles in the south were mainly in Hunan. With the support of its new air force, Jiang's GMD Central Army struck first, with several major offensives. Feng's Northwest Army, being the strongest in the coalition, crushed Jiang's forces in Gansu at the end of May, but the Northwest Army could not capitalize on its victory, as the Yan's Shanxi Army was unable to join it in time. This led the Northwest Army to go on the defensive. Later, in Kaifeng, the Northwest Army repulsed Jiang's counterattack and nearly surrounded his forces. In August the Shanxi and Northwest Armies had a major battle with Jiang's forces while attacking Xuzhou. Losses for both sides exceeded two hundred thousand. Again, the Northwest Army did not receive support from the Shanxi Army in time and fell short of complete success. The Shanxi Army retreated from Jinan and took heavy casualties while crossing the Yellow River. After defeating the Guangxi Army in Hunan, Jiang decided to launch a major counteroffensive on Shandong. Landed in Qingdao, Jiang's forces retook Jinan on August 15. Jiang's army then gathered in Gansu and Shanxi Provinces to prepare for an all-out offense. At this point, Zhang Xueliang had not taken sides.

At age twenty-nine, Zhang became the key to success for both sides. He was the eldest son of twelve children of Zhang Zuolin, who had control over the three provinces that made up Manchuria. His army totaled over four hundred thousand, with large stocks of munitions, including naval units, an air force, and an armaments industry.

He integrated a large number of local militias into his army and thus prevented Manchuria from falling into the warlord struggle chaos. Although Manchuria officially remained a part of the Republic of China, actually it was an independent kingdom isolated from the rest of China by its control of the only pass connecting the Great Wall to the sea, which could be closed against invaders. Zhang pocketed all the tax revenue and in 1922 took control of the only rail link, the Beijing-Shenyang Railway, north of the Great Wall.

Manchuria shared a long border with Soviet Russia. The Chinese Eastern Railway, which was under Russian control, ran through northern Manchuria, and the land immediately on either side of the tracks was Russian territory. From 1917 to about 1924, the newly empowered Comitern in Moscow was having such difficulties establishing itself in Siberia that often it was not clear who was in charge of operating the Eastern Railway on the Russian side. Zhang avoided a showdown with the Soviets, and after 1924 the Soviets managed to reestablish their dominance.

The Japanese, however, posed more of a problem. After the Russo-Japanese war of 1904 to 1905, Japan had gained two important outposts in south Manchuria. The so-called Guangdong Leased Territory consisted of a 218-square-mile peninsula in the southernmost part of Manchuria and the ice-free port of Dairen, which became the main link to Japan. Reaching northward from the territory, the South Manchurian Railway passed through Shenyang, linking up with the Chinese Eastern Railway in Changchun. The Japanese Army controlled the land on either side of the railway. This army maintained up to fifteen thousand men in Manchuria, tolerating and being tolerated by Zhang Zuolin's army although he kept up a war of words, playing on the anti-Japanese sentiments in the Chinese public.

The Japanese believed that Zhang's son, Xueliang, who was known as a playboy and an opium addict, would be much more pliable to Japanese influence than his father would. Thus they choose to assassinate the father. Surprisingly, the younger Zhang proved to be more independent than anyone had expected. With the assistance of an Australian adviser, he overcame his opium addiction and declared his support for the Nanjing GMD government. One of the first things he did was to rid of his staff of Japanese influence. At a New Year's banquet he hosted in January 1929, several prominent pro-Tokyo officials were invited, and they were executed in front of the assembled guests. Zhang then immediately reassigned the Japanese sympathizers' troops or departments to his trusted people, who carried out the next-level purges, to consolidate his control.

When the conflicts raged between Jiang and the Beijing coalition, Zhang was busy trying to wrestle control of the Chinese Eastern Railway from the Soviets. His troops were defeated by the Soviet army led by none other than Galen, the Russian military mentor to the Jiang's Whampoa officers. Zhang's troops suffered heavy casualties, and he had retreated to the south of the Great Wall. At this point, Zhang had to decide whether to support Jiang Jieshi or the Beijing coalition. In spite of Zhang's doubt about Jiang's motives, he decided that Jiang had the best chance of uniting China against both the Soviet and the Japanese. He also thought if the coalition were to defeat Jiang, China would lapse into another chaotic warlord era. Naturally, he knew he was in the best position to bargain for the continued independent control over Manchuria, the railways in Hebei, and the customs revenues from the port city of Tianjin. After consulting with his Australian adviser, he then held a conference with his key civilian and military leaders until early morning the next day. He wired Jiang and declared the terms of his support.

Jiang agreed, and on September 18, 1930, Zhang announced his support of Jiang by wires to the others. Two days later Zhang's army entered the Shanhai Pass. This turn of events resulted in the Beijing Coalition collapsing almost immediately. The Shanxi Army withdrew to the north of the Yellow River, while the Northwest Army was defeated. On November 4 Yan Xishan and Feng Yuxiang announced their retirement. Yan fled to Dalian and Feng to Jehol. Zhang absorbed Feng's troops. The conflict was now over. The so-called Central Plains War was the biggest armed conflict inside the GMD party. The war affected many provinces, and the sides committed over 1.3 million troops, suffering over three hundred thousand casualties combined. As a result, the Nanjing government was nearly bankrupt. Jiang deployed troops originally tasked with destroying the Red army, which prevented Jiang from carrying out his plan to exterminate the CCP.

❖ ❖ ❖

Jiang celebrated his victory with Meiling in Shanghai with her family and received his baptism as a Methodist in accordance with his marriage promise to the Soong family. He then returned to Nanjing to deal with Hu Hamin, who advocated civilian control over the military, now that the northern warlords had been dealt with. Jiang countered that the CCP remained to be disposed of, and he proposed revising the constitution to accommodate such an exigency. Jiang invited Hu to his house for dinner, and supposedly the two argued until early morning and Hu stayed overnight. The next day Jiang announced that Hu had taken ill and had to go to a nearby resort for recovery. Many of the GMD elders were upset with such treatment of Hu, including Wang Jingwei and Sun Yatsen's son from his first marriage, Sun Fo. Again, they called for the suppression of Jiang. Such opposition had no real teeth, and Jiang just chose to ignore them and revised the constitution to provide the president with the power to appoint the five-yuan branches of the government. In June of 1930, he became president and the chairman of the executive yuan that gave him the overall control of the military.

Finally, Jiang Jieshi was able to turn his attention to the extermination of the CCP. He had always practiced realpolitik with his enemies, such as the northern warlords Feng, Yan, and Zhang and GMD politicians Wang and Hu. Jiang had collaborated with them and then attacked them. To Jiang, there was only one enemy, the CCP, that he would never cooperate with since it posed the greatest existential threat to him. He believed the CCP had the popular support and appeal as Sun Yatsen's original GMD, which, given the opportunity, would eventually defeat him.

In the spring of 1928, the GMD army attacked Mao's base in Jiangxi, and Mao had to flee with his ragtag army and joined with a CCP regiment led by Zhu De and Lin Biao, a Whampoa graduate and GMD officer in the Northern Expedition. They united their forces and attempted to retake Jinggangshan. Initially the CCP army was successful, but the GMD army counterattacked and pushed the Red Army back. Over the next few weeks, they fought an entrenched guerrilla war in the mountains. The CCP Central Committee again ordered Mao to march to south Hunan, but he refused. Contrastingly, Zhu De complied, leading his armies away from the approaching enemy. The GMD army attacked Mao's base, and his troops fended them off for twenty-five days. In retreat, Mao was able to join with Zhu De's army and returned to Jinggangshan. Joined by a defected GMD regiment and other Red Army forces, the CCP group had outgrown the small mountainous area. However, it suffered badly from food shortages over the winter.

In January 1929, Mao and Zhu evacuated their base and took their armies south, to the area around Tonggu and Xinfeng in Jiangxi, which they consolidated as a new base together with three thousand men. The evacuation, however, led to a drop in morale, and many troops became disobedient. This worried the Central Committee, which ordered Mao to disband his army into small autonomous units to spread the revolutionary message instead of armed combat. Mao refused, and in February, he created the Southwest Jiangxi Provincial Soviet government in the region under his control. In November Mao received the news with much sadness and pain that his wife and sister were captured and beheaded. Mao also faced internal opposition from members of the Jiangxi Soviets accusing him of being too moderate and hence antirevolutionary. In December, Mao executed many of his opposition and replaced them with his royalists. The CCP Central Committee moved to Jiangxi and proclaimed it the Soviet Republic of China, an independent communist state. Although Mao became chairman of the Council of People's Commissars, his power diminished, with Zhou Enlai taking over control of the Red Army.

In October of 1930, Jiang adapted a strategy of encirclement and annihilation to deal with the Red Army; he launched forty thousand troops to attack Jiangxi. Outnumbered, Mao responded with guerrilla tactics prescribed by the works of Sun Tzu, and by the end of December, he had defeated the GMD army and captured and brutally executed its commander. In a second campaign led by He Yingqin with one hundred thousand troops, which was ambushed by Red Army and had five hard-fought battles over two weeks, He's army suffered twenty thousand casualties and lost over twenty-five hundred rifles and other weapons. It was He's first defeat in a major battle. As a result, the area under Mao's control had trebled. Angered at this failure, Jiang personally arrived to lead a three-pronged offensive with a hundred fifty thousand fresh troops. Jiang was able to score initial successes by pushing Mao back to his original area. Jiang halted his campaign at this point to block any movement of the Guangdong faction to return to Nanjing and the more-pressing issue of the Japanese encroachment. Given a breather from Jiang's attack and having gained additional territory, Mao proceeded with his land reform program along with education programs and female political participation. In November of 1931, the CCP Central Committee moved from its hiding place in Shanghai to Jiangxi and proclaimed itself the Republic of Soviet China.

After the CCP established its headquarters in Jiangxi, Mao's status within the party declined. In response, Mao claimed a need to eliminate alleged GMD spies and anti-Bolsheviks operating inside the Jiangxi Soviets. He began a purge with torture and guilt by association. The campaign continued until the end of 1931, killing approximately a hundred thousand people and reducing the size of the Red Army from forty thousand to less than ten thousand. Zhou Enlai, the nominal leader of the CCP at the time, originally supported Mao's purges as necessary. After he arrived in Jiangxi in December 1931, Zhou criticized Mao's campaigns as against anti-Maoists more than legitimate threats to the party, for the campaign's general senselessness, and for the widespread use of torture to extract confessions. Following Zhou's efforts to end Mao's ideological persecutions, Mao's campaigns gradually subsided in 1932. In December of 1931, Zhou replaced Mao Zedong as secretary of the First Front Army and chief political commissar of the Red Army. Other party leaders, including Lin Biao, criticized Mao's tactics at the August 1932 CCP congress. The most senior leader to support Mao in 1932 was again Zhou Enlai, who had become disillusioned with the strategic leadership of other senior members in the party, including Zhu De. Zhou's support was not enough, and Mao was demoted to a figurehead in the Soviet government until he regained his position later, during the Long March.

❖ ❖ ❖

The Japanese economic presence and political interest in Manchuria had been growing ever since the end of the Russo-Japanese War (1904–05). The Treaty of Portsmouth that ended the war had granted Japan the lease of the South Manchuria Railway branch (from Changchun to Lüshun) of the China Far East Railway. The Japanese government, however, claimed that this control included all the rights and privileges that China granted to Russia in the 1896 treaty, as enlarged by the Kwantung Lease Agreement of 1898. This included absolute and exclusive administration within the South Manchuria Railway Zone. Japanese railway guards were stationed within the zone to provide security for the trains and tracks; these soldiers frequently carried out maneuvers outside the railway areas.

There were many reports of raids on local Chinese villages by bored Japanese soldiers, and the Japanese ignored all complaints from the Chinese government. In early 1931, the Japanese Army devised a plan to invade Manchuria by generating a major incident that became the pretense for such an invasion. The plan was to sabotage the rail section in an area near the Chinese garrison under the command of Zhang Xueliang. The Japanese hoped to alert Chinese troops by an explosion and then blame them for having caused it, which would be a cause for a formal Japanese intervention. The explosives were detonated as part of the plan on September 18. The damage, however, was minor and caused no delay in rail traffic on that day. Nevertheless, on the following morning the Japanese artillery opened fire on the Chinese garrison as a response. The Japanese destroyed Zhang Xueliang's small air force, and his soldiers fled their barracks as five hundred Japanese troops mounted a savage surprise attack against the Chinese garrison of around seven thousand. The Chinese troops were no match for the experienced Japanese troops and their advanced weaponry. By the evening the fighting was over, and the Japanese had occupied Mukden at the cost of five hundred Chinese and two Japanese lives. The Mukden incident was the precursor to the Second Sino-Japanese war.

Having recently lost a major military conflict against the USSR, Zhang Xueliang did not respond with reinforcement. Zhang claimed he was under implicit instructions from Jiang Jieshi to adhere to a nonresistance policy. Japanese troops proceeded to occupy and garrison the major cities around the area. Although they faced some independent Chinese resistance, the Japanese Army occupied all major towns and cities in the provinces of Manchuria: Liaoning, Jilin, and Heilongjiang. Chinese public opinion strongly criticized Zhang Xueliang for his nonresistance. While the Japanese presented a legitimate threat, Jiang continued to focus on eradicating the CCP. Many charged that Zhang's Northeastern Army of nearly a quarter million could have withstood the Japanese Army of only eleven thousand men. In addition, his arsenal in Manchuria was considered the most modern in China, and his troops had tanks, around sixty combat aircraft, four thousand machine guns, and four artillery battalions.

Zhang's seemingly superior force was undermined by several factors. One was that the Japanese Army had a strong reserve force easily moved by railway from Korea, which was a Japanese colony, directly adjacent to Manchuria. Second, more than half of Zhang's troops were garrisoned at south of the Great Wall in the Hebei Province, while the troops north of the wall were scattered throughout Manchuria. Zhang's troops could not have been deployed fast enough to fight the Japanese in any concentration north of the Great Wall. Finally, most of Zhang's troops were out of the typical warlord mold, undertrained, poorly led, had questionable morale, and had dubious loyalty compared to their Japanese counterparts. Japanese secret agents had permeated Zhang's command because of his and his father's past reliance on Japanese military advisers. The Japanese knew the Northeastern Army very well and were able to conduct operations with ease and to exploit its weaknesses.

In the summer of 1931, a great flood occurred from the Yangtze, causing the surrounding provinces and the hundreds of millions of residents to face homelessness, crop failure, famine, and diseases. Heavy rain caused the Grand Canal to spill over, and two hundred thousand were killed. The Yellow River also crested its bank, resulting in more disasters. By the end of August, it affected over one hundred fifty million people. Clearly this was another urgent issue confronting the Jiang government. The shock of the Mukden Incident and the great flood caused Jiang to halt his extermination effort of the CCP, and he reverted once more to national unity.

In late 1931 Jiang released Hu Hamin from house arrest and met him, Wang Jingwei, and Sun Yatsen's son, Sun Fo, in Shanghai to call for party reconciliation and national reconstruction. On November 20, in a conference convened in Nanjing, the Guangzhou faction of the GMD insisted that Jiang Jieshi step down to take responsibility for the Manchuria debacle. On December 15 Jiang resigned as the chairman of the GMD government and was replaced as premier of the Republic of China (head of the executive yuan) by Sun Fo, who was a graduate of the University of California, Berkeley, with a master's degree from Columbia University. Boqun knew him well from the 1920s when Sun Fo worked with Boqun on communication matters, especially the rail network in Shanghai and later in Guangzhou. Sun's credibility was in being Sun Yatsen's son rather than because of the merit of any accomplishments. He had no real power base of any sort. In fact, upon his appointment, Sun Fo asked Boqun how he could get started and Boqun suggested to ask Jiang, Wang, and Hu to form a committee and let them deal with the national emergencies. Sun agreed and immediately wired the three to that effect. At the time Jiang was already in negotiations with Wang, trying to set aside their last five years of differences. In January of 1932, Wang and Jiang met in Hangzhou and called Sun to join them. Wang told him that he was ready to be the head of the government and Jiang could be the head of the military. Then they returned to Nanjing, went to Sun Yatsen's tomb and solemnly pledged their cooperation and best efforts to deal with the crisis at hand.

Few Chinese had any illusions about Japanese desires for China. Hungry for raw materials and pressed by a growing population, Japan initiated the seizure of Manchuria in September of 1931 and established the last Qing emperor, Puyi, as head of the puppet state of Manchukuo in 1932. The loss of Manchuria, and its vast potential for industrial development and war industries, was a blow to the GMD economy. On September 19, 1931, the Nanjing government turned to the League of Nations for a peaceful resolution. The Chinese Foreign Ministry issued a strong protest to the Japanese government and called for an immediate stop to Japanese military operations in Manchuria. On October 24 the League of Nations passed a resolution mandating the withdrawal of Japanese troops by November 16.

Japan, however, rejected the league's resolution and insisted on direct negotiations with the Chinese government. Negotiations went on intermittently without many results. On January 7, 1932, US Secretary of State Henry Stimson proclaimed the Stimson Doctrine, stating that the United States would not recognize any government that was established by Japan in Manchuria. On January 14, a League of Nations commission arrived in Shanghai to evaluate the situation. On October 2 the commission published its report rejecting the Japanese claim that the Manchurian invasion and occupation was an act of self-defense, although it did not assert that the Japanese had perpetrated the initial bombing of the railroad. The report ascertained that Manchukuo was the product of Japanese military aggression in China, while recognizing that Japan had legitimate concerns in Manchuria because of its economic ties there. The League of Nations refused to acknowledge Manchukuo as an independent nation.

On January 18, 1932, in Shanghai, agitated Chinese civilians beat five Japanese Buddhist monks near a Japanese factory as part of the protest against the Japanese takeover of Manchuria. Two were seriously injured, and one died. Over the next few hours, a group burned down the factory in response to the Shanghai Municipal Police's aggressive antiriot tactics in the aftermath of the beating of the monks. One police officer was killed and several hurt when they arrived to quell the disorder. This caused an upsurge of anti-Japanese and anti-imperialist protests in the city and its concessions, with Chinese residents of Shanghai marching onto the streets and calling for a boycott of Japanese-made goods. The situation continued to deteriorate over the next week.

By January 27 the Japanese military had deployed some thirty ships, forty airplanes, and nearly seven thousand troops around the shoreline of Shanghai. The Japanese justification was that it had to defend its concessions, businesses, and citizens. The Japanese also issued an ultimatum to the Shanghai Municipal Council demanding public condemnation and monetary compensation for any Japanese property damaged in the monk incident and demanding that the Chinese government take active steps to suppress further anti-Japanese protests in the city. On January 28, the Shanghai Municipal Council agreed to these demands.

Throughout this period the GMD's Nineteenth Army was stationed outside the city and took no action, which caused consternation to both the civil Chinese administration of Shanghai and the international concessions. The Nineteenth Army was generally viewed as little more than a warlord force, posing as great a danger to Shanghai as the Japanese. In the end, Shanghai merchants donated a substantial bribe to the Nineteenth Army, hoping they would leave and not incite a Japanese attack. On the midnight of January 28, however, Japanese carrier aircraft bombed Shanghai in the first major aircraft carrier action in the Far East. Three thousand Japanese troops proceeded to attack various targets, such as the northern train station, around the city and began an invasion of the Japanese settlement in areas north of Suzhou Creek. In what was a surprising about-face for many, the Nineteenth Army, instead of leaving after being paid, stayed on to put up a fierce resistance.

Though the opening battles of the conflict took place in the Hongkew district of the International Settlement, this soon spread outward to Chinese-controlled Shanghai. The majority of the international settlements remained untouched by the conflict. The foreigners would watch the war from the banks of Suzhou Creek and even visit the battle lines. Shanghai, being a metropolitan city with many foreign interests invested in it, other countries, such as the United States, Britain, and France, attempted to negotiate a cease-fire between Japan and China. Japan refused and continued to mobilize troops in the region. On February 12 American, British, and French representatives brokered a half-day cease-fire for humanitarian relief to civilians caught in the crossfire. On January 30 Jiang Jieshi decided to relocate temporarily the capital from Nanjing to Luoyang as an emergency measure since Nanjing's proximity to Shanghai could make it an easy target.

On February 12 the Japanese issued another ultimatum, demanding that the Chinese Army retreat twenty kilometers from the border of Shanghai concessions, a demand promptly refused by the Chinese forces. This only intensified fighting in Hongkew. The Japanese were still not able to take the city by the middle of February. The Japanese increased their troops to nearly ninety thousand supported by eighty warships and three hundred airplanes. Finally, on February 14, Jiang sent his Fifth Army into Shanghai, which brought the total Chinese forces up to fifty thousand against the Japanese force of over a hundred thousand. On February 20 the Japanese increased their bombardments to force the Chinese away from their defensive positions near Miaoxing, while commercial and residential districts of the city were set on fire.

Outnumbered and outgunned, Chinese defensive positions deteriorated rapidly without naval and air support. In contrast, Japanese forces backed by both aerial and naval bombardments steadily advanced. On the twenty-ninth the Japanese landed behind Chinese lines. The defenders launched a desperate counterattack but were unable to dislodge the Japanese. On March 3 both the Nineteenth Army and the Fifth Army retreated from Shanghai, marking the official end of the battle. On March 4 the League of Nations passed a resolution demanding a cease-fire, even though sporadic fighting persisted. On March 6 the Chinese unilaterally agreed to stop fighting, although the Japanese rejected the cease-fire. On March 14 representatives from the League of Nations arrived at Shanghai to facilitate a cease-fire. While negotiations were going on, intermittent fighting continued in both outlying areas and the city itself. On May 5 China and Japan signed the Shanghai Cease-fire Agreement, which made Shanghai a demilitarized zone and forbade China to garrison troops in areas surrounding Shanghai, Suzhou, and Kunshan, while allowing the presence of a few Japanese units in the city. The Chinese were to keep only a small police force within the city. To many Chinese this was foreign colonization all over again.

After the cease-fire, Jiang reassigned the Nineteenth Army to suppress the CCP insurrection in Fujian. The Nineteenth Army won some skirmishes against the CCP and then negotiated peace with them. On

November 22 the Nineteenth Army revolted against the GMD government and established the independent Fujian People's Government.
In January 1934 Jiang's army easily crushed the new Fujian government, which did not have the support of all elements of the CCP. The
leaders of the Nineteenth Army escaped to Hong Kong, and the GMD
army either disbanded or reassigned their army to units of the GMD
army.

After the Shanghai disaster, both Wang Jingwei and Zhang
Xueliang resigned all their respective GMD government positions.
Jiang somehow was blameless, and he stepped into the power vacuum and become the successor to Zhang, who stated that he would
go abroad to study and then settle in France. Wang decided to go to
Hamburg, Germany, for treatment of his diabetes. Jiang resumed his
attention back to the CCP in Jiangxi. He deployed a hundred and forty
thousand troops to seal off the province's eastern and southern borders and a hundred thousand troops to face the sixty-five thousand–
man Red Army. With the support of Jiang's new air force, he won some
battles, and the Red Army suffered heavy casualties at the beginning.
Later the Red Army won the next few battles with exceptional and
unexpected mobility. At this point Jiang called an end to the campaign, and the two sides were at a standstill at the end of 1932.

CHAPTER 12

1928-1932

BOQUN'S SECOND CAREER AND MARRIAGE

中國國民黨第五屆中央執行委員會第五次全體會

**GMD's Fifth National Congress, Nanjing, 1928
(Boqun, second row, second left from Jiang, center;
He Yinggin, first row right, eighth from Jiang)**

In October 1928, after the successful Northern Expedition, Jiang Jieshi as the president assumed the position of the head of the executive yuan. He appointed all the heads of the ministries. Boqun was appointed as the as a member of GMD Political Committee, the minister of communication, president of National Communication

University, and chairman of National Mercantile Committee. In spite of his doubts about Jiang's national leadership, he was convinced he could still contribute to the revolution and the republican movement and then move on to a second career in education. Since his student days in Japan, Boqun had been keenly interested in the communication system of a nation as the backbone for modernization. That was his specific interest shared interest with Sun Yatsen, and Sun had given him the job of planning and development of an overall communication system for the unified republic. Boqun had been working on this since he left Guiyang in 1918 to join Sun in Shanghai and followed him to Guangzhou. He continued the work among the political upheavals and the Eastern and Northern Expeditions as Jiang Jieshi's point man for communications. Due to Boqun's head start, the Ministry of Communication was among the three only ministries ready to go in mid-1927. The others were Foreign Affairs and Finance. Five other ministries were started a year later in 1928.

Boqun faced a Herculean task in both transportation and communication when he started to work on a unified nationwide system. In 1912 the nation had a total of fifty five hundred miles of railway and hardly any modern highway. Foreigners and foreign contractors managed most communication and custom offices, as were shipping and merchant marines. There was no civil air transport other than a few airports built by foreign countries dedicated to their diplomatic and military usage. Telegrams were available to most large cities, and telephone connections were extremely sparse and limited to just a few cities. There were no commercial radio stations. The provinces were responsible for the development of their own system, and there was no nationwide consideration in the planning. No national regulation for the development and the utilization of such systems existed at the time.

The first task for Boqun was to recruit a core group of young Western college–trained people to manage each function under the ministry: highway, railway, air transport, shipping and inland water-ways, post, and telecommunications. Additionally two other support functions needed to be established: the Bank of Communication and University of Communication and Transportation. The latter was to train Chinese replacements of the foreign nationals and to staff new positions; foreigners were working in various functions, and they enjoyed preferential treatment over the Chinese. Finally he had to develop and implement a nationwide communication system for tele-phone, air travel, railroads, and highways as well as regulation and tax collection for such a system.

Boqun's objectives by 1932 were to build additional ten thou-sand miles of railways and twenty thousand miles of paved high-ways; to take over completely the management and staffing of all post and telegraph offices from the British, French, and Swiss com-panies; and to form a national airline. With the right people already identified, Boqun was able to take over the management of the postal system from the French and the opium-import control from the British by 1930. By the end of 1930, an automatic telephone system was established in Shanghai, Wuhan, Beijing, and Nanjing. An airway joint venture was started with a US company for domestic air travel, and discussions started with Germany for international air travel. By the time Boqun left the ministry in 1932, it had been fully and well staffed. Although there were, still foreigners in certain posi-tions, the unequal treatment was eliminated. The government par-tially approved legislation for management and development of the national communication system. Most of the provinces were inte-grated into a nationwide system of post and telegraph, telephone, and postal saving.

In late 1924 Boqun commuted between Shanghai, where he continued his residence, and Guangzhou, where he worked for Sun Yatsen's republican government. A group of professors led by Ou Yuanhuai, a graduate of Southwestern University and Columbia

University in the United States, approached Boqun to become the chairman of the first private university, the Great China University in Shanghai, which had a student body of about three hundred. They named the university from a famous Chinese saying of "China Ever Bright." Since Boqun had always had an interest in education dating back to his Tokyo days, he accepted the appointment and led a fundraising effort for building its own campus. Boqun personally contributed seventy thousand yuan for a total of three hundred thousand yuan. The work of building the campus started in 1929 and was completed in 1930 on three hundred acres of land with a small brook running through it. The campus consisted of lecture halls, an auditorium, science laboratories, a library, a gymnasium, health care facilities, dormitories for men and women, a dining room, and teaching staff living quarters.

❖ ❖ ❖

Bao Zhining was from Nantong, Jiangsu, located on the northern bank of the Yangtze River, near the river's mouth. Nantong is a vital river port bordering Yancheng to the north, Taizhou to the west, Xuzhou and Shanghai to the south across the river, and the East China Sea to the east. The Bao name is unusual for Chinese Hans, and it is a Chinese version of a Mongol name dating from the Yuan dynasty. The Bao family can trace their ancestors to the reign of Kublai Khan, Genghis Khan's grandson and founder of the Yuan dynasty, when his army defeated the Southern Song dynasty and secured the Yangtze Delta in 1297.

Zhining's grandfather, Bao Shaopu, passed the provincial examination and become a Juren, served as a Jiangsu provincial government official, and later transferred to Shangding Province as the director of its library. He was a close friend of Sun Baoqi, who was the premier and foreign minister under Yuan Shikai in 1916 briefly and then again served under Cao Kun in 1924. Through his connection with Sun, Bao was eventually transferred to Beijing and worked as a secretary in the premier's office till late 1924, when he retired and brought his family back to Nantong.

Zhining's maternal grandfather was even more impressive. Zhang Jian was from Haimen County, Jiangsu Province. He was the first of the national imperial examinations and awarded the title of the exemplar of the state (Zhuangyuan) in 1894. He served in the famed Hanlin Academy, an academic and administrative institution founded in the eighth century. Membership in the academy was confined to an elite group of scholars who performed secretarial and literary tasks for the court. One of its main duties was to decide on interpretations of the Confucian classics, which formed the basis of the imperial examinations.

Zhang Jian

In 1909 Zhang was elected the chair of Jiangsu provincial parliament. In 1912, Zhang drafted the abdication edict for Puyi, the last emperor of China. He became the minister of enterprise of the provisional government of the Republic of China. In 1913 Zhang became the minister of industry and commerce and minister of agriculture and forestry in the Yuan Shikai government. In 1914, he served as the director of the State Administration of Water Resources. After Yuan accepted the twenty-one demands of the Japanese in 1915, Zhang resigned all his government posts, returned to Nantong, and focused his interest in education and business. He founded the first teacher school in modern China, Nantong Normal College. He established the first private museum of China, Nantong Museum. His well-known motto was, "Enterprise as father, education as mother," which had a profound impact on modern

Chinese society. In his lifetime he founded over twenty companies and over three hundred schools and made a significant contribution to the industrialization and education of modern China.

Zhining's father, Bao Junhao, was born the same year as Boqun. He went to Japan at the Qing government's expense to study English and political science. He was fluent in English and returned as a teacher. He married Zhang Jian's daughter, who was a passionate proponent of Western education and Chinese traditional culture. Bao Junhao joined the foreign services of the GMD government in Guangzhou and later in Nanjing. He served in various overseas assignments. Since Junhao was traveling overseas on a regular basis, his wife stayed at home alone to raise their children. Her mother had a great influence on Zhining, who was the first female in the family without bound feet and had the aspiration of higher education and a professional career. She finished her high school education at the boarding college preparatory school in Nantong in 1928. She passed the entrance examination for the most prestigious private college in Shanghai, the University of Shanghai. It was established by American Baptist Missionary Union and Southern Baptist Convention by combining two separate colleges into one university in 1911. Out of several hundred who applied, Zhining was among the only hundred accepted.

Bao Junhao had two brothers and a sister. Zhining become very close to the youngest brother, Junjian, who she affectionately referred as Uncle CJ. CJ graduated from Beijing University and then won a government scholarship to Columbia University for his doctorate in international political science and foreign policy. He met and married an American lady, Editha, who had been studying Chinese language and culture at nearby Barnard College. In spite of both families' consternation over the interracial marriage, the couple was well suited for each other. When Zhining first laid eyes on her, she could not believe she was so tall, so blond, and spoke Chinese in perfect Mandarin. In 1928 CJ and his wife had settled in Shanghai, where he was the Education Department director of the city. They were Zhining's substitute parents. She stayed in their house while in attendance at the university and was part of their house parties during weekends. Her aunt had given her the English name Elizabeth and made her feel as if she were her own sister. They spent long evenings together learning about each other's culture, and Zhining learned a lot about America.

As Zhining completed her first year at the University of Shanghai, she realized the emphasis of her studies was on English, which was just the right thing for her since she did not have enough of it in her preparatory school in Nantong. On the other hand, Zhining felt there was insufficient time spent on her main interest of Chinese literature and social studies. Her feeling was exacerbated by the decision to leave the university of her roommate and best friend. During the summer vacation, she met one of her best friends from the Nantong school and enrolled at the Great China University. She thought Zhining would be happier there. Zhining visited the campus of Great China and spoke with several teachers and students. The leaders at Great China impressed her: Boqun's work and accomplishments in the revolutionary movement and Ou Yuanhuai's reputation in the higher education field. In addition, Ou and CJ had been good friends since their Columbia University days, and Zhining liked Ou and his wife from meeting them at various social functions. Upon the approval of her parents, Zhining transferred to Great China for her second year.

❖ ❖ ❖

Zhining's college days at Great China were very happy ones. Her roommate was a very pretty and gregarious young woman from Guangzhou, fluent in English, and into all sort of arts and music. She was from a wealthy merchant family with many connections with the Shanghai café society. By her third year, Zhining was involved in various extracurricular activities, such as volleyball, tennis, and drawing. Another was Chinese opera, which would become her life passion. It had roots going back to the third century and evolved, in time, into several regional varieties. Her main interest was in Kunqu, which was one of the three oldest extant forms of Chinese opera. UNESCO selected it as one of the Masterpieces of the Oral and Intangible Heritage of Humanity by in 2001. The most famous example was *The Peony Pavilion* composed

Zhining (L) and roommate

during the early Ming dynasty. Zhining's favorite was *The Peach Blossom Fan* for its political and historical context. She would sing parts of it right up to her eighties. She joined a very popular Kunqu club founded by some sophisticated young women. She took singing lessons from a famous teacher-performer and was good enough to perform in club-staged performances.

Boqun attended one of her performances and was struck by her beauty, poise, and artistry. The next day Boqun sent flowers to her on behalf of the university with a personal note to express his pride and appreciation. In Zhining's junior year, she was elected by the student body as the "Flower of Great China," which was for the student most accomplished in her studies, her extracurricular activities, as well as her personal conducts. Again, she received her award directly from Boqun, with another personal note of congratulations and best wishes. Both of these occasions were the highlight of Zhining's university days, but unbeknownst to her, Boqun was captivated by her charm as he had been by no other woman in his life.

In the summer of 1930, Zhining was home in Nantong with her mother and brothers for vacation while her father was abroad. She received a telegram from CJ asking her to return to Shanghai for a very important matter. Zhining arrived in Shanghai in late July and stayed at her uncle's home. CJ then told her that Ou Yuanhuai had called on him and told him that Boqun was interested in Zhining for marriage and asked CJ for a formal introduction and the Bao family's permission to court her. Ou further advised that Boqun was forty-five years old and lost

Boqun 1929

Zhining, 1929

his first wife in 1928 and a son from that marriage had died in 1927. In their previous contacts at public events, Zhining was favorably impressed by not only Boqun's youthful physical appearance but also his sincerity and cultured manners and the depth of his conviction and commitment to the revolution led by Sun Yatsen. She admired the personal and familial sacrifices he had made for his beliefs that were well known to the students. She was a popular student and had a lot male students pursuing her attention; she found them to be rather immature and boring. She was surprised and

241

flattered by Boqun's interest; she also felt that the age difference of twenty-four years would not be an issue for the union to produce children. She was certain children would be as important to Boqun as to her since he was childless. Thus, she agreed that they should meet and get more acquainted.

After several dinners with Ou, CJ, and their wives, Boqun and Zhining were able to spend some time together without chaperones on several outings. On the very first outing, Boqun told Zhining that that he had fathered a boy with a Japanese woman in Tokyo in 1912 who was born after he had left Tokyo. Boqun also told her that he'd had a concubine in Shanghai since 1911 when he returned from Tokyo to work in that city. As the practice of the time, Boqun set up a household for the concubine and brought his son back from Tokyo to be raised by her. He gave the boy the Wang name and set up a trust fund for him but did not give either the concubine or this son any inheritance rights to his estate. He further promised Zhining that if they were married, he would sever his relationship with this concubine. Boqun formally disclosed this information to CJ since he had to conduct a thorough research of Boqun's familial situation to ascertain his marital status and to ensure there were no possible estate inheritance entanglements. CJ actually interviewed the concubine and asked lawyers to review the document she signed foregoing all claims to Boqun's estate.

After such due diligence, CJ pronounced that Boqun was eligible to marry Zhining. In August Boqun proposed, and Zhining then informed her parents. CJ's wife was extremely excited about Boqun's interest, and she encouraged Zhining and the Bao family to accept Boqun's proposal. Zhining's parents' initial concerns about the age difference were overcome by Boqun's ministerial position in the government as well as his revolutionary roles after Zhining convinced them Boqun was the husband for her. On September 9, 1930, Zhining and

Boqun were engaged. Zhining gave Boqun a small photograph, and he wrote his feelings on the back:

> She who gave me her photo,
> Is tall, strong, and slender,
> Yet her manner is quiet, harmonious, and serene.
> Immediate mutual attraction and becoming close,
> On shared beliefs and future vision of togetherness.
> We are now like shadows of each other,
> Both realize the need for hard work ahead.
> Trust is the bond of two different souls,
> No earthly event can separate the joined hearts.
> I wish to fly with you in the sky and run in the land,
> Even if I live until one hundred, all be with you.
> The past ten years have brought me sadness and despair,
> Now I wish to join a happy life with you.
> We shall have our place of quiet and peace,
> Away from the busy and chaotic world around us.
> We shall learn from each other, and pass us to our children.

In 1930, as it is now, there were plenty of so-called tabloids in Shanghai, and they had a field day with the Wang-Bao engagement. The most persistent story was that Boqun had to agree to three pre-nuptial conditions. First, he had to put up a deposit of hundred thousand yuan as guarantee that his estate was not encumbered, second, he had to build a new mansion in Shanghai's most fashionable French quarter, and last, he had to allow and pay for Zhining to go abroad for graduate studies. None of these was true. Zhining and Boqun both wanted to start a family as soon as possible. Since Boqun was commuting between Nanjing and Shanghai, he had only rented his residence for all these years while his work was in Shanghai. Boqun and Zhining had talked about where to build a house for their family. They decided their new home will be built in Shanghai, where Boqun would continue to work full time with the much-expanded Great China as its president after his retirement from his cabinet post in Nanjing.

Zhining and Boqun's Marriage, 1931
The Bao family on left and the Wang family on the
right except CJ's wife, on the right of Zhining

On June 18, 1931, Zhining and Boqun were married. He was a forty-six-year-old cabinet minister and the president of Great China University and held the position of Guizhou representative to the parliament. She was a twenty-two-year-old honor graduate with a degree in social sciences from the same university. Boqun had taken out announcements in each newspaper in Shanghai stating both the couple's backgrounds and emphasizing the fact that he was widower and the union had the blessing of both families. The wedding day was full of bright sunshine and a light breeze. Several hundred guests and relatives attended the wedding. Her maternal grandmother, father, mother, oldest brother, Johnson, and two uncles and their wives, including the blond Editha and several cousins, represented Zhining's family. All the Bao family was dressed in Western clothing except for the two older women. Zhining was in a Western white traditional dress and Boqun in a typical formal long Chinese gown. The Wang family included Boqun's mother, two sisters, He Yingqin's brother, and several cousins, all in formal Chinese attire. Jiang Jieshi and He Yingqin both sent their congratulations and regrets, for they were both dealing with a national crisis with the CCP and the Japanese.

After the formal wedding ceremony, Zhining changed into a traditional red qípáo and attended a banquet of over forty tables. Many made wedding toasts, glasses were clanged, and fine foods were consumed. Following the tradition, Boqun brought Zhining to his residence, where his mother formally accepted her into the household. Boqun's mother, Liu Xianqing, was extremely pleased that Zhining had married into the Wang family.

She said to the happy couple,

> Heaven has finally granted the Wang family a just reward for all the sacrifices it has made. Zhining is from such a refined and cultured family; her becoming a member of this family will help fill the voids of our lost sons. She will bring worthy male offspring to the Wang family and provide the guidance for them be leaders and contributors for our nation. Boqun will finally receive the love and joy of a family that he so well deserved after spending all

his life for the benefit of clan and country. I, represent-ing the Wang and Liu families, hope you will enjoy each other and your offspring for a thousand years.

Not all the Wang family had welcomed Zhining with such open arms and boundless affections. Many thought Boqun should have chosen a Guizhou native or at least a southwest Han Chinese instead someone with Mongol blood. Nevertheless, Boqun's three sisters and their husbands all shared their mother's feelings about Zhining, espe-cial He Yingqin and his wife. When Boqun told them he had decided to marry Zhining, Wenxiang, his sister and He's wife, asked him what was so special about her. Boqun had answered first with all the usual acco-lades, but he concluded, "She is such a generous spirit; one would be embarrassed to behave in a petty manner around her."

The honeymoon lasted for three days in Shanghai, and then Boqun had to return to work in Nanjing. He took Zhining by train to his offi-cial Nanjing government residence. Zhining liked the house, which was large and airy, with a garden surrounding the house. Boqun's work days started at seven. He returned home for lunch and was usu-ally back home by six. Many evenings there were working dinners or guest entertainment. Zhining quickly became a good host and took charge of the small household staff since she was brought up in such a household and was well trained in such things. On the weekends Boqun would take Zhining sightseeing in Nanjing, a city well known in Chinese history and culture. It is located in the lower Yangtze River drainage basin known as the Yangtze River Delta. Nanjing has long been one of China's most important cities. It is recognized as one of the four great ancient capitals of China. Its history dates back to 500 BCE, when a fort was built by the state of Wu of the Three Kingdom period. The first Ming emperor rebuilt the city in 1368 after he had overthrown the Mongol Yuan dynasty. It took two hundred thousand laborers over twenty years to rebuild the city. Nanjing's city walls are the longest in the world and remain standing today. Boqun knew the city and its surroundings well, and Zhining was anxious to see and to learn about Nanjing's many wonderful antiquities and sights.

In early 1930, construction began on number 31, Lane 1136, Yuyuan Road, in the French quarter of Shanghai for the Wang residence. The house was designed by a Shanghai architect, Lui Yingshi, in the Gothic Renaissance style of the Middle Ages. The main building consisted of three floors and a full basement, for a total of 21,500 square feet, and sat on piece of land of over ten acres. In addition to the main building, there was a green house, garages, and a guardhouse for the front entrance. The main building faced a garden of fifty thousand square feet dotted with trees, flowers, and stone sculptures. There were bridges over streams and several garden sitting areas. Boqun had personally designed the garden and selected most of the flowers and trees. The glass greenhouse kept the family supplied with fresh flowers all year around. The interiors were limestone, European mosaic tiles, various hardwood, and marble. It had over forty rooms. The first floor consisted of several living rooms, an entertainment room, several dining rooms, a library, an office, bathrooms, and a grand main entrance. The second floor was the living quarters for Boqun, Zhining, and the children. It consisted of five bedrooms of various sizes, each with its own bathroom. It also contained a calligraphy studio for Boqun. The third floor was the living quarters for Boqun's mother and other relatives with a similar layout as the second floor. Each floor had its own balcony overlooking the garden. The kitchen and the servant's quarters were located in the basement.

❖ ❖ ❖

In January of 1932, Boqun officially resigned from his cabinet post of the minister of communication but remained in the GMD congress as representative from Guizhou. Many from Guizhou wished him to return as the governor, but Boqun declined since he was fully committed to the Great China. He would indicate that he had been away from Guiyang too long and it would be better for one who had been in the province to serve in that position. In addition, deep down Boqun had lost all interest in politics where power intrigues were required.

In May of 1932, Japan and China finalized a cease-fire, but Jiang's struggle with the CCP continued. Jiang was also concerned about the southwest provinces, Yunnan, Guizhou, and Sichuan, which had remained independent from Nanjing's control. Since Boqun was from that area and knew the power players better than most, Jiang asked him to be his personal representative to those provinces with the objective of ascertaining their current position and possibly obtaining their cooperation against both the CCP and the Japanese. Boqun accepted the assignment but stated what he considered the probable scope of success.

> Yunnan's Long Lun is a soldier and a patriot. I have no doubt he will join in the effort of defending the nation against the Japanese. I am not certain he will spill blood against the CCP; some of its top military men are his friends. I will feel him out as to what can motivate him to do so. As you know, Long Lun will also have major influence over how Guizhou will act. Guizhou will most probably follow Yunnan's lead. It is necessary to help Guizhou to be independent from Yunnan. Moving some troops from Hunan to Guizhou will help in that regard. I will attempt to persuade Long to stay out of any power struggle in Guizhou. Sichuan is a different situation with no less than five different warlords, and the control of their respective territories is always fluid. I believe you did the right thing in naming Liu Xiang as the governor even though he does not control the whole province. I think his uncle, Liu Wenhui, needs to be brought into the same camp as well. My objective is to bring them together without wasting their resources fighting each other. Maybe through the

elders of the clan, the uncle will have his own province of Xikang instead contesting Sichuan. Liu Xiang will most likely do what he can to support the anti-Japanese effort, but he will be neutral toward the CCP at best.

Jiang agreed with Boqun's assessment, and Boqun left in June for Chongqing by ship. Zhining was eight months pregnant and decided to leave Nanjing for Shanghai. While the new house was under construction, Zhining was comfortable in the rental house with Boqun's mother and sister, Wenbi. The birth of a boy on July 1, 1932, brought much joy to both Wang and Bao families. Boqun received the good news by wire in Chongqing, and he named his son Zucheng, which meant ancestor's heritage. The child has two dimples, as Zhining noted was the Bao family trait, since her father and her grandmother both had two dimples, but the child was also generally beautiful, and she gave Boqun credit for that.

Boqun's assignment in Sichuan was successful to the extent the Liu clan elders stopped the uncle and nephew from fighting and agreed to the plan suggested by Boqun. Liu Xiang was unhappy, for he felt that he could have finished off his uncle and become the master of both Sichuan and Xikang. Yunnan and Guizhou both had promised cooperation in confronting the Japanese and were non-committal about the CCP. Boqun made a personal trip to Chengdu, Sichuan, where his friend Dai Kan had committed suicide on July 16, 1917. Boqun went the temple outside of the ancient city south gate where Dai died and paid his respects, and with tears from his eyes, he left these words:

> Gone are my elder brother and mentor
> So long ago on our journey to Japan,
> East wind of summers past carried away the hero's remain.
> How the true patriots are now few and chaos reign,
> Will our dreams ever be gained?

Boqun departed in September to return to Nanjing, and when he disembarked in Hankow, the usual inspection of his boat found opium on board that was strictly forbidden by law. Since the boat carried only Boqun and his small staff, it became an embarrassment for Boqun even though he and his staff were not opium users. Rumors indicated that Liu Xiang had placed the opium on the boat to cause Boqun trouble since he had prevented him from eliminating his uncle. This event caught Boqun by surprise, and he was more convinced than ever to stay out of politics, especially carrying out any assignment for Jiang Jieshi.

Boqun reported to Jiang Jieshi in Nanjing. Jiang congratulated him on his efforts in Sichuan and his confirmation about the intent of Yunnan and Guizhou. Jiang did not mention the opium affair. Boqun stated to Jiang that he had done his last assignment for the central government in order to devote full time to the Guizhou provincial affairs and the Great China University. He resigned all his government positions save for representation of Guizhou. Jiang thanked Boqun for his service over the years. Boqun left the presidential building looking forward to seeing his newborn son and his loving mother in Shanghai. He felt that a heavy burden had been lifted from his shoulders, and he was much lighter on his feet.

CHAPTER 13

1933-1935

LONG MARCH, XIAN INCIDENT, AND UNITED FRONT

At the start of 1933, Japan continued to exploit internal conflicts in China to increase its territorial gains in China. The Japanese realized the political and military power of Jiang Jieshi's Nanjing government was limited to just the area of the Yangtze Delta, and the other sections of China essentially remained in the hands of local warlords. Japan sought out Chinese collaborators to help them establish friendly relationships with the warlords in the northern and northeastern provinces. The northern provinces affected by this policy were Inner Mongolia (Chahar and Suiyuan), Hebei, Shanxi, and Shandong. It was most effective in Inner Mongolia and Hebei. In 1935, under Japanese pressure, Jiang agreed to prohibit GMD from conducting political party operations in Hebei and Chahar. By the end of 1935, the Chinese government practically had abandoned northern China. By May of 1935, Japan had set up puppet governments for each province, providing all necessary military and economic control and support.

He Yingqin, 1935

When the Mukden Incident took place in Manchuria, Jiang Jieshi had made a decision to deal with Japan with compromise and appeasement while focusing his military resources to exterminate the CCP threat. Jiang sent He Yingqin to replace Zhang Xueliang as chairman of the Beijing Military Committee, which was the supreme organ in charge of the GMD military forces of northern China. Jiang gave this position to He because of his personal friendship with several key commanders of the Japanese Army, and He had sworn to Jiang that he would do his best to negotiate with the Japanese rather resorting to armed conflict. Subsequently He had to sign several agreements with the Japanese to that aim. In June of 1935, the He-Umezu Agreement provided for a total withdrawal of all Chinese forces from Beijing and Hebei Province. In late 1935 He returned to Nanjing and resumed his previous position as chief of staff of the army.

In addition to Manchuria, Jiang had withdrawn almost two hundred thousand troops from northwest China to boost his campaign against the CCP. The Japanese also attacked the Chinese economy and provided opium to undermine the Chinese. It smuggled various Japanese manufactured goods into as far as Nanjing, undercutting the local producers and depriving Jiang's government of much-needed tax and customs revenues. They set up hundreds of opium dens in Beijing and other areas under their control while Japanese navy ships transported the prohibited substances to Shanghai and other cities on the Yangtze.

At the end of 1933, Jiang Jieshi and his wife, Meiling, traveled to Hangzhou to meet Zhang Xueliang, who had returned from their European trip accompanied by his Australian adviser, William Henry Donald, an Australian newspaperman who worked at various Western news journals in China from 1903 through World War II. He moved to Shanghai, where he became a key editor to the economics monthly, *Far Eastern Review*. At the same time, he befriended Charlie Soong, the very wealthy publisher, businessman, and father of the Soong sisters. He quit the *Review* after it became more pro-Japanese and became an adviser to Sun Yatsen and later Zhang Xueliang. He also helped to cure Zhang and his wife's opium addiction and advised them on their European trip. Donald had impressed the Jiangs, in particular

Meiling, with his straightforward worldliness and his intelligence. The next day Jiang appointed Zhang as the deputy commander-in-chief of the Bandit (CCP) Suppression Army for Hebei, Henan, and Anhui Provinces. Zhang, based in Wuhan, at Donald's urging began a campaign for social reform there and moved the remnants of his northeast army to drive out the CCP from their positions within the three provinces.

In the beginning of 1934, Jiang returned to his campaign against the CCP with his new German military adviser, who had rebuilt the German army after the end of WWI. Sparing no expense, which the government could ill afford, Jiang marshaled his Central Army at five times the size of the CCP troops. He finally forced the CCP to fight a relatively static battle by using the so-called block house strategy of containment, which involved building fortified outposts along strategic points to contain the Red Army.

In early 1934, the Jiangxi base was no longer sustainable by the CCP. Its Standing Committee appointed Zhou Enlai to organize the evacuation to a nonspecific northwestern remote area, out of Jiang's reach. Zhou made his plans in complete secrecy since GMD had its spies everywhere. Even senior leaders were informed only at the last moment of troop movements. The withdrawal began in early October 1934. Zhou's agents identified a large section of the GMD blockhouse line manned by troops of a Guangdong warlord known to prefer preserving his troops to fighting. Zhou negotiated and bribed for safe passage for the Red Army to pass through various nominally GMD-provinces under the warlord's control. The CCP group consisted of more than ninety thousand troops, eleven thousand administrative personnel, and thousands of civilian porters and families, which successfully completed the crossing of the Xinfeng River and marched through Guangdong and into Hunan.

There it encountered the last of the GMD army's blockhouse fortifications at the Xiang River, where it was intercepted by regular Whampoa-led and -trained GMD troops and suffered heavy casualties.

Of the eighty thousand in the CCP group who attempted to break out of Jiangxi, only thirty thousand successfully escaped. The conditions of the CCP's forced withdrawal demoralized some leaders, but Zhou remained calm and retained his commanding presence and perseverance. Zhou had reconsidered his plan to meet up with another Red Army in Hunan, but it became obvious that would the most expedient route and Jiang would have set an ambush for them. Mao Zedong, now serving on Zhou's staff, suggested they should head toward Sichuan via Guizhou, where the GMD's sway was questionable and the local military typically led by self-serving warlords.

In a meeting of the CCP Central Committee on December 12, 1934, near the border between Hunan and Guizhou, Zhou endorsed Mao's proposal and overruled the objections of others and CCP's new German adviser. The Red Army reached the mountains of southeast Guizhou; they continued west through Zunyi and north toward Sichuan, hoping to establish a base area there. On January 1, 1935, Zhou proposed that the Central Committee approve all military plans and operations. The proposal was accepted and became effective immediately, which prevented any military leader from acting independently. On January 15 the Red Army captured Zunyi, the second-largest city in Guizhou. As Mao had predicted, the city was poorly defended and was too far from GMD forces to mount a counterattack. By the time the CCP Army occupied Zunyi, it had only about ten thousand troops left. The CCP Zunyi Conference lasted from January 15 until January 17, 1935, and resulted in a reshuffling of the party structure. Mao became one of three members of the Military Affairs Commission, headed by Zhou Enlai. Within this group, Zhou was empowered to make the final decisions on military matters, while Mao was Zhou's assistant. When the army resumed its march northward to reach the remote province of Shanxi, Jiang's forces blocked the direct route to Sichuan. The CCP contingent spent the next several months maneuvering to avoid direct confrontation with hostile forces but still attempting to move north to join other CCP forces.

When Jiang Jieshi realized the CCP had taken a new route, he and Meiling flew to Sichuan to organize defense and to ensure the loyalty of the ruling Liu family who controlled large portions of the province. The Jiangs established their home base in Chongqing. At the front, Jiang had sent for his most able general, Xue Yue, born to a Hakka peasant family in Guangdong; he was in the first graduating class of Whampoa and one of the most effective GMD commanders of the Northern Expedition. During the CCP's long march, his forces chased the retreating Red Army all the way to Sichuan and Guizhou. The Red Army retreated across the great swamplands and finally escaped to Shaanxi Province. He then turned his forces around, marched unstopped to central China, and defeated the famed Red Army commanders in the areas they controlled and forced them out of these strongholds after reducing their forces by more than half.

On March 24, 1935, the Jiangs flew to Guiyang, Guizhou, to direct the battle at Zunyi between the chasing GMD Army and Red Army rear guard. Against overwhelming numbers, the Red Army rear guard was completely wiped out. Due to the weather, Jiang was not able to use his air force to do damage to the main CCP group. He then engineered a military coup against the local warlord in Guiyang and replaced with him with one of his subordinates. In April Jiang reported to Nanjing that the Zhou and Mao–controlled CCP had been defeated and he was turning his attention to Zhang Guotao, who was a founding member of CCP and senior to both Mao and Zhou in the party hierarchy. Zhang had established another CCP base in Sichuan in 1932 with his Fourth Red Army of eighty thousand. Instead of crossing grasslands where Jiang had planned an ambush, Zhang attempted to take over Chengdu. A combined force of GMD and local Liu armies defeated him and caused him to retreat to the upper Yellow River. Zhang then gathered up additional CCP troops to face Xue Yue's GMD forces but suffered another defeat. He then retreated to the far west, where he faced battles with the local Muslims and had to march further west away from the GMD's reach.

Avoiding the main populated areas and enemy troops in Sichuan, the main group of the CCP Army under Zhou and Mao headed for the high country of the Great Snow Mountain range at fourteen thousand feet. It was an arduous and epic journey against nature and attacks from the indigenous Tibetans and chased by the GMD troops. On June 12, 1935, the main CCP group united with the Fourth Red Army, led by Zhang Guotao. Zhang arrived with his eighty some thousand troops in relatively good condition. The fact that he had control of superior forces gave him the power to challenge the authority of Zhou and Mao.

Zhang and Mao disagreed with the direction of the march. Zhang insisted on going southwest, while Mao wished to go northward, toward Shaanxi. The two armies eventually split, each going their separate way. Zhang's Fourth Red army traveled south, then west, and finally north toward the Muslim Qinghai Province. On the way Xue Yue's GMD Army and his Chinese Muslim allies destroyed a large portion of Zhang's forces. The remnants of Zhang's forces later rejoined elements of the Second Red Army before eventually linking up with Mao's forces in Shaanxi.

The Muslim forces attacked Mao's First Red Army, traversing several swamps. All along the way, the Red Army confiscated property and weapons from local warlords and landlords while recruiting peasants and the poor. Mao and his group finally arrived in Shaanxi in October 1935 and joined with local CCP forces there, who had already established a CCP base in Yenan at northern Shaanxi. Only some seven thousand men under Mao's command made it out of the original hundred thousand who had started the march. A variety of factors contributed to the losses, including fatigue, hunger and cold, sickness, desertion, and military casualties. During the retreat, membership in the party fell from three hundred thousand to around forty thousand. It took another year for the Second Red Army to reach Yenan, where CCP had established its base. This completed the famed CCP Long March.

❖ ❖ ❖

Boqun had looked forward to the year of 1933 as a beginning of a new life in earnest. He had tried to shed all his revolutionary dreams and sorrows to take up a happy life with a beautiful young wife and an adorable new son. He and Zhining were scheduled to move into the new Shanghai house in the fall; Boqun enjoyed in the decoration and finishing of the interior and even shopping with Zhining. He had more time to devote to his passion of calligraphy, especially his specialty, the seal script, an ancient style of

Liu Xianqing and daughters

Chinese calligraphy. It evolved organically out of the Zhou dynasty script, arising in the warring state of Qin about 400 BCE. The Qin variant of seal script became the standard and was adopted as the formal script for all of China in the Qin dynasty and was still widely used for decorative engraving and seals (name chops or signets) in the Han dynasty through the present. Boqun was an expert in his own time, and many friends and even strangers would ask him to write scrolls of their favorable poems, quotes, etc. Boqun loved doing it and now that he had the time, he would usually spend an hour or more writing each day.

Although Boqun's duties as president at the Great China University kept him fully occupied, almost each week he had visitors from his political and revolutionary past for his advice and offering for him to serve on various positions. He declined all such offers and refrained as much as possible from political discussions. Boqun was known as a true disciple of Sun Yatsen in GMD circles. He was extremely concerned about the Japanese encroachment and the factional split within the GMD. He was careful in sharing his views about the Jiang-led government in Nanjing, even with his trusted brother-in-law He Yingqin and his wife, Boqun youngest sister, Wenxiang. As in all-important family issues, he only could speak his mind with his mother and Zhining. His mother, Liu Xianqing, now seventy-one, still kept up with the current events and political landscape, as she always had done all her life. She continued to read the newspapers and continued to surprise Boqun with how current she was with the news of the day. During one of their frequent discussions, Boqun lamented about how he should broach his views about state of the nation with He Yingqin and his wife. His mother offered,

> First of all, I think you can depend on Yingqin's personal loyalty to you. You, Dilun, and I agreed that is the keystone of his personality, and we can depend on him as a part of the family. It is difficult for anyone to pass judgment on Jiang's policies and strategy, but the man is an ambitious egotist and opportunist in spite of his professed devotion to Sun's principles and considers them impractical. He considers the nation to be a family, with himself as the father and all others his children who need his guidance to survive. Does that

sound familiar? Jiang is just like all the emperors of our past, even those supposedly enlightened ones. At this point of our history, Jiang may be just the man to take us to the next stage of a true republic. In any case, what Jiang has accomplished thus far is remarkable and borders on miraculous; but what about the future? Is he laying the groundwork? Does he have a plan other than his obsession to exterminate the CCP? What alternative do we have?

In early April Boqun family accompanied him for the traditional Qingmin or tomb clearing days to Dilun's tomb in Hangzhou. Dilun had picked out the site, located on shore of the famous and beautiful West Lake, where he had remodeled a small house. The grave had two stone tablets with writings by Boqun and He Yingqin praising Dilun's accomplishments in his short life. Boqun was visibly in deep sorrow as he swept the gravesite and buried incense. He then stood silently for over half an hour while his wife and son left him alone. They stayed in the house for three nights, visited all the sites, and enjoyed the famous Hangzhou seafood fit for any emperor. Boqun had tried to make a sad occasion for himself into a joyous outing for his family, and Zhining was deeply touched, as she noted in her dairy.

In June Boqun's sister, Wenxiang, came to Shanghai from Beijing for a medical checkup, and Boqun's family accompanied her back to Beijing. Many of Boqun's friends and comrades of the revolution who came as far as Tianjin greeted them. He Yinggin took time off, and with his wife along with close friends, He escorted the Wang family around the sights of Beijing and the surrounding area. Zhining was surprised by how good the food was, especially the famous Beijing duck served at the family restaurant that had catered to emperors over the years. Wenxiang made sure during the sightseeing there were always several women of Zhiling's age so they could share the latest fashions and manner of Beijing society mixed with a bit of the latest gossip. They were guests of the famous Beijing opera for several nights, and both enjoyed the performance.

Boqun received a wire while in Beijing in early July stating that Dilun's concubine had died in Shanghai. Although they were never married, after the death of Dilun's wife, to avoid further friction with the Liu family, both Boqun and his mother considered her family. She was only seventeen when Dilun took her in, and she was pregnant when he was assassinated. A daughter was born three months later. She knew about the assassination and had kept it from Dilun's mother all these years, as requested by Boqun. She had raised her daughter called Eighth Sister, on her own and tried to take care of her mother-in-law and her household needs. Boqun's mother and sisters liked her, and they were very sad over her passing, as was Boqun, since her death also brought up his feelings of how much he missed his brother. She was buried in the Wang family plot in Shanghai, as was Boqun's first son, Fusen.

At the end of September, the new house was ready for occupation. Zhining had asked Boqun's older sister, Wenbi, to consult the Chinese lunar calendar for the most auspicious date for the move in. On October 13 the official move started, and it took two days to move Boqun's family, his mother, Wenbi, a widow, plus all the servants. Boqun personally conducted the move from six in the morning till seven the next evening. It then took another couple of weeks for the family to settle in. Zhining was happy and envied by her friends, but she felt a bit intimidated by the size of the house, all of Boqun's extended family under the same roof, and her responsibility as the mistress of such a household. Boqun, sensing her apprehension, took her into his arms and assured her that she would do a great job as the mistress since he trusted her judgment, intelligence, and knowledge. Boqun made sure that he continued to offer assurances through the next year, and his mother did the same. By the end of year, Zhining felt comfortable and confident to be the mistress of house and even enjoyed her position

Wang Boqun house, Shanghai.

In the beginning of 1934, both Boqun and Zhining had gone through a period of minor sickness, but by March they both had recovered and enjoyed life once again. Their son, Zucheng, was a year and half old and in good health, with baby teeth started to come through. He walked and chased his nurse around the house. He also like to talk and to engage others with his obviously above-average intellect. In mid-March he had the symptoms of a cold, with fever and coughs. Friends had recommend a pediatrician trained in England, and his diagnosis was measles. It had affected his lung and heart. Injections and medicine did not improve his condition. He lapsed into a coma, and out of desperation Boqun brought in the best Chinese medicine doctor in Shanghai, and he was unable to revive Zucheng either. He died in the afternoon of March 24, 1934, only two weeks after he had contracted the disease. The whole extended family was deeply in mourning, and Boqun and Zhining were inconsolable. Zucheng was buried in the Wang family plot in Shanghai next to his half-brother, Fusen.

Zhining was seven months pregnant, and Boqun was concerned for her health and the unborn child, so he decided to take her for a short respite to Suzhou, a city founded in 514 BCE. It has over twenty-five hundred years of rich history, and relics of the past are abundant. The city's canals, stone bridges, pagodas, and meticulously designed gardens have contributed to its status as one of two most beautiful cities in China. There is ancient Chinese saying, "Above there is heaven, on earth there are Xu and Hang," which referred Xuzhou and Hangzhou. Since the Song dynasty, it had been an important center for China's silk industry. UNESCO

Zucheng. 1934.

added the classical gardens in Suzhou its list of the World Heritage Sites in 1997 and 2000. Suzhou is dubbed the Venice of the East or Venice of China. They stayed with one of Boqun's best friends with a traditional Chinese house on the ancient Pingjiang Street along the Grand Canal. The list of China's "famous history and culture streets" includes Pingjiang Street, which features elegant bridges, flowing waters, and unique historical architecture. The Grand Canal, at over eleven hundred miles, is the longest man-made river in the world. Starting at Beijing, it passes through Tianjin and the provinces of Hebei, Shandong, Jiangsu, and Zhejiang to the city of Hangzhou, linking the Yellow and Yangtze Rivers. The oldest parts of the canal date back to the fifth century BCE, although the various sections were finally combined during the Sui dynasty.

Boqun wanted to take Zhining away just for a couple of days so both of them could have a change from Shanghai, where Boqun had mourned the death of his beloved Dilun and both sons. He did not wish to stay longer due to Zhining's condition. Of all the wonderful sights of Suzhou, Zhining's favorites were the gardens. Out of the eight most famous gardens, there were four classical gardens. Each represented the style of the Song, Yuan, Ming, and Qing dynasties and are currently the UNESCO World Heritage sites. The couple chose to visit the Yuan (Mongol)-style Lion Grove Garden with caves, grottos, ponds, structures, and bridges connecting the various garden sections. The plum blossom forest was in full bloom, and the walkway was paved with fallen flowers. Boqun held Zhining's hand and walked to see all the exotic plants and flowers while birds and animals chanted in a world of their own. Their friends took them to dine the famous Suzhou dishes, such as cherry pork, slow-cooked with cherries for seven or eight hours, sweet and sour Mandarin fish, stir-fried crackle eels, broad beans stir-fried with spring onions, chicken stewed in watermelon, and mushrooms with shepherd's purse greens. They also enjoyed the famous and incomparable bafei soup made from liver and meat of the barbel fish. For few hours, the wonderful sights and delicious food pushed their sorrows into the back of their consciousness. The next day they visited a famous temple near the house and enjoyed a moment of solitude before taking a train back to Shanghai.

On May 15, 1934, an eight-pound son was born was in perfect health to Zhining and Boqun. The parents and the extended families were overjoyed. Each in their own way paid thanks to heaven for their good fortune so soon after the tragic death of Boqun's son. It is customary for Chinese families to use two characters for the name. The first character denotes the child's generation in the family, and the second is to be unique for the specific child. Since Zu was the first character of the first child now deceased, Boqun decided on De (virtue) to be the first character and Fu (induce) as the second. After the birth, Zhining

263

devoted most of her time to taking care of the child. In her dairy, she remarked that she felt guilt about being a bit obsessed about Defu after the death of her first son and for not spending enough time with Boqun, even though he never complained.

Boqun's mother had been visiting her daughter, Wenxiang, in Beijing since March, and Boqun had not told her of Zucheng's passing. In early June Boqun and Zhining went to the train station to meet her. She noted Zucheng's absence, and Boqun told her, "He is with his other grandmother in Nantong because of the birth of Defu." His mother asked him to invite Zhining's mother to visit them in Shanghai and bring Zucheng with her. Eventually Boqun had to tell his mother the truth. She was so upset that she would not eat for two days. Zhining overheard her cries to heaven as to what crime the family committed to cause the loss of so many male offspring. Liu Xianqing, the Wang matriarch, become ill soon thereafter, and in spite the finest medical care from both Western and Chinese doctors, she died on September 16, 1934 at age seventy-two and was buried in Shanghai with her two grandsons. She had been the guiding light for Boqun all his adult life and for rest of the family when her husband died in 1904 at age forty. She backed her sons in their political differences with her younger brother and the rest of the Liu family. In retrospect, as Zhining noted in her diary, perhaps Boqun was right not to tell her about Dilun's assassination since that gave her some element of hope to live on and enjoy her grandchildren. Otherwise she might have died then out of grief for him twelve years earlier.

In March of 1935, Zhining's father and her eldest brother, Johnson, returned to Shanghai from Paris after her father's three-year Foreign Ministry assignment in France. It was a most happy reunion when the rest of Bao family joined them in Shanghai, and the whole family stayed at the Wangs' new house for a week. In April Zhining's father became the very first Chinese council-general for Vancouver in western Canada, which would require moving the entire Bao family there. Zhining was not happy about the turn of events since she would sorely miss all of her family for several years. In May Boqun and Zhining bid farewell to her parents and three brothers when they embarked on a steamship for Vancouver. Zhining could not help but feel a sense of lost so soon after she had lost her firstborn and all of her immediate family was gone to a faraway land across the great ocean.

When Boqun resigned his ministerial post, he still wanted to serve the country where he felt that he could contribute. Thus, he continued to be a member of GMD and the Central Executive Committee as well as a Guizhou representative to the legislative yuan, which meant he needed to be in Nanjing on a monthly basis. In October of 1935, Boqun had to attend several meeting in Nanjing, and he took Zhining and Defu with him. Boqun rented a house when he resigned as the minister of communication in 1932 and vacated the government-owned ministerial house. The rental was located in a quiet, tree-lined residential area close to shopping and the main city park so the family could occupy themselves as Boqun attended to his business. There were also a lot of social dinners and events Zhining would attend with Boqun and that kept the couple busy in the evenings.

❖ ❖ ❖

On November 12, 1935, at 9:00 a.m., Boqun attended the opening session of the GMD Central Executive Committee multiday conference chaired by Wang Jingwei and attended by all the key members, including Jiang Jieshi, Zhang Xueliang, and He Yingqin. After conclusion of the morning meeting, a photo session was set up, but Jiang chose to leave to speak with the general meeting of provincial delegates. After the photo session, the committee started to leave, an shots rang out and hit Wang Jingwei in his cheek, chest, and arm. He was bleeding from his mouth as well as his bullet wounds. Jiang rushed back and help carry Wang to the ambulance. Zhang and another attendee pinned down the assassin. He was a sergeant in the Nineteenth Army, and he insisted that he was acting on his own in protest against the Japanese appeasement. Wang was rushed to the local hospital and then was transferred by train to Shanghai. Out of fear for his life, he resigned his government posts and departed for Paris for medical reasons. Back at the conference, Jiang received 495 out of 515 in the election for key position of chairman of the Central Executive and Supervisory Committees. Now with Wang Jingwei practically retired and Hu Hanmin sidelined in Guangzhou, Jiang had secured his leadership position. Boqun was shaken that evening as he told Zhining what happened and remarked that Wang probably took the bullets for Jiang since he was the man behind the Japanese appeasement.

❖ ❖ ❖

Boqun traveled to Nanjing almost on a monthly basis and sometime twice a month, and he liked to have Zhining and Defu with him. The rental in Nanjing was a bit small for the family, and they decided to build a small Western-style house in the same district as the rental. The couple spent much time again on planning and selecting the furnishings for the new house, and Boqun got involved in the design of the garden. The house was complete at the year's end, and the family started to use the house in beginning of 1936.

By 1936, the Great China University was known for excellence in its curriculum and teaching staff. Students came from many provinces, even some foreign countries, to study Chinese language, history, music, and politics. It had more than fourteen hundred undergraduate students and some seven hundred graduate students. As president, Boqun had a full-time job of managing the organization and the all-consuming fundraising. His days started at eight in the morning, and most days he would arrive home after seven in the evening. Zhining would host many entertainment functions. They both had their days full and fulfilling. On August 27, 1936, Zhining gave birth to her first daughter, DeXiang, in Shanghai. Zhining was a little surprised by Boqun reaction of joy instead of disappointment, as the traditional father would have in the birth of a daughter instead of a son.

While the family was in Nanjing in September 1936, Boqun's older sister, Wenbi, became seriously ill in Shanghai. The family returned to Shanghai immediately by night train. Wenbi lived with the family, and she did not take care of her own health and had smoked since a young age. She lost her husband in her twenties and had a son who was married. Zhining liked her for her carefree attitude and being a bit of an eccentric. She always had heart problems and but did not want to be treated by Western doctors, in spite of Boqun's constant suggestions to consult Western specialists. Wenbi died just two weeks after at age fifty-five. The family buried her in the family plot in Shanghai. It was a difficult loss for Boqun since he was closer to her then the two younger sisters due to their much younger ages. She often sat in on the discussions the Wang brothers had with their mother over the years. Zhining tried to console Boqun through this poignant year of both births and deaths of all his dear ones in the family, yet she knew how much sadness he had to carry through these difficult days.

In October Zhining's uncle CJ and Boqun's good friend and confidant was appointed as the ambassador to Greece stationed at Athens. Zhining had developed a special relationship ever since her university days in Shanghai with his wife, Editha, who loved Chinese culture and spoke Mandarin like a native. Zhining helped her shopping for Chinese painting and antiques for the embassy, and materials and designs of Chinese dresses for her to wear on the usual diplomatic functions. At the end of the month, Boqun and Zhining saw them off by steamship. Zhining could not help the tears of farewell as she done in the send-off of her own family, but on the other hand, she was grateful the she had a loving husband two wonderful, healthy children.

❖ ❖ ❖

At the end of 1935, as the CCP had settled into Yenan, Jiang Jieshi ordered Zhang Xueliang to move from his base in Wuhan up north to Xian, the capital of Shaanxi for the contentment of the CCP and preparation of the final extermination. Zhang was to join up with the Northwest Army lead by Yang Hucheng, a former associate of Feng Yuxiang, who taken over the army from Feng when he retired after the Great Plains War against Jiang. Nominally, Zhang was in charge of the combined forces.

Hu Hanmin died of a heart attack in Guangzhou in the summer 1936 amid demonstrations against the Japanese appeasement policy adapted by Jiang Jieshi. The independent warlords also were concerned about Jiang's assertion of troops into their provinces against the CCP; five hundred thousand GMD troops had taken up positions in Hunan, Yunnan, Guizhou, and Sichuan. Jiang commenced an opium trade blockade at the coastal and border southern provinces that undercut their revenues. On June 1, 1936, the Guangdong-Guangxi Anti-Japanese National Salvation Army led by Li Zongren advanced into Hunan. Jiang had used his favorite weapon, the silver bullet, for the last five years to bribe various southern military commanders. The ensuing defections from Li's army made the uprising more difficult than Li had anticipated. On August 11 Jiang flew to Guangzhou with Meiling and Donald, who had left Zhang Xueliang and joined Jiang as an adviser. Jiang met with Li and his key associate and offered generous terms to save face without having to fight the hundred thousand troops lined up against them. Against such overwhelming GMD forces, Li accepted an income to Guangxi of 2 million yuan per month, and Jiang promised to fight the Japanese. The brief rebellion ended by September 1, 1936

❖ ❖ ❖

Having pacified the southern uprising, Jiang pressed his campaign of CCP extermination. The Jiangs flew to Xian to meet with Zhang Xueliang on the battle plan. Xian was the capital of Shaanxi, the province where the CCP had established their base after the Long March. Jiang instructed Zhang to adapt the blockhouse strategy of building forts and roads to press on against Yanan, but most of his troops were eager to go home and fight the Japanese in Manchuria. Zhang, after his European visit, was convinced that Japan was the enemy, not the CCP. His own contact with the CCP had shown they were of the same mind.

He spoke to Jiang in private, but it fell on deaf ears.

> GMD is risking loss of popular support and will promote its own demise if it takes territory inch by inch in a civil war while losing large chunks of its territory to the Japanese province by province. Like you, I have fought the CCP and find them to be a formidable opponent, and I can't help but feel there must be a way to join hands with them and form a united front against the Japanese.

Mao Zedong had sent Zhou Enlai to Zhang, urging him to form a united front against the Japanese, who had murdered his father and taken Manchuria from him. After a meeting with Zhou, Zhang refused openly break with Jiang Jieshi but agreed to take a neutral position. He also agreed that China needed a united government and civilian control of the military, as Sun Yatsen had envisioned. He allowed the CCP to set up a liaison office in Xian. Zhang then informed his senior staff, including Yang Hucheng, and they all supported Zhang's position.

On October 22, 1936, the Jiangs flew to Xian personally to implement his CCP suppression plan. Both Zhang and Yang stated their neutral position. Jiang angrily threatened to send Zhang's army to faraway Guangdong, and Yang's army integrated into the GMD army at the CCP front and flew back to Nanjing. When Zhang and Yang ignored his order, Jiang Jieshi came to Xian again on December 4, 1936, accompanied by a group of GMD military officers to direct the suppression campaign. In the interim between these two visits, the Japanese-backed Inner Mongolian Army had tried to invade Suiyuan Province, now part of Inner Mongolia. Yan Xishan's Shanxi Army defeated the invaders in late 1936 and drove them out of Suiyuan. Yan's success had shown the Chinese that it was possible and necessary to resist the Japanese.

After their unsuccessful attempts to persuade Jiang to join forces with the CCP against the Japanese aggression, Zhang and Yang decided to take matters into their own hands. In the early hours of December 12, 1936, Zhang's bodyguards arrested Jiang and his entourage. During the arrest, several in Jiang's group were killed, including Jiang's nephew. Although the world believed the event was a coup, Zhang and Yang had decided to force Jiang to negotiate with the CCP for a united front against the Japanese. When the news reached Nanjing, there was confusion and disagreement within both the GMD and the CCP on how to handle the incident. Rumor was that Jiang was killed along with some of his group. The GMD government decided to appoint He Yingqin, then the minister of war, in charge of deciding what action to take. He and the army general staff decided to attack Xian and to rescue Jiang if he was still alive. Jiang's wife, Meiling, desperately sought a peaceful solution, fearing an attack would cause Jiang's death. Independents such as Li Zongren and Yan Xishan who opposed Jiang did not want him to die, leaving China without national leadership at the time that would only benefit the Japanese. They sent a wire to Zhang and Yang in support of Jiang. Additionally, the Western powers, such as the United States and the United Kingdom, preferred a peaceful resolution to the incident, for they regarded Jiang as the only leader who could lead a united China against the Japanese aggression.

In the CCP there were two opinions as well. Most of the leaders, such as Mao and Zhu De, proposed the execution of Jiang. Others, such as Zhou Enlai, realized it could bring more damage to the anti-Japan movement if Jiang died since he had become a symbol of national revolution and unity. Meanwhile the GMD Army began marching toward Xian to rescue Jiang, and the GMD bombers flew over the city, threatening air attack. On December 14 Meiling decided to send Donald, who had previously been Zhang's adviser and close friend, to Xian in preparation for a visit by Meiling to negotiate Jiang's release.

Stalin also helped Jiang. He believed Jiang's execution would not be beneficial to either Chinese resistance to Japan or Soviet interests in the Far East. Desperately in need of Soviet aid, Mao relented to Stalin's position and agreed for peace talks. On December 14, 1936, the CCP delegation, led by Zhou, met with Zhang and Yang in Xian to find a peaceful resolution. On December 22, 1936, Meiling and her elder brother, TV Soong, flew to Xian to meet the CCP delegation and their hosts. Zhang met them at the airport and greeted them warmly. The Soong family had befriended Zhang when he was a playboy in Shanghai in 1925; he actually had dated Meiling and was considered suitable marriage material. On December 24, 1936, the parties reached an agreement to establish a united front against Japan and to release prisoners accused of inciting anti-Japanese riots. The next day Zhang released Jiang and his entourage. To show his good faith and continued loyalty to Jiang and the GMD, Zhang escorted him back to Nanjing, against the strong advice of Zhou that he would not be freed or worse be put to death. Zhang ignored Zhou's warning, and upon arrival in Nanjing, Jiang had Zhang put under house arrest. He was moved, along with the GMD capital, to Chongqing, and later in 1949 when the CCP took over China, Zhang was transported to Taipei, Taiwan, where he remained for the next forty years.

❖ ❖ ❖

In captivity Zhang spent his time studying Ming literature and the Manchu language and collected Chinese fan paintings, calligraphy, and other works of art by illustrious artists. Sotheby's auctioned

Zhang's collection of more than two hundred works with tremendous success on April 10, 1994, for millions of US dollars. He and his wife, Edith Chao, became devout Baptists and regularly attended Sunday services at a Methodist church with Jiang's family. After Jiang's death in 1975, his freedom was restored officially in 1991. In 1993 Zhang and his family left Taiwan to take up residence in Hawaii. There were numerous invitations from the People's Republic of China (PRC) for him to visit mainland China and accept a position in the government, but he refused, citing his loyalty to the GMD. He died at the age of one hundred on October 14, 2001, and was buried in Hawaii. The leaders of the People's Republic of China hailed him as a great patriot. Jiang Zemin, then the leader of PRC, called him a "hero for eternity."

❖ ❖ ❖

Once Jiang was safely back in Nanjing, the GMD army entered Xian, and the Zhang and Yang armies moved north to fight the Japanese under the GMD's command as directed by Jiang. Having been through the chaos caused by his kidnap and the lack of a successor, Jiang named Chen Cheng as his successor. Chen, a Zhejiang native as Jiang, graduated from Baoding Military Academy in 1922 and entered Whampoa Academy as an instructor. He had successes in both the Northern Expedition and the CCP suppression. Chen had accompanied Jiang to Xian and gained Jiang's trust by their shared experience. On the other hand, He Yingqin, as the minister of war, advocated more-aggressive action and became less trustworthy in Jiang's mind since his proposal risked Jiang's safety. The Xian incident had made Jiang a hero all over the country and silenced all of his previous critics, including the CCP, but it also made him more self-centered and less willing to delegate authority. He Yingqin had hoped to become Jiang's successor, and Jiang's decision to the contrary caused him great consternation. In a private discussion with Boqun, he considered following Boqun into retirement from politics.

Boqun responded,

I wish Dilun was here to lead the country, truly unite the factions, and defeat the Japanese. I understand your frustration with Jiang and his clique of gangsters and money grabbers, but I also believe that for this very critical movement, there is no one who can step into his position. Besides, anyone else would require time to unite the country, and by then the Japanese would have overrun our motherland. I hope that after the Xian incident Jiang will become more aggressive against the Japanese even though he did not sign any agreement to the effect.

As for retirement, you are not in same position as when I retired. I finished all I could have done, and others can carry on just as well. You are a good military leader, and China needs you in the forthcoming all-out war against the Japanese. Jiang knows that, and that is why he has not pushed you out of his inner circle. My advice is to stay in your current position or ask for a frontline command to show Jiang that he can trust you again. Dear Yingqin, I also feel for your place in history, you must show that you are not a quitter in the face of battle.

CHAPTER 14

1936-1940
JOURNEY TO AND
LIFE IN GUIYANG

In spite of the continued turmoil caused by power struggles, natural disasters, and Japanese encroachment, the "Nanjing Decade" of 1928–37 was one of consolidation and accomplishment under the leadership of the GMD. Improvements were made in the economy, social progress, infrastructure, democracy development, and cultural renewal. Foreign concessions were moderated through diplomacy. In May 1930 the government regained the right to set its tariffs from foreign nations. Although Jiang Jieshi got most of the credit, many of the accomplishments were the work of others in the government like Boqun. The most significant among this group of officials were two of Jiang's relatives: Soong Ziwen, brother of the Soong sisters, and Kong Xiangxi, husband of the oldest Soong sister.

TV Soong

Soong Ziwen, known as TV, was educated at Harvard and Columbia and was recruited by Sun Yatsen for financial planning of the Guangdong government. After the Northern Expedition, he served as governor of the Central Bank of China and minister of finance. He resigned in 1933, protesting against Jiang's appeasement of Japan. Kong Xiangxi served as the minister of industry and commerce and later succeeded

Soong as the minister of finance. The significant reforms by Soong and Kung were to institute a national fiat currency, the yuan, and to balance the national budget in 1927. This led to price stabilization and debt amortization, which enabled reforms in taxing authorities and banking. With a stabilized tax base, the government was able make strides in education and industrial production. Efforts were also made to standardize the Chinese language. Newspapers, magazines, and book publishing flourished, and the expansion of communications facilities further encouraged a sense of unity and pride among the people. The GMD government also modernized the legal and penal systems, built railroads and highways, improved public health facilities, legislated against narcotics, and augmented agricultural production. Laws were passed and campaigns initiated to promote the rights of women. The Rural Reconstruction Movement was one of many that took advantage of the new freedom to raise social consciousness.

During this time a series of massive wars took place in western China, including the Kumul Uyghur Rebellion in Xinjiang (1931–1934), the Sino-Tibetan War (1930–32), and the Soviet invasion of Xinjiang in 1934. Although the central government was nominally in control of the entire country during this period, large areas of China remained under the semiautonomous rule of local warlords, provincial military leaders, or warlord coalitions. GMD rule was strongest in the eastern regions around the capital of Nanjing, but regional militarists such as Feng Yuxiang and Yan Xishan retained considerable local authorities.

❖ ❖ ❖

The year 1937 began with another tragedy for the Wang family. Zhou Shouyua, husband of Boqun's second sister, Wenxiao, died on January 22 at age forty-three in Shanghai. Zhou was a graduate of the Kunming Law School and served under Dilun in the National Protection Movement. He married Boqun's second sister, Wenxiao, in 1918, and had two boys and three girls; the youngest girl was about the same

Zhou Shouyuan Family 1935

age as Defu. Zhou had worked in the communication ministry under Boqun since 1927 after returning from the Northern Expedition. At the time of his death he was the chief of the Telecommunications Bureau of Shanghai and Suzhou. He was also helping Boqun in various provincial mat-

ters of Guizhou. Boqun thought highly of him and grieved by his passing. He spent much time and effort with Wenxiao and her children to help her through a difficult period with such young children.

❖ ❖ ❖

At the start of 1937, all the areas north, east, and west of Beijing were controlled by Japan. Under the terms of the Boxer Protocol of September 7, 1901, China had granted nations with legations in Beijing the right to station guards at twelve specific points along railways connecting Beijing with Tianjin. This was to ensure open communications between the capital and the port. After a subsequent addendum of July 15, 1902, these forces were allowed to conduct maneuvers unilaterally, without informing the authorities of other nations or China. By July of 1937, Japan had expanded its forces, estimated at fifteen thousand, mostly along the railways. This number of men and amount of material was several times the size of those detachments deployed by European powers and greatly in excess of the limits set by the Boxer Protocol. The Marco Polo Bridge, located in the southwest of Beijing, was the choke point of the Beijing-Wuhan Railway and guarded the only passage linking Beijing to GMD-controlled areas in the south. Prior to July 1937, the Japanese had repeatedly demanded the withdrawal of all Chinese forces stationed in this area and had attempted to purchase nearby land to build an airfield. Jiang Jieshi's government, in a rare demonstration of opposition to the Japanese aggression, refused since Japanese control of the bridge would completely isolate Beijing from the GMD-controlled south.

In June of 1937, Japanese troops carried out intensive military training maneuvers in the vicinity of the western end of the Marco Polo Bridge every night, and the Chinese government requested that advance notice be given so local inhabitants would not be disturbed. The Japanese agreed to this condition. On the night of July 7, 1937, however, Japanese maneuvers were carried out without prior notice, and the local Chinese forces, thinking an attack was underway, fired in self-defense. This caused an exchange of fire, resulting in a missing Japanese soldier. The subsequent search for the missing Japanese soldier escalated into armed conflict for the control of the Marco Polo Bridge and the towns nearby. The occupation of the bridge changed hands several times before the Japanese military and members of the Japanese Foreign Service began negotiations in Beijing with the Chinese government. It resulted in a truce and cease-fire. Both sides continued the hostilities and in fact rushed in more reinforcements of their respective military forces. Four divisions of Chinese troops moved to the border, with three on the Japanese side. Throughout July of 1937, skirmishes were fought around the bridge and the surrounding areas. Several additional attempts at negotiation proved futile, and on August 9, 1937, a Japanese naval officer was shot in Shanghai, causing a full-scale war between China and Japan.

The Japanese imperial government in Tokyo initially was reluctant to escalate the conflict into a full-scale war, being content with the gains acquired in northern China following the Marco Polo Bridge Incident. Jiang Jieshi, however, believed that the breaking point of Japanese aggression had been reached and his credibility as the leader of China would be compromised if he continued his appeasement policy. He quickly mobilized the GMD government's military forces and placed them under his direct command. Jiang ordered an attack on Japanese Marines in Shanghai on August 13, 1937, leading to the Battle of Shanghai. The Japanese then had to commit over two hundred thousand troops, along with numerous naval vessels and aircraft, to capture the city. After more than three months of intense fighting, Shanghai fell in November 1937.

❖ ❖ ❖

When the war had spread to Shanghai in August 1937, Boqun was in Nanjing attending an emergency meeting of the government. Zhining was left in Shanghai with the two young children. The Japanese had initiated air raids to soften up the defense, and the situation was extremely tense. Boqun had decided that Zhining should take their two children to Hong Kong, where his sister Wenxiang had already moved as a precaution. Travel by steamship to and from Shanghai was very much restricted, and Boqun had to contact the British Council General in Shanghai and the American ambassador in Nanjing to secure passage

Boqun, Zhining, Defu, Dexiang,

for his family. Finally the Wang family was able to book passage on the first British ship to leave Shanghai. Zhining's mother and her two younger brothers, Channing and Gerson, were on the same ship embarking from Nantong. The Wang family joined the Bao family on August 25, 1937, for their journey to Hong Kong. Even with her family surrounding her, Zhining still felt a great sense of loss for the beautiful house Boqun had built for her and the community of friends she had to leave behind. Zhining was pregnant and would most likely give birth to her fourth child in a strange land and a temporary home.

Upon arrival in Hong Kong, the Wang and Bao families were met by Wenxiang and her daughter, Ruby, who escorted them to their relatively small rental house. Zhining decided that her family should rent a different house nearby to be on their own and not to crowd out Wenxiang's family in their place. The families moved in with one of the Bao family's best friends, who was a rich Hong Kong merchant with a large house, which was able to accommodate all of them. In the general neighborhood, there were many American and British children, and the two children had a great time playing with them. Zhining lost a lot weight because she was not used to the Cantonese food until Zhining's mother taught the cook how to prepare Shanghai food. That made life better for the Wang family.

Meanwhile Boqun was in Nanjing working in part helping He Yingqin with the defense of the southwestern provinces and with the transfer of Great China University to Guiyang. The latter required raising money from the Education Ministry and private sources for relocation to Guiyang with most of the faculty and students. In October Boqun had to travel by ship to Macao to meet with funding sources, and he then flew to Hong Kong to see his family. Zhining and Wenxiang met his plane at the Kowloon airport, and Zhining welcomed him into her arms. She heard the news that the campus of the Great China had been destroyed in part by Japanese air raids and the classes were now suspended. It was such sad news about the war and its unthinkable consequences.

Boqun had to leave after only a few days for Guiyang to manage the Great China transfer. Soon after, Defu was taken ill with pneumonia, and he was treated at the Hong Kong General Hospital for over a week with high fever. All the family was relieved when he finally recovered. In November Zhining's father had wired to ask her mother and the two younger brothers to join him in Vancouver, Canada. After much discussion among Zhining, her mother, and Boqun, it was decided that the middle brother, Channing, should remain and attend the Great China in Guiyang since he already began studying there in Shanghai. In addition Zhining thought Channing would be helpful in accompanying her in the trip to Guiyang. Another girl, Deann, was born on December 3, 1937. Boqun arrived in Hong Kong shortly thereafter to see his new daughter and to prepare his family for their long journey to Guiyang.

After seeing Zhining's mother and youngest brother, Gerson, depart for Canada on a British steam ship, the Wang family, now including Boqun, Zhining, Channing, Zuma (the maid), and three children, boarded their own ship for Haiphong, Vietnam, on January 1, 1938, en route to Kunming. Boqun was taken ill immediately upon arrival in Haiphong and had to seek medical treatment. It took two weeks for him to be pronounced fit for travel. On January 13, 1938, Boqun flew to Kunming to prepare lodging for the family. The rest of the family then transferred to Hanoi and took the Hanoi-Kunming railway to Kunming. Boqun and several of his good Yunnanese friends awaited them at the train station.

Since the Kunming hotels were a bit substandard, Boqun arranged an entire floor in a hospital set up for the family. The family were wined and dined by Long Yun, Governor of Yunnan, and his family. Long was a comrade-in-arms of Dilun and He Yingqin in the National Protection Movement. In the next day, the family had dinner given by mutual friends with Cai E's wife and son. Boqun remarked on how much the son looked like his famous father, and he urged him to carry on in his father's steps. The family stayed in Kunming for about a month for Boqun as a representative of Jiang Jieshi to ensure Long Yun's support of a coordinated defense of Southwest China against the Japanese. Since Yunnan bordered on Indochina and Burma, it was now a most important strategic city in the war. Long Yun assured Boqun that it would provide all possible support against the enemy.

Boqun took Zhining and Channing sightseeing in Kunming, a city of combined Chinese and French cultures. It had many natural sights, such as the Black Dragon Pool and the unique Stone Forest, as well as ancient temples and palaces. Boqun also showed them the building where the instigators of National Protection Movement signed in blood on December 19, 1915, to invocate the movement against Yuan Shikai. Boqun was very emotional in pointing out those who had served and died for what they believed; he singled out especially Cai E, Dai Kan, and of course, Dilun. He wept for them out of respect and sorrow. Both Zhining and Channing were moved as well. On February 12, 1938, the Wang family finally was driven to Guiyang through Xingyi. Along the route they were welcomed by officials of cities, relatives, and friends. They were entertained in Xingyi by relatives of the three famous families of Liu, Wang, and He, and friends for two nights before departing for Guiyang. Zhining and Channing were very impressed that Boqun had commanded such respect and friendliness among all sorts of people, from lowly peasants to high officials.

Boqun's Guiyang house was one of three buildings in the Wang compound perched on the high point of the National Protection Road in honor of the Wang family's role in the movement. Both Dilun and Boqun each had a modern-style house, and in between was a Chinese-style house for their mother and grandmother. Dilun's daughter and other relatives were in one of the Western-style houses, and Boqun's family moved into the other, while Boqun's sister, Wenxiao, and her family moved into the Chinese-style house in the middle. The three houses shared a central courtyard and had their respective entrances. The open side of the courtyard was closed off by a covered gallery, which served to close the courtyard with an ornate door.

The whole compound was surrounded by a large garden extending to the main entrance with a guard house, garages, horse stable, and servants' quarters. It had a high wall enclosing the entire compound. The Boqun house was small compared to the Shanghai house. It had three floors with a round tower in one of the corners of the house. The first floor served as formal living and dinner areas and a round study for Boqun; the second had a round master bedroom with its own anteroom, two small bedrooms for the children, and a common sitting room for the whole family; and the third had a round guest room, Zuma's room, and storage. The house was not grand, the stair was narrow, and the rooms were relatively small, but Zhining felt comfortable and almost more homey there than the grandeur of the Shanghai house.

Zhining had been concerned about Boqun's wealth since he had been having stomach pain and passing blood in his stools, sometime with a high temperature. Although the temperature would return to normal and the bleeding would stop, the condition often recurred from time to time, particularly when he was under stress. Zhining's concern was exacerbated by the busy and extraneous life he faced upon his return to his native land after a twenty-year absence. He had many old friends calling, many dinner receptions, local government officials' consultations, on top of his official duties in the national government, now relocated to Chongqing, Sichuan, and managing the crisis of moving and reestablishing the Great China. In April, while attending a meeting in Chongqing and staying with He Yingqin's family, Boqun was ill again and had to stay in the hospital for over one month. In the meantime, their second daughter, Deann, was ill, and Zhining was unable to visit Boqun in Chongqing. She much regretted that. Boqun finally returned to Guiyang after almost a two-month absence. Zhining found him to be much thinner, but he seemed to be as fit as before, which served to calm her.

As Boqun continued with his work with Great China, Zhining received an invitation from Jiang Jieshi's famous wife, Soong Meiling, to serve in the Chinese Women's National War Relief Society as the chairwoman for Guizhou. It was Soong Meiling's ambitious social welfare program to establish schools for the orphans of GMD soldiers. The orphanages were unusually well appointed, with playgrounds, swimming pools, a gymnasium, modern and well equipped classrooms, and dormitories. Soong was deeply involved in the organization and even selected all of the teachers herself. There were two Nanjing schools, one for boys, and one for girls, built on a thousand-acre site at the foot of Purple Mountain. She referred to these children as her war orphans and made them a personal cause. The fate of the children of fallen soldiers became a much more important issue in China after the beginning of the war with Japan in 1937. In order to provide a decent living and education for these children, she established the Chinese Women's National War Relief Society. She made frequent mention of her war orphans in her many campaigns for foreign aid. The provincial chair was usually given to the wife of the provincial governor, but because of Boqun's revolutionary stature and Zhining's social science education, she was given the honor and the position. In their first business meeting, Zhining was very positively impressed by Meiling in her sincerity of doing well for the children. Thus, she agreed to help.

With Boqun's connections, Zhining established two such schools. Both were formally temples that had to be completely remodeled for the needs of the orphans. The government funded about 50 percent of the cost, and Zhining had to raise the rest from the citizens and the businesses of the province. She had to recruit the staff for teaching,

Soong Meiling

medical, and other auxiliary services. She was involved in many details, even the design of the uniform. Fortunately, she was able to elicit many of her friends to help in a large and complex assignment. Still, with this position in addition to her already busy schedule of managing the household and taking care of the children, Zhining felt there was little time left for her and her husband to be together. She and Boqun realized this was their sacrifice and duty for the war effort.

❖ ❖ ❖

Unlike Japan, China was unprepared for total war and had little military-industrial strength, no mechanized divisions, and few armored forces. Up until the mid-1930s, China had hoped that the League of Nations would provide countermeasures to Japan's aggression. In addition, the GMD government was mired in a civil war against the CCP, as Jiang was quoted, "The Japanese are diseases of the skin; the Communists are a disease of the heart." Even under these extremely unfavorable circumstances, Jiang realized that to win support from the United States and other foreign nations, China had to prove it was capable of fighting. Knowing a hasty retreat would discourage foreign aid, Jiang resolved to make a stand at Shanghai, using the best of his Whampoa-trained divisions to defend China's largest and most industrialized city from the Japanese. The battle lasted over three months, saw heavy casualties on both sides, and ended with a Chinese retreat toward Nanjing but proved that China would not be easily defeated and showed its determination to the world. The battle became an enormous morale booster for the Chinese people, as it decisively refuted the Japanese boast that Japan could conquer Shanghai in three days and China in three months.

Afterward Jiang adopted the strategy of trading space for time. The Chinese army would put up fights to delay the Japanese advance to northern and eastern cities, allowing the home front, with its professionals and key industries, to retreat west into Chongqing. Building on the hard-won victory in Shanghai, the Japanese captured Nanjing and Northern Shanxi by the end of 1937. These campaigns involved approximately three hundred fifty thousand Japanese soldiers and considerably more Chinese.

Three hundred thousand Chinese civilians were mass murdered and tortured and tens of thousands of women raped during the notorious Nanking Massacre after the fall of Nanking from December 13, 1937, to late January 1938. Even today some Japanese deny that the massacre occurred. When Japan captured Nanjing, the Chinese shifted their headquarters and industries to Wuhan. Thus Wuhan virtually became the political, economic, and military center at the time and the wartime capital of China at the onset of the engagements in Wuhan. It is located halfway up the Yangtze River and was the second-largest city at the time, with a population of two million. The city was divided by the Yangtze River and Hanshui River into three regions: Wuchang, Hankou, and Hanyang. Wuchang was the political center, Hankou was a commercial district, and Hanyang was the industrial area. Due to its rail and sea connections, Wuhan was a major transportation hub in China.

In January of 1938, the Japanese army in China disregarded its Tokyo headquarters' directive for a one-year truce and pursued the

Li Zongren 1938

Chinese army retreating from the Shanghai-Nanjing Theater, driving northward into Jiangsu, Shandong, and Henan Provinces. These were the areas of operation of the joint GMD and CCP forces. The Japanese planned to fight through the Jinpu Railway from the north and south, regrouping at Xuzhou. From there, they would attack Wuhan and force the GMD into surrender. At this time, the Japanese armies were very powerful, so this operation should have been done with relative ease. As a result, the commanders did not deploy their full forces to complete the task. The Chinese army, led by Li Zongren and Bai Chongxi, scored the first major victory in April 1938 over the Japanese at the battle of Taierzhuang, located on the eastern bank of the Grand Canal. It was a frontier garrison northeast of Xuzhou. Bai, a Muslim Hui, and Li both graduated from the Cai E–led Guangxi Military Cadre Training School in Guilin. Li and Bai shared power in Guangxi and for the most part kept their independence from Jiang Jieshi. This was also the first CCP and GMD united front against Japan. The CCP formed the New Fourth Army and the Eighth Army and placed them under the nominal control of the GMD army during the battles.

The Japanese operation started on March 24. Li Zongren's army disguised themselves to be farmers and refugees, cut communication lines and supplies, diverted streams, and disabled rail lines. Supplies and fuel were being dropped from airplanes to Japanese troops, but the quantities were insufficient, which caused the Japanese to retreat in the first attempt at Taierzhuang. The Japanese then attempted to tunnel under the city wall, but they were caught and killed on March 29. Over the next week, both sides skirmished near the city and surrounding area, and many were killed in small arms battles. Finally the Japanese attacked frontally and were caught in a Chinese encirclement on April 6, resulting in a major Japanese defeat. The Chinese captured almost a thousand Japanese soldiers and large quantities of military supplies. It broke the Japanese military invincibility and provided a tremendous boost to Chinese morale.

After the eventual fall of Xuzhou in May 1938, the Japanese planned an extensive invasion of Hankow and the takeover of Wuhan, intending to destroy the main force of the combined GMD-CCP Army. The Chinese, on the other hand, were prepared for the defense of Wuhan. They managed to gather up more than one million troops, around two hundred planes, and thirty naval ships. On April 29, 1938, the Japanese air force launched major air strikes with over five hundred planes on Wuhan to celebrate Emperor Hirohito's birthday. This was one of the most intense air battles of the Second Sino-Japanese War. The Chinese air force shot down twenty Japanese planes at a loss of twelve. In an attempt to win more time for the preparation of the defense of Wuhan, the Chinese opened up the dikes of the Yellow River on June 9. The flood, known now as the 1938 Yellow River Flood, forced the Japanese to delay their attack on Wuhan, but it also caused somewhere around half million civilian deaths. The Japanese finally captured Wuhan on October 27, 1938, forcing the GMD government to retreat to Chongqing, but Jiang refused to negotiate unless the Japanese agreed to withdraw to pre-1937 borders. By 1938 the Japanese had captured Guangzhou and effectively completed its blockade of ocean ports of China except for Nanning, Guangxi, and most strategic supplies had to be brought in through roads from Burma and Indochina.

Chongqing is a city in Sichuan Province perched on high cliffs at the junction of Yangtze and Jialing Rivers. It had been an imperial city in 340 BCE, and it had been home to defeated emperors and pretenders over the centuries in Chinese history. Sichuan, the largest Chinese province at the time, is located beyond Yangtze's great gorges and ringed by the protective mountains, with its area larger than France. It is a backward province, but it has all the natural resources and fertile land one would need to live on. Jiang Jieshi had stated, "Even if we had lost fifteen out of the eighteen provinces but kept Sichuan, Guizhou, and Yunnan, we could defeat our enemy, recover our lost land, restore our country, and accomplish the revolution."

❖ ❖ ❖

At the end of 1938, Wang Jingwei decided that Jiang's leadership could not defeat the Japanese, and he was tired of being marginalized. He and his staff flew to Kunming, Yunnan, and from there to Hanoi, Vietnam, then a part of French Indochina. He then called for peace talks with the Japanese and narrowly escaped another assassination attempt, which killed his secretary. He was so outraged and changed his mind to retire to France but instead decided to go back to occupied China. He and his followers would claim that he was acting in the best interest of China by seeking a peaceful solution to end Jiang's resistance. This fit well into the Japanese goal of a pan-Asian order, which would include China but of course with Japan pulling all the strings. Wang was set up by the Japanese as the head of a "reformed" puppet government in Nanjing, though he spent most of his time in Shanghai, where he confiscated the newly built house of Boqun and Zhining as his residence and office.

Wang Jingwei had clearly seen Jiang's precarious position even though he had dictatorial powers, but his GMD Army had all but ceased to exist as effective fighting force. Conscription and training of replacements were slow, and the military equipment was antiquated. Additionally the cohesion of his officers was highly suspect due to Jiang's insistence of having direct control instead of a command structure, and he put obedience above ability in his commanders. All of Jiang's personal characteristics heightened his belief in his infallibility and promoted faction infighting among his top officers.

❖ ❖ ❖

As one of Jiang's closest associates over the years, He Yingqin was powerful in his own right because of his extensive connections through the Whampoa graduates. He was not trusted by Jiang after the Xian Incident, and he was not named as Jiang's successor. He was not given the command of a large military force, but he had been chief of staff since 1927 and minister of war since 1935. Over the years He was responsible for the planning of military operations and supplies procurement for all military requirements. He and his wife, Wang Wenxiang continued to be close to Boqun and his family. After Boqun had retired from Jiang's government, their respective positions of power and influence had effectively switched, where Boqun now needed his brother-in-law to help him in many instances as he did twenty years ago for him. Boqun could not help but notice a gradual change in He since 1931, when He suffered the defeat of the Fourth Encirclement Campaign against the CCP in Jiangxi and lost forty thousand of his troops. Boqun noted to Zhining,

> He Yingqin is like a brother to me, and over the years I have watched him grow and evolve. Regrettably, history had not been kind to him for what he has done since the dreaded CCP campaign where he lost the battle so badly, along with so many of his men. Then there was the Xian incident, where he lost Jiang's trust and set him up in rivalry with Cheng Chen, whom I actually like. Yingqin's talents were more suited for administration rather than commanding an army, and his Japanese military training molded him into a man of obedience at all cost. Dilun would have been a better role model for him and would have guided him into a better place in history. With Jiang setting his environment for him, he had no choice but find his own niches wherever possible. He is becoming as paranoid as Jiang about the CCP, and he is probably not above making money from his current position. He now owns more land than the Wang family. It is amazing to me that a leader can mold a follower by his own example…It is just too bad and sad for me to see.

❖ ❖ ❖

Through 1940, the GMD Army adopted the concept of attracting advancing Japanese troops to ambushes, flanking attacks, and encirclements in major engagements. The most prominent example of this tactic was the successful defense of Changsha, Hunan, in 1939, in which heavy Japanese casualties were inflicted. Local Chinese resistance forces, organized by both the CCP and GMD, continued their resistance in occupied areas to attack the enemy and make their administration difficult over the vast land area of China. In 1940 the Red Army launched a major offensive in north China, destroying railways and a major coalmine. These constant harassment and sabotage operations deeply frustrated the Japanese Army and led them to employ the "Three Alls Policy" (kill all, loot all, burn all). It was during this period that the bulk of Japanese war crimes were committed after the Nanjing Massacre.

After 1940, as predicted by Jiang, the Japanese encountered tremendous difficulties in administering and garrisoning the seized Chinese territories and tried to solve its problems by implementing a strategy of creating friendly puppet governments, such as Manchukuo under the last Qing Emperor, Puyi, in Manchuria. As part of this strategy, the Japanese created the most prominent, the Nanjing Nationalist Chinese government headed by former GMD premier Wang Jingwei. Wang's Nanjing government was not particularly effective as in Manchukuo due to atrocities committed by the Japanese Army and Japanese refusal to delegate any real power. The only success the Japanese had was the ability to recruit a large police force to maintain public security in the occupied major cities, such as Shanghai, Beijing, Nanjing, and Tianjin. Despite Japan's steady territorial gains in northern China, the coastal regions, and the rich Yangtze River Valley in central China, they were unable to control the rest of the north and eastern China. The uneasy alliance began between GMD and CCP started to break down by late 1938, partially due to the CCP's aggressive efforts to expand their military strength by absorbing Chinese guerrilla forces behind Japanese lines. Chinese militia who refused to switch their allegiance were often labeled as collaborators and attacked by CCP forces. This obviously caused concerns among the GMD commanders.

Prior to the outbreak of the war, Germany and China had close economic and military cooperation, with Germany helping China modernize its industry and military in exchange for raw materials. More than half of German arms exports during its rearmament period were to China. Nevertheless, the proposed thirty new German-trained divisions in the GMD Army failed to materialize after Germany withdrew its support in 1938, when Adolf Hitler formed an alliance with Japan against the Soviet Union. After the signing of the Anti-Comitern Pact between Germany and Japan, the Soviet Union hoped to keep China in the war as a way of deterring the Japanese from invading Siberia, thus saving itself from the threat of a two-front war. In September of 1937, the Soviet leadership signed the Sino-Soviet Non-Aggression Pact and provided a Soviet volunteer Chinese air force, training personnel, and military supplies.

As part of this secret operation, Soviet technicians upgraded and ran some of China's transportation systems. Bombers, fighters, supplies, and advisers arrived, including Soviet general Vasily Chuikov, the future victor of the Battle of Stalingrad. Prior to the entrance of the Western allies, the Russians provided the largest amount of foreign aid to China, totaling some US$250 million in credits for munitions and other supplies. In April of 1941, Soviet aid ended as a result of the Soviet-Japanese Neutrality Pact and the beginning of the Great Patriotic War between Germany and the Soviet Union. This pact enabled the Soviet Union to avoid fighting against Germany and Japan at the same time. In total 3,700 Soviet advisors and pilots served in China, and 230 of them died fighting the Japanese. From December 1937 events such as the Japanese attack of the gunboat USS *Panay* in Nanjing harbor and the Nanjing Massacre swung public opinion in the West sharply against Japan and increased their fear of Japanese expansion. This prompted the United States, the United Kingdom, and France to provide loan assistance of war supplies to China, although real help did not commence until 1941.

❖ ❖ ❖

In the beginning of 1939, the Japanese began their bombing of Guiyang, which was another adjustment of daily life that the Wang family had to endure. The Wang family built a bomb shelter in the compound, and drills were conducted to get the family to the shelter immediately when the bomb siren went off. Even though none had struck the compound, the closeness of death and destruction posed an ever-present danger. Boqun went to Chongqing in January, and Zhining brought Defu to join him there later to attend Wenxiang's birthday party, which had many guests at the He residences. During the party, news came regarding the worst Japanese air raid to hit Guiyang. Although their children in Guiyang were safe, the couple couldn't return immediately since Boqun had important Great China funding matters he had to conclude. Upon their return, they found the destruction of the city beyond their imagination. They were relieved that their family did not suffer and the family compound was intact.

❖ ❖ ❖

On September 1, 1939, Nazi Germany invaded Poland. On September 3 France and Britain declared war on Germany. On September 17, after signing a cease-fire with Japan, the Soviets also invaded Poland. Poland's territory was divided between Germany and the Soviet Union. The Soviets invaded Finland in November 1939. France and Britain, treating the Soviet attack on Finland as tantamount to entering the war on the side of the Germans, responded to the Soviet invasion by supporting the USSR's expulsion from the League of Nations. The Soviets and Germany entered a trade pact in February 1940, pursuant to which the Soviets received German military and industrial equipment in exchange for supplying raw materials to Germany to help circumvent the Allied blockade. In April of 1940, Germany invaded Denmark and Norway. Denmark immediately capitulated despite Allied support, and Norway was soon lost. British discontent over the Norwegian campaign led to the replacement of Prime Minister Neville Chamberlain with Winston Churchill on May 10, 1940.

Germany launched an offensive against France, Belgium, the Netherlands, and Luxembourg on May 10, 1940. The French-fortified Maginot Line and the Allied forces in Belgium were circumvented by flanking German troops through the thickly wooded Ardennes, and the bulk of the Allied armies found them trapped and were annihilated. British troops were forced to evacuate the continent at Dunkirk, abandoning their heavy equipment by early June. On June 10 Italy, under Benito Mussolini, invaded France, declaring war on both France and Britain. Paris fell on June 14, 1940, and eight days later France surrendered and was soon divided into German and Italian occupation zones. In June, during the last days of the Battle of France, the Soviet Union forcibly annexed Estonia, Latvia, and Lithuania and then annexed the disputed Romanian region of Bessarabia as well. Meanwhile, Nazi-Soviet political rapprochement and economic cooperation gradually stalled, and both countries began preparations for war. In the rest of 1940, Britain had its hands full defending against German invasion attempts and intensive strategic bombing campaigns, which came to be known as the Blitz against major British cities, including London. Elsewhere Britain had to extend itself against Italy when it seized British Somaliland, attacked British-held Egypt, and then invaded Greece in October 1940.

Throughout this period, the neutral United States took measures to assist China and the Western Allies. In November of 1939, the Allies began to purchase strategic material from the United States by amendments of the American Neutrality Act. In 1940, following the German capture of Paris, the United States significantly expanded its navy in both personnel and ships. In September the United States further agreed to a trade of American destroyers for British bases. Still, a large majority of the American public continued to oppose any direct military intervention into the conflict well into 1941. Although President Franklin Roosevelt had promised to keep America out of the war, he nevertheless took concrete steps to prepare for that eventuality. In December 1940 he accused Hitler of planning world conquest and ruled out negotiations as useless. He called for the United States to become an "arsenal for democracy" and promoted the passage of lend-lease aid to support the British war effort. Roosevelt also began secret high-level talks with the Churchill to determine how to defeat Germany should the United States enter the war.

❖ ❖ ❖

What was happening in Europe left China virtually alone in its fight against the Japanese. Particularly in July 1939, negotiations between Japanese and the British led to an agreement by which Britain obtained a Japanese promise not to attack its Asian territories in return for recognizing Japanese conquests in China as legitimate. Britain was obliged to close the Burma Road, which runs from Rangoon to Kunming. It, along with the Indochina Road, which ran from Haiphong to Kunming, were main strategic supply routes for China from the West. In June of 1940, the fall of France allowed the Japanese to occupy French Indochina in September; it set up military bases there and closed the Indochina Road as well. The only road into China still open was by way of Soviet Russia.

The Burma Road, thus thrown into the world's spotlight, started at Rangoon, paralleled the railway to Lashio, and then snaked through wild and remote country along the route of the Old Tribute Road, toward Chongqing through Kunming, a total distance of twenty-one hundred miles. Marco Polo took the same trail some six hundred years ago. The Chinese government began rehabbing the road to the Burma in late 1937, after the Japanese invasion. It replaced chain-and-plank bridges with concrete spans, laid a quick-draining gravel surface, and rolled it with huge boulders drawn by water buffaloes. The total of unpaid conscripted workers at one time exceeded a hundred twenty thousand. Russian munitions, British oil, American trucks, and railway equipment flowed to China from the West.

At the same time, the US government extended a trade agreement with Japan. Under the agreement, Japan purchased trucks, machine tools, petrol and petroleum, and various other much-needed supplies for its war against the Chinese. To make matters worse for China, Japan invaded and occupied the northern part of French Indochina in September 1940 to prevent China from receiving the ten thousand tons of materials delivered monthly by the Allies via the Haiphong-Yunnan Railway line. At the end of September 1940, the Tripartite Pact united Japan, Italy, and Germany to form the Axis Powers. The pact stipulated that any attack of any Axis Power would be forced to go to war against all three. At this point, Britain realized its mistake and reopened the Burma Road in October 1940.

In November of 1939, the Japanese attacked and occupied Nanning, the capital of Guangxi, effectively severing foreign aid and supplies to China's war efforts by the sea, rendering Indochina, Burma Road, and the air lift over the Himalaya known as the "Hump" the only means to supply China. The Japanese then proceed to capture the key point of Kunlun Pass and threatened the Chinese rear base that protected Chongqing. In spring 1940 Bai Chongxi, in charge of the defense of Guangxi, told Jiang Jieshi that unless he got some real help, the American airbase and training centers would be at risk. Jiang dispatched the Fifth Corp, the most elite unit and the only unit in the Chinese army with tanks and armored vehicles, from Hunan to Guangxi. Its soldiers were combat-hardened veterans from winning previous battles against the Japanese troops, and its morale was high. Two divisions attacked the Japanese-held Kunlun Pass. Another division had cut off Japanese reinforcements from the rear and killed the Japanese commander. The most elite unit of the Japanese Fifth Division—the Twenty-First Brigade—was wiped out in the battle. The brigade had also participated in the Russo-Japanese War, and it was nicknamed the "unbreakable sword." The

Japanese commander admitted in his diary that the Chinese soldiers' fighting ability had surpassed the Russians his brigade had encountered in Manchuria. This campaign was the first major victory of the Chinese Army since the Battle of Taierzhuang, where Bai and Li Zongren had led a force of the United Front with the participating Red Army.

❖ ❖ ❖

Both government and Great China University affairs would take Boqun to Chongqing at least monthly. In early October 1939, while Boqun was away, the second daughter of Dilun had a reoccurrence of bone cancer. She passed away on October 26, 1939, at age eighteen. Boqun was very upset, for she was a small, spunky girl and had many of Dilun's traits. Boqun thought 1939 was not a good year for the Wang family's karma, and he was happy to have it to come to its end.

After a couple of tough years of struggling against Japan, China could see a possible light at the end of a long tunnel in that the West and especially thought the United States might be willing to lend a helping hand. The year 1940 was better for the Wang family as well, even though the bombing continued and most Chinese adjusted their lives to live through the war as the Wang family. The only death in the family was Zhining's second uncle, Bao Junzheng, in Chongqing at age fifty-three. He was a graduate of the Beijing University, spoke fluent English, and served in Finance Ministry for most of his life. He first wife died at age thirty and had two daughters. His second wife had three daughters. Zhining was not as close to him as Uncle CJ, but she appreciated his strong character, and he could be funny at family gatherings.

The site for the new Great China situated outside of Guiyang to avoid the air raids and the higher costs of the city. The most-challenging task was the funding for the project. The Wang family life in 1940 was more tranquil, and there were no illnesses most of the time. The family frequently went to family burial grounds about twenty miles just outside of the city, and Boqun would go there on horseback, which was one of his passions. The rest of the family would follow by car and pack a picnic of food offerings for the dead. After the incense lighting, burning of paper money, and food offerings, the family would eat the food offerings and enjoy the natural beauty of the surroundings of the burial site. It was a respite from the days of bombing and its aftermath.

CHAPTER 15

1941-1943

TURNING POINT OF THE WAR

The year 1941 did not start well for the war against the Japanese. The New Fourth Army Incident ended any cooperation between the GMD and the CCP. It was unclear which side started the hostile action, but on January 5, 1941, the CCP New Fourth Army was surrounded and attacked in Maolin, Anhui, by a GMD force of eighty thousand. After days of fighting, the CCP incurred heavy losses, including many civilian workers who staffed the Red Army's political headquarters. On January 13 only two thousand CCP troops out of the original nine thousand were able to break out. Jiang Jieshi ordered the New Fourth disbanded on January 17, but the CCP disregarded the order and reorganized the army and set up the general headquarters in Jiangsu in conjunction with CCP Eighth Route Army. Together they comprised seven divisions and one independent brigade, totaling over ninety thousand troops. Regardless of who started the conflict, the united front against the Japanese was no more.

As the war unfolded in Europe and Asia, Americans began to see the advantage of funding the British war against Germany while staying out of the hostilities themselves. Nine months before the United States entered the war in December 1941, President Roosevelt signed the Lend-Lease Bill on March 11, 1941. It permitted him, "To sell, transfer title to, exchange and lease, lend, or otherwise dispose of, to any such government whose defense the president deems vital to the defense of the United States, any defense article." In April this policy was extended to China and in October to the Soviet Union. Roosevelt approved in lend-lease a total of fifty billion dollars' worth of supplies: thirty-two billion to Britain, eleven billion to the Soviet Union, three billion to France, two billion to China, and smaller sums to other Allies. This served to be the turning point of the World War II.

By 1941 Japan held most of the eastern coastal areas of China and Vietnam, but guerilla fighting continued in these occupied areas. Japan had suffered high casualties from unexpectedly stubborn Chinese resistance, and neither side could make any swift progress. On June 22, 1941, Germany attacked the Soviet Union. Notwithstanding non-aggression pacts or trade connections, Hitler's assault threw the world into a frenzy of political realignment and strategic revisions. On July 21 Japan occupied the southern part of French Indochina against a 1940 agreement not to invade southern French Indochina.

From bases in Cambodia and Southern Vietnam, Japanese planes could attack Malaysia, Singapore, and the Dutch East Indies. As the Japanese occupation of Northern French Indochina in 1940 had already cut off supplies from the West to China, the move into Southern French Indochina was a direct threat to Britain and Dutch colonies as well. On July 24, 1941, President Roosevelt requested Japan to withdraw all its forces from Indochina. Two days later the United States and Britain began an oil embargo; two days after that, the Netherlands joined them. This was a decisive moment in the Sino-Japanese War. The loss of oil imports made it impossible for Japan to continue operations in China on a long-term basis. It set the stage for Japan to launch a series of military attacks against the Allies, including the air attack on Pearl Harbor on December 7, 1941.

As part of a general Pacific campaign to secure all the ports in Southeast Asia, the Japanese launched an assault on Hong Kong on the morning of December 8, 1941. Japanese forces raced down the New Territories and Kowloon and crossed Victoria Harbor on December 18. British, Canadian, and Indian forces, supported by the Hong Kong (mainly Chinese) Volunteer Defense Forces attempted to resist the rapidly advancing Japanese but were heavily outnumbered. Finally defeated, on Christmas day, 1941, the British surrendered. The brutality of the Japanese continued as shown in the St. Stephen's College incident when drunken Japanese soldiers entered St. Stephen's College, which served as a hospital, shot two volunteer doctors to gain entry, and bayoneted all the wounded soldiers who were incapable of hiding. This ushered an almost four years of brutal imperial Japanese administration of Hong Kong.

❖ ❖ ❖

In late August of 1941, the Foreign Ministry promoted and recalled Zhining's father, Bao Junhao, from Vancouver, Canada, and the family, including his wife and youngest son, Gerson, had to relocate to Chongqing. Zhining's mother and Gerson, left for Hong Kong while her father stayed in Vancouver to complete the transfer. Gerson had finished his first year at the University of British Columbia and wished to continue at the University of Hong Kong instead of going with his parents to Chongqing. His mother left Gerson with friends to attend school, and she left for Guiyang to visit Zhining and her family. Gerson had a great time in Hong Kong until the Japanese takeover in December. Hong Kong relatives and friends help Gerson to leave, and he arrived in Guiyang several months later. Gerson stayed with his brother, Johnson, and his new Chinese-Canadian wife, May (Ye Meizhou). May was from a Chinese immigrant family and was born and educated in Vancouver. Johnson and May met and married there before returning to China in 1940. Johnson was now a lecturer at the Great China, where both his younger brothers, Channing and Gerson, were now enrolled.

❖ ❖ ❖

Within a few days of the Japanese surprise attack on Pearl Harbor on December 8, 1941, China formally declared war against Japan,

Germany, and Italy. Almost immediately Chinese troops achieved another decisive victory in the Battle of Changsha, which earned the Chinese government much prestige and proved to the Allies that the Chinese Army was capable to do its job. The Battle of Changsha (September 6–October 8, 1941) was Japan's second attempt at taking the city of Changsha, the capital of Hunan Province. The offensive was carried out by more than a hundred twenty thousand Japanese troops, including supporting naval and air forces. The Chinese Ninth Army Group under the command of General Xue Yue conducted a response that included street fighting inside Changsha city. The Japanese suffered over ten thousand casualties and retreated. Thereafter President Roosevelt referred to the United States, United Kingdom, Soviet Union and China as the world's "Four Policemen," elevating the international status of China to an unprecedented height after a century of humiliation at the hands of various imperialistic foreign powers. China continued to receive lend-lease supplies from the United States as the Chinese conflict become part of the Asian theater of World War II.

In mid-1941 the US government financed the creation of the American Volunteer Group nicknamed the "Flying Tigers" to replace the Soviet volunteers and aircraft withdrawn from China earlier. The Flying Tigers did not enter actual combat until after the United States had declared war on Japan, but they did conduct pilot training for the Chinese based in Kunming and Nanning. It was organized and led by Claire Lee Chennault, who began his career in the Army Air Service during World War I and became the chief of Pursuit Section at Air Corps Tactical School in the 1930s. In the mid-1930s Chennault led and represented the first Army Air Corps aerobatic team the Three Musketeers. He resigned from the USAF as a captain in 1937 and went to China with several American civilians as trainer for the Chinese air force. He developed a good working relationship with both Jiang Jieshi and his wife, Meiling, who led the Air Force Commission for the government. Chennault became the chief air force adviser to Jiang Jieshi throughout the war.

By early 1941 President Roosevelt sent P-40 Tomahawk fighters enough for three air squadrons to the Chinese under the American lend-lease program. Chennault recruited some three hundred American pilots and ground crew. They were mercenaries and some idealists motivated by adventure in and salvation for China. They developed into a crack fighting unit under Chennault, always facing superior Japanese forces. Their early combat success of three hundred kills against a loss of only twelve of their shark-painted fighters earned them wide acclaim and much love of the Chinese people at a time when the Allies were suffering heavy losses on several fronts. The United States Army Air Forces in all other theaters adopted the Flying Tigers' dog-fighting tactics.

The Japanese invaded and occupied Bangkok, Thailand, in December 1941. As they had done in China, they tried to instigate a local uprising against the British in Burma. The Japanese objective in Burma were initially limited to the capture of Rangoon, the capital and principal seaport. This would close the overland supply line to China and provide a strategic bulwark to defend Japanese gains in Malaysia and the Dutch East Indies. Also, the Japanese knew rubber from that area was one of the few vital resources that the United States was not self-sufficient in. It was thought critical that the Allies be denied access to Southeast Asian rubber supplies if they were ever to accept peace terms favorable to Japan. Japan invaded Burma in January 1942, and the combined British and Chinese forces were no match for the Japanese. Rangoon fell on March 7. The Allies retreated to the north and hoped to make a stand with reinforcement of additional Chinese troops, but the Japanese defeated the Allies, forcing them to retreat into India. Sea routes to China and the Yunnan-Vietnam Railway had been closed since 1940. Therefore, between the closing of the Burma Road in 1942 and its reopening as the Ledo Road in 1945, foreign supplies were largely limited to what could be flown in over the Himalaya, referred to as the Hump by the Allied pilots, a death-defying feat back in those early days of air travel.

By 1942 most of China's industry had already been captured or destroyed by Japan, and the Soviet Union refused to allow the United States to supply China through Kazakhstan into Xinjiang. For these reasons, the Chinese government never had the supplies and equipment needed to mount major counteroffensives. Despite the severe shortage of weapons and materiel, the Chinese were successful in 1943 repelling of major Japanese offensives in Hubei and Chengde, Hunan. Jiang was named by the Allies as the Allied commander-in-chief in the China Theater in 1942. Roosevelt and his army chief of staff George C. Marshall appointed General Joseph Stilwell as the chief of staff to Jiang and served as the commander of the China Burma India (CBI) Theater responsible for all lend-lease supplies going to China and later was deputy commander to Jiang as well. Stilwell served three tours in China, where he became fluent in Chinese. Just prior to World War II, Stilwell was the top corps commander in the army and was initially selected to plan and to command the Allied invasion of North Africa. When it became necessary to send a senior officer to China to keep that country in the war, Stilwell was selected, over his personal objections since he was concerned about Jiang as a leader and the political situation he would be stepping into. In his earlier career, Stillwell had the nickname "Vinegar Joe" due to his caustic personality. Later, as a commander, his leadership style that emphasized concern for the average soldier and minimized ceremonies and organizational structure earned him the nickname of "Uncle Joe" from his troops.

Stilwell's assignment in the CBI was extremely difficult. He had geographical administrative command on the same level as the

Joseph Stilwell, 1942.

commands of Dwight D. Eisenhower and Douglas MacArthur over their own respective European and Asian theaters. Unlike the other theaters, the CBI was never a theater of operations and did not have an overall American operational command structure. The China Theater came under the operational command of Jiang Jieshi while the Burma India Theater came under the operational command of the British, whose supreme commander was Admiral Lord Louis Mountbatten. The British and the Chinese were ill-equipped and more often than not on the receiving end of Japanese offensives. Jiang was interested in conserving his troops and Allied lend-lease supplies for use against any sudden Japanese offensive in China, as well as against the CCP after the war. Jiang's wariness increased after observing the disastrous Allied performance against the Japanese in Burma. After fighting and resisting the Japanese for five years, many in the GMD government, including He Yingqin, his chief of staff, felt that it was time for the Allies to assume a greater burden in fighting the war.

When Stilwell had arrived in the embattled Chinese capital of Chongqing in March 1942, the Japanese were already driving into Burma, capturing the capital, Rangoon on March 6. Stilwell took command of two Chinese divisions and in cooperation with the British and Indians, tried to stem the Japanese onslaught. Defeated, he and his staff endured a rugged, 140-mile hike over jungle-covered mountains to India. "We got a hell of a beating," Stilwell told the crowd of reporters in Assam, India. It was May 1942, and he was chafing at failure in his first command in the field. By occupying Burma, the Japanese had not only gained access to vast resources of teak and rubber, but they had also closed the Burma Road, seven hundred miles of dirt highway that represented China's last overland link with the outside world. The reopening of an overland route to China would be the major Stilwell goal, indeed obsession, in the CBI throughout Stilwell's tenure.

Stilwell first objective for his assignment was the training and reformation of the Chinese army. These reforms clashed with the delicate balance of political and military alliances in China, which kept Jiang in power. Reforming the army meant removing men who maintained Jiang's position as commander-in-chief and put them under Stilwell's control. While Jiang gave Stilwell technically overall command of some fifty thousand Chinese troops, Jiang was concerned that the new American-led forces would become yet another independent force outside of his control. Since 1942 members of the Jiang's staff had continually objected to Chinese troops being used in Burma for the purpose of returning that country to British colonial control. Jiang therefore sided with the Flying Tigers Chennault's proposal that the war against the Japanese could be won largely using existing Chinese forces supported by its enhanced air forces augmented by the Flying Tigers. The dilemma forced Chennault and Stilwell into competition for the valuable lend-lease supplies arriving over the Hump from British-controlled India. George Marshall, in his biennial report covering the period of July 1, 1943, to June 30, 1945, acknowledged he had given Stilwell "one of the most difficult" assignments of any theater commander.

Based on his previous military experience in China, Stilwell was convinced that the Chinese soldier was the equal of any given proper training and leadership. He established a training center at Ramgarh, India, two hundred miles west of Calcutta, for two divisions of Chinese troops under Sun Liren from forces that had retreated from Burma. Sun was a graduate of Purdue University and Virginia Military Institute and had demonstrated bravery and leadership in the Battle of Shanghai. Stilwell's training program met resistance from the British, who feared that armed, disciplined Chinese would set an example for Indian insurgents, and from Jiang Jieshi, who did not welcome a strong military unit outside of his control.

From the outset, Stilwell's first goals were the opening of a land route to China from northern Burma and India by means of a ground offensive in northern Burma, so that more supplies could be transported to China. His second was to train a modernized and competent Chinese army that would fight the Japanese in the CBI. Stilwell argued that the CBI was the only area at that time where the possibility existed for the Allies to engage large numbers of troops against their common enemy, Japan. Unfortunately, the airborne logistical train of support from the United States to British India was still being organized, while supplies being flown over the Hump were barely sufficient to maintain Chennault's air operations and replace some Chinese war losses, let alone equip and supply an entire army. Additionally, critical supplies intended for the CBI were being diverted due to various crises in other combat theaters. Of the supplies that made it over the Hump, certain Chinese and American personnel diverted some of it into the black market for their personal enrichment. As a result, most Allied commanders in India were short on supplies and only able to focus on defensive measures.

Stilwell's leadership and his tenacity did lead to several key combat successes for the Chinese forces. The most laudable was the battle of Yenangyaung, Burma, where on April 17, 1942, Sun Liren led his Chinese 113th Regiment with only eight hundred to rescue over seven thousand Allied troops pinned down by the Japanese in extreme heat of over 110 degrees. Later King George VI rewarded Sun with the Order of the Commander of the British Empire and honored other officers with medals as well. Sun's division, retrained and reequipped in India, confirmed Stillwell's respect for the Chinese soldier and ultimately spearheaded Stilwell's 1943 drive to recapture North Burma and reestablish the land route to China by the Ledo Road, also known as the "the Stilwell Project."

The Ledo Road was started in December 1942 under the direction of General Stilwell; it was intended to be the primary supply route to China. It became a highway stretching from Assam, India, to Kunming, China, for about twelve hundred miles. On January 12, 1945, the first convoy of 113 vehicles left Ledo. They reached Kunming, China, on February 4, 1945. In the six months following its opening, trucks carried a hundred thirty thousand tons of supplies from India to China. Twenty-six thousand trucks carrying the cargo were handed over to the Chinese as well. The road was built by fifteen thousand American soldiers and thirty-five thousand local workers at a cost of US$150 million. Eleven hundred Americans and many more locals died during the construction. As most of Burma was in Japanese hands, it was not possible to acquire information as to the topography, soils, and river flow metrics before construction started. This information had to be acquired as the road was constructed. It was indeed a Herculean effort for the engineers as well as the laborers.

❖ ❖ ❖

The year 1941 did not start well for the Wang family. Boqun continued to work hard on both the affairs of the government in Chongqing and the Great China University funding in Guiyang and at the same time struggled with his chronic stomach problems. Zhining in her third month of pregnancy had a miscarriage, which turned out to be a male. She was extremely disappointed, for she felt the family was short on male children, and she had hoped to bring another into the world. Boqun tried to console her in expressing his feeling that they already had enough children and it was not worth risking her health to have another. Zhining wrote in her dairy that she really appreciated his concern.

In late August 1941, Zhining's father, Bao Junhao, and her mother had returned from Canada for his promotion in the Foreign Ministry in Chongqing. En route they visited Zhining's family in Guiyang. The family had a festive reunion for both the Bao and Wang families. All of Zhining's brothers were now in Guiyang and either teaching or studying at the Great China. Channing had decided to stay in Guiyang and attend the Great China in preparation for study in America at Cornell University for his master's in civil engineering. The next day Zhining took her parents to visit both the war orphan schools she had established. They were impressed by the healthy and happy children, who enjoyed Junhao's talk about serving as a diplomat in Canada and about how life is different in the Western world. At the end of his talk, the children asked many interesting questions and showed their appreciation by a big round of applause. Junhao was delighted with his visit and told his daughter that he was very proud of what she had accomplished under the war-torn conditions.

In the next days, Boqun and Zhining showed her parents around all the usual sites of interest around Guiyang. Junhao also had the opportunity to spend some alone time with all his sons. Gerson recounted his escape from Hong Kong and how well he had done at the Great China. Channing assured his father he would do his best at Cornell and make the Bao family proud. Johnson and May brought his parents up to date on their married life, his teaching career, and his desire to follow his father's footstep in the foreign services. Junhao and his wife also enjoyed quality grandparent playtime with Zhining's three children. After a two-week visit, he left for Chongqing to return to his work at the Foreign Ministry. His wife stayed behind with Johnson till he settled their living quarters in Chongqing.

Johnson, May, Gerson, Channing.

Zhining was happy to see both of her parents after such a long absence. The both seemed to be in good health and fine spirits. It was a happy occasion for all the Bao family to be together.

On September 19, 1941, Boqun reached his fifty-seventh year and his sister, Wenxiang, had come to his birthday celebration in Guiyang. Boqun had not wish to have festive celebrations in a time of war, but so many friends and relatives had traveled many miles to

309

visit him in Guiyang, so he relented to have a party. For the occasion, Wenxiang and Zhining arranged a lunch of twelve tables and dinner of nineteen in total for three hundred some guests. Later Boqun thanked Zhining for such a grand party, and he enjoyed himself in spite of his misgivings.

Boqun received a call on October 21 from He Yingqin, who told him that Bao Junhao had died in his hotel in Chongqing

Bao Junhao and wife 1941

and police report indicated he had died of a heart attack. In the next days, the Wang family, along with Zhining's mother, Johnson, and Uncle CJ and his wife had arrived from Greece. He Yingqin had requested further investigation of the cause of death, and it was concluded that there might be foul play of robbery gone bad. The family decided Junhao would be buried in Chongqing and transferred to Nantong when the war was over. Zhining was very sad, for her father had worked all his life representing China in foreign lands, often without his family, and finally he would be settled down in one place with his family and now he would not have that chance. Zhining's mother was grief stricken, but the presence of all the family members around her greatly consoled her.

After her father's death, Zhining recalled that in 1938 she had heard about a famous fortune teller in Guiyang, and out of curiosity she took Channing with her to pay him a visit. After the fortune teller was given her birth sign and date as well as an examination of her palms and thumbs, he pronounced that she would have long and good life. He saw her under a beautiful tree in full bloom with old and a young spirits. He said the older spirit was from Boqun's family and the young spirits were her children. He predicted that within three years, Zhining would be in mourning for her father unless she could keep him away from temples. He also read Channing's fortune and pronounced that he would travel far to live a long, fruitful life but gave him the same warning about his father as well. The fortune teller could have guessed that they were related since the siblings looked alike, thus the same prediction.

Zhining told Boqun what she had been told, and Boqun confirmed that the man was very well known in Guiyang and many people in Guiyang actually confirmed his predictions to be true. On the other hand, Boqun teased Zhining that for two well-educated persons to seek out and to believe a fortune teller was incredulous and she should not give him a second thought. Zhining had forgotten the fortune-teller, but in recalling the prediction, she realized she had taken her father to the war orphan schools, which were converted temples. She did not discuss this with Boqun but talked to Channing, who told her to forget about the prediction which was more than likely just a coincidence since many public buildings were converted temples in wartime. Although Zhining agreed, there was still a doubt in her mind that she might have caused her father's death.

Since 1924 when Ou Yuanhuai convinced Boqun to join in the effort of starting the Great China University, Ou had become a close friend and trusted confidant to both Boqun and Zhining. Ou had left his wife, who was a citizen of Germany and a university professor in Shanghai, to join Boqun in his effort to reestablish Great China in Guizhou. Ou had spent much time at the Wang's house and had impressed Zhining with his earnestness as well as his expertise in education; she told Boqun that he was lucky to have Ou by his side. Boqun agreed and he recommended him for a position as the Commissioner of Education for the Guiyang City government which helped Ou's financial position. Ou once told Zhining that Boqun was the only person for whom he would have left his family for the sake of an institution.

In mid-March 1943 Boqun went to Chongqing and met with He Yingqin, who had been unofficially working for the Great China cause. He told Boqun that the Education Ministry wanted to appoint him as the president of the Guizhou University and incorporate Great China into it; He thought Boqun would not accept such a position and abandon the Great China name after he worked so hard over twenty years for it. The next day Boqun met with the minister and told him that he would not accept changing the name, and he further commented that would be like selling reputation for money, which he could not do. Upon his return Boqun worked long hours with Ou Yuanhuai and the rest of the staff to ask alumni throughout the world to write to the Education Ministry in support of keeping the name. This also became a fundraising effort in case the government would not provide funding. On April 21 Boqun got the good news that Great China would remain Great China, and it would still receive partial funding from the government in the amount of five hundred thousand yuan. This good news took a lot pressure off Boqun, who was using his own money as well as money from personal loans. After the Education Ministry's approval of Great China's funding, Boqun continued to solicit additional private funds. The most substantial source was from the Kong Xiangxi family and friends. Kong was married to the eldest Soong sister, Ailing, which thus made him brother-in-law to both Sun Yatsen and Jiang Jieshi. Kong served at various times in the GMD government as premier and minister of finance. Kong has been a good friend to Boqun since they were introduced by Sun Yatsen in the earlier days of the republic.

Zhining become pregnant in March 1942, and in the second month she became ill and the doctors recommended that she should have an abortion to prevent serious health issues. Boqun agreed with the doctors and told Zhining he would not want even a son if that would mean risking her life. Zhining agreed to the abortion attempt but it was not successful, and another daughter, Dezen, was born in November, three months ahead of schedule. Due to her health and difficult birth, Zhining resigned her position as the provincial chairwoman of the

Chinese Women's National War Relief Society. Zhining regretted that she had to resign, for she had great empathy for the children and developed a close relationship with many of the staff. Soong Meiling came to the farewell dinner for Zhining, delivered a speech praising her efforts over the years in establishing and managing the program, and presented her with a silver plaque to that effect. Boqun sat at the head table, and he was extremely proud of his lovely wife and added his own admiration to Soong's speech.

At the start of 1943, Boqun spent two months in Chongqing finalizing Great China funding. There was a budget shortfall of a hundred thousand yuan the previous year and the projected deficit of current year would be even more. Boqun was seeking additional government funding for the shortfall in a tough financial year for China. Boqun got sixty thousand yuan, which still left him with work to do from private sources. While Boqun was in Chongqing, Uncle CJ was back to take on the position of counsel general in New Delhi, India. Zhining and Johnson went Chongqing to visit him and to attend the birthday festivities of Wenxiang as well. January 21 was Wenxiang's birthday, and there were many parties attended by old friends and colleagues. Zhining, Boqun, and Johnson then accompanied CJ to his brother's gravesite and had a good lunch after the sad visit. The highlight of the entertainment was a dinner at TV Soong's house. Soong was the brother of the Soong sisters and then the foreign minister after serving as the premier. The dinner guests included He Yingqin, Wenxiang, and other high GMD friends. The menu was French, and it was definitely as fine as anything from Paris and conversation was in both Chinese and English. It was indeed a cosmopolitan evening; both Boqun and Zhining enjoyed it tremendously.

In mid-March Jiang Jieshi came to Guiyang. Boqun attended several functions in his honor, and on one such occasion, Jiang asked about Great China and Boqun talked about the funding difficulties and the importance of education, especially in times of turmoil, that can set back a nation's development. He cited the Taiping Rebellion as an example of how education has been shortchanged and the nation had suffered from it. Jiang listened carefully and empathetically; he promised to look into additional funding. When Boqun returned home, he could hardly contain his joy when he related to Zhining how Jiang had reacted to his plea. Nothing ever came of the conversation, and Boqun was deeply disappointed knowing how much waste and corruption there was in the government.

In April 1943 all four of the Wang children had come down with measles. Fortunately, all of them came through without complications. It was a great relief for their parents after what they had been through with their firstborn. Zhining was pregnant again, and she was glad her mother was just minutes away whenever she needed her. After her father died, it took her mother over one year to regain her composure and gone back to her bubbly self. Johnson and Channing were scheduled to leave for India to visit Uncle CJ and to send Channing off to America for his advanced education at Cornell. Gerson stayed with his mother in Guiyang while he finished his studies at Great China. Zhining's mother was by her side when she had her fifth child, a girl, Delin, born on December 12, 1943. The child was healthy, and the birth was without complications.

Wenxiang and her daughter, Ruby, came to Guiyang in late July for Boqun's fifty-eighth birthday. He really did not want to have a big, festive celebration while the Japanese continued to bomb Guiyang. It was just five tables for the family. Zhining felt bad about how Boqun had been working so hard yet could not have the kind of celebration they had in years past, especially in Shanghai. Boqun returned to Chongqing, along with his sister and niece, to attend the annual GMD party congress. Boqun was honored by his selection for a eighteen-member group of most important GMD elders, which included such people as Sun Yatsen's widow, Soong Chingling, Feng Yuxiang, and Li Liehchun.

❖ ❖ ❖

Throughout 1943 Stilwell would press Jiang Jieshi and the British to take immediate actions to retake Burma. Jiang demanded large amounts of supplies before he would agree to take offensive action, and the British refused to meet their previous pledges to provide naval and ground troops due to Churchill's "Europe-first" strategy. Stilwell began to complain openly to President Roosevelt that Jiang was hoarding US lend-lease supplies because he wanted to keep Chinese forces ready to fight the CCP after the end of the war. Jiang reasoned that since China had already suffered tens of millions of war casualties, Japan would eventually capitulate in the face of America's overwhelming industrial output and military strength. Thus the Allies gradually lost confidence in the Chinese ability to conduct offensive operations from the Asian mainland and decided to concentrate their efforts against the Japanese in the Southwest Pacific area.

At the end 1942, Soong Meiling suffered a whole list of aliments and went to America for treatment. She stayed at the Harkness Pavilion Medical Center in New York City on an entire floor. Once her treatment was completed, she rested at the Roosevelt's house at Hyde Park for two weeks as she regained her usual energy and drive. She then decided to take up Wendell Willkie's suggestion to promote the Chinese cause in the war. Willkie was the Republican candidate, defeated by Roosevelt in the presidential election of 1940. He was sent by Roosevelt on a world tour in the interest of bipartisanship in the time of war. On his Chongqing visit, Willkie was treated like the American president, and it was said he had a fling with Meiling. With heavy promotion by Henry Lace, the publisher of *Time* and a strong supporter of the Jiangs, Meiling set out to win American support and promote herself as a world-class leader.

The tour began in February 1943. She started by staying at the White House for two weeks and getting President Roosevelt to send more military aid. She praised Chennault and got him all the supplies he needed but criticized Stilwell for his incompetence and contemptuous attitude. She then became the first Chinese and the first woman to address a joint session of Congress, where she received a four-minute standing ovation before she even opened her mouth. A White House state dinner was held in her honor, and she charmed hundreds of reporters at a joint press conference with Roosevelt. She addressed a rally of twenty thousand at Madison Square Garden. Luce put her on the cover of *Time*, and she was written up by American newspapers and journals as the angel of an indomitable China. From New York Meiling went to Boston, Chicago, Hollywood, and San Francisco as her United China Relief Fund collected large sums of money wherever she spoke at rallies. There was no doubt she touched the Americans' heartstrings, but her grandstanding drove many American officials crazy, including the president.

In July Meiling returned to Chongqing with a massive treasure trove of American and European personal goods acquired in the United States. She then resumed her place next to Jiang as his equal partner in power. Meiling saw herself as a world figure and intended to establish her status, even if it meant provoking a family feud against her older brother, TV, who was Jiang's point man in Washington and had ambition to replace his brother-in-law, H. H. Kong, as the Chinese premier. TV had the support of the most capable generals, Cheng Chen and Xue Yue; both had come to realize the need for military, political, and financial reform.

Unbeknownst to Stilwell, he had become a pawn in the power struggle between the Soong siblings. Knowing Jiang's feelings regarding Stilwell and Cheng, TV proposed a plan to replace Stilwell with Cheng, and he told Roosevelt that if Stilwell was not replaced, Chinese cooperation in the war could not be assured. He cabled Jiang and told him that Roosevelt was considering such a proposal. Upon hearing this Meiling, with her older and more manipulative sister, Ailing, who hoped to put her husband, H. H. Kong, into Jiang's position, called Stilwell to a meeting and they told him they were concerned about the state of the Chinese army and asked for his input. The meeting concluded with the idea that Meiling would become the minister of war, replacing He Yingqin, whom both Meiling and Stilwell detested. The family feud reached a two-day climax at Jiang's home. Though Jiang was for the Stilwell recall, he much preferred the more agreeable Kong running the government instead of TV, who certainly had more credibility to replace Jiang himself. Others remembered Jiang's comment about TV on more than one occasion that "TV has spent so much time in America, he looks like an American and thinks like an American." This ended the Soong family feud for the moment. Stilwell pieced things together later when Cheng Chen lost his command of Y force, and although He Yingqin survived, he was scolded by Jiang for the slow pace of troop training and replacement.

One of the most significant conflicts to emerge during the war was between Stilwell and Chennault, the commander of the famed Flying Tigers and who later became the Chinese air force commander. As adviser to the Chinese air force, he proposed a limited air offensive against the Japanese in China in 1943 using a series of forward air bases. Stilwell insisted that the idea was untenable and that any air campaign should not begin until fully fortified air bases were protected by an established large infantry base. Stilwell then argued that all air resources should be diverted to his forces in India for an early conquest of North Burma.

Jiang, Roosevelt, Churchill, Meiling, 1943, Cairo.

Following Chennault's advice, Jiang rejected the Stilwell proposal. British commanders sided with Chennault, knowing they could not launch a coordinated Allied offensive into Burma in 1943 with the resources then available. During the summer of 1943, Stilwell's head-quarters concentrated on plans to rebuild the Chinese Army for an offensive in northern Burma, despite Jiang's insistence on support for Chennault's air operations. Stilwell believed that after opening a supply route through northern Burma by means of a major ground offensive against the Japanese, he could train and equip thirty Chinese divisions with modern combat equipment. A smaller number of Chinese forces would transfer to India, where two or three new Chinese divisions would also be raised. This plan remained only theoretical at the time since available airlift capacity for deliveries of supplies to China over the Hump barely sustained Chennault's air operations and were wholly insufficient to equip a new Chinese army.

In late November 1943, an Allied summit was held in Cairo. Jiang and Meiling were invited to attend, and they had private meetings with both Roosevelt and Churchill. China's was thus confirmed as one of the four great powers of the world. Stalin chose not to attend since the Soviets had a nonaggression pact with Japan and insisted on having another meeting with Roosevelt and Churchill in Teheran. Unfortunately, Jiang's Cairo attendance did not change the desperate status of China. Most of army remained inadequately equipped, ill-trained, and with a lack of motivation and able leadership. More than half a million of them had switched to the collaboration regime of Wang Jingwei. Inflation soared to over 200 percent, and the economy was aggravated by counterfeit money printed by the Japanese. Drought hit the south, with over a million deaths, and a quarter of the population in areas controlled by the GMD was homeless. Yet Jiang somehow had maneuvered himself into the one of the top leaders of the world. Meiling turned out to be the attraction of the Cairo meeting; her presence and bilingual ability impressed both Roosevelt and Churchill. The photo of the four of them was widely distributed in China as the proof of Jiang's eminence.

The main issue at Cairo was to confirm the Allied united front against Japan and the return of territories taken from China. Jiang got an American promise for money and weapons and to regain Manchuria and Formosa (Taiwan) after Japan was defeated. The Jiangs flew back to Chongqing without Stilwell, who would go with Roosevelt and Churchill to meet with Stalin in Teheran. Stalin agreed to declare war on Japan after Germany had been defeated. The Allies agreed that the priority of the war was the cross-channel invasion of France and landings from the Mediterranean, which would take all the available landing craft, and thus the Burma invasion would have to be postponed again. Jiang, after being informed of the delay of the Burma invasion by Stilwell, decided to go it alone to show the Allies that the Chinese could fight as well as any Allied troops. He ordered Stilwell to take charge of the fifty thousand Chinese X forces he had trained to commence the invasion with American air support as agreed to in Cairo. Stilwell was ecstatic as he led his men into north Burma in mid-December 1943.

CHAPTER 16

1944-1945

BOOUN'S FINAL JOURNEY

AND THE WAR ENDS

The Allies established the new Southeast Asia Command in August 1943. Joseph Stilwell was the deputy supreme Allied commander under Admiral Lord Louis Mountbatten. Stilwell took command of various Chinese and Allied forces in the CBI, including a new US Army special operations unit known as Merrill's Marauders. Stilwell also built up his Chinese forces for an eventual offensive in northern Burma. On August 17, 1943, the Allied leaders met in Quebec and finally agreed to the invasion of northern Burma. On December 21, 1943, Stilwell assumed direct control for the invasion of northern Burma, and in April 1944 Stilwell launched his offensive to capture the Burmese city of Myitkyina. The town was strategically important not only because of its rail and water links to the rest of Burma but also because it was located on the planned Ledo Road. In mid-May the Marauders joined up with the Chinese X Force Army under Sun Liren from India and took the Mitkyina airfield, the largest in Burma. The Japanese repelled subsequent attacks of the heavily defended town. In early August, after an eighty-day siege, the combined American and Chinese forces finally captured Myityina and thus allowed the construction of all-important Ledo Road to proceed.

In mid-April of 1944, the Japanese launched their biggest single offensive of the war in China, Operation Ichigo, which consisted of over half million men with the objective of taking the air bases in eastern China, which were home of the American bombing attacks of Japanese homeland, and to open a land route to French Indochina. Japanese forces began by crossing the Yellow River into Henan and routed the Chinese defenders. Jiang refused to send in the First Army, which served to block CCP forces, and the Japanese quickly took three air bases and the key railroad. Luoyang was captured by end of May. The Japanese then proceeded south from Wuhan to Hunan, which was defended by the famed Xue Yue and his Tenth Army. With no reinforcements or supplies from Jiang, Xue had to withdraw from Changsha after holding off three waves of attacks. Jiang had ordered Xue to move west toward Sichuan, but Xue moved south to defend Hengyang, which was the key to halting the Japanese advance toward Guangxi.

The American Fourteenth Air Force with the Flying Tigers and Chinese pilots bombed the Japanese supply lines intensely, causing the enemy to be short on fuel and ammunition. The Japanese pulled back in mid-July, opening up a window for the Chinese to regroup. Jiang still refused to send supplies, but he did send in reinforcement troops, which were poorly equipped, sick, and tired. The lack of coordination and cooperation for self-serving interests was not limited to the Chinese but affected the Americans as well. Stilwell refused to send in supplies and fuel when requested by Chennault. On August 8, 1944, Hengyang fell after holding out for seven weeks. At the time the Japanese were exposed to encirclements and flanking attacks. If Stilwell had responded to the call for help for supplies, Chennault's air power could well have turned the tide for the Chinese side. Without the air support, the Japanese destroyed half of the crack Tenth Army of Xue. It was a lost opportunity for Stilwell, who professed to be a proponent of strong Chinese Army like the Tenth Army.

After a month of rest and regrouping, the Japanese army launched its second wave of offense toward Guilin and Liuzhou in Guangxi. The Chinese troops defending the area were mainly the remnants from the Battle of Hengyang and the Guangxi troops under the command of

Bai Chongxi. On November 1, 1944, when the Japanese started their attack, only twenty thousand Chinese troops were available to defend Guilin. Most civilians had fled weeks before, and Guilin was heavily scorched by enemy bombing and artillery. Stilwell went to great pains to send American munitions to Bai's forces. After ten days of intense fighting, the Japanese occupied Guilin, and on the same day, they entered Liuzhou as well. Fighting continued sporadically as Chinese forces made their rapid retreat. By November 24 the Japanese were in control of 75 percent of Guangxi, and killed two hundred thousand and wounded more than four hundred fifty thousand civilians, including hundreds of thousands of women and children.

In December 1944 Japanese forces reached French Indochina and achieved the purpose of Operation Ichigo. Nevertheless, there were few practical Japanese gains. US air forces moved inland from the threatened coastal bases. The operation also forced British commandos working with the Chinese to leave China and return to Burma. Japan continued to attack US airfields up to the spring of 1945, causing a series of the airfield relocations. One affected airfield had been part of Operation Matterhorn, the B-29 bombing mission of the Japanese homeland conducted by the Twelfth US Air Force. Although this affected the operation for a short time, the Twelfth was able to resettle on Marianas Islands. Thus Operation Ichigo had minimal effect on the defense of the Japanese homeland.

By capturing Guangxi, the Japanese successfully cut off Chongqing from its supply route of the ocean and the rivers. With the rapid deterioration of the Chinese front after the Japanese launched Operation Ichigo in 1944, Franklin Roosevelt was extremely concerned about the situation in China. He sent an ultimatum via Stilwell to Jiang threatening to end all American aid unless he placed Stilwell "in unrestricted command of all your forces." An exuberant Stilwell immediately delivered this letter to Jiang despite pleas from Patrick Hurley, Roosevelt's special envoy in Chongqing, to delay delivering the message and work on an arrangement that could achieve Roosevelt's aim in a manner more acceptable to Jiang. Seeing this act as a move toward the complete subjugation of China, Jiang gave a formal reply in which he said that for him to stay as the head of state of China, Stilwell had to be replaced immediately and he would welcome any other qualified US general to fill Stilwell's position. He even sent a list of such generals accepted by him along with his reply.

Roosevelt realized he had no viable alternative to Jiang in China, and he could replace Stilwell with another that could possibly work out better with Jiang. Hurley further indicated if Stilwell stayed, America ran the risk of losing China due to Jiang's possible capitulation to the Japanese. Roosevelt recalled Stilwell from his command on October 19, 1944. The recall was officially based partly on the controversy concerning the casualties suffered by US forces in Burma and due to the continuing difficulties Stilwell had in working with the British and Chinese commanders, especially Jiang. In November 1944 Stilwell departed from Chongqing for the United States after he refused the highest Chinese decoration, the Special Cordon of the Blue Sky and White Star, from Jiang. Stilwell met with Soong Qingling, who wept on his withdrawal; TV Soong and He Yingqin accompanied him to the airport. Stilwell's return to the United States did not have the usual ceremony. Upon his arrival two army generals met him at the airport, who told him that he was not to answer any media questions about China whatsoever.

Stilwell never fully realized his plan to train and modernize thirty Chinese divisions in China in addition to the three divisions of X forces already in India. As Chennault had predicted, supplies carried over the Ledo Road at no time approached the tonnages of supplies airlifted into China. In July 1945 seventy thousand tons of supplies were flown over the Hump compared to only six thousand tons using the Ledo Road. The airlifts continued until the end of the war. Stilwell's drive into north Burma, however, allowed the air transport command to fly supplies into China more quickly and safely using a more southerly route without Japanese fighter harassment. American airplanes no longer had to make the dangerous route over the Hump and thus allowed the delivery of more supplies.

Stilwell was replaced by General Albert Coady Wedemeyer, a skillful desk general who spent two years at the German Staff College. He was an expert of German war strategy and authored the victory plan adapted for the Allies in defeating Germany. He was also involved in planning the Normandy Invasion and was on Jiang's list of the Americans acceptable to him. General George Marshall on October 27, 1944, directed Wedemeyer to proceed to Chongqing and to assume the position of chief of staff to Jiang and commander of all US forces, replacing Stilwell. Wedemeyer later recalled his initial dread over the assignment, as service in the Chinese theater was a graveyard for American officials, both military and diplomatic. When Wedemeyer actually arrived at Stilwell's office, he was dismayed to discover that Stilwell had intentionally departed without seeing him. Stilwell did not leave a single briefing paper for his guidance. Searching the office, Wedemeyer could find no record of Stilwell's plans or records of his former or future operations. General Wedemeyer then spoke with Stilwell's officers but learned little from them because Stilwell, according to the staff, kept everything in his "hip pocket."

❖ ❖ ❖

In March 1944 Boqun traveled to Chongqing for his usual business and for He Yingqin fifty-fifth birthday. To avoid the usual celebration, He and his wife took Boqun on a boat around the coast to a hot spring, and they hiked the surrounding area together in peace and quiet. It happened to be a time without Japanese bombing, and the three of them enjoyed the view and bird songs just like in peacetime so long ago. Boqun complimented He that at the advanced age of fifty-five, he still maintained his military bearing and general good health, in spite of the assassination wounds and his slight permanent limp. They returned to the city and enjoyed a fine meal in one of the He's favorite restaurants. Three of them agreed that they should find time to enjoy such peaceful outings more often as in their younger days in Xingyi, Beijing, and Shanghai.

During the monthly government meeting in May at Chongqing, Jiang presented Boqun with the Order of Blue Sky and White Sun with Grand Cordon. In his acceptance speech, Boqun stated,

> I am extremely humbled by this honor. It makes me think about all the people who had paid the ultimate price in the revolution that gave birth to this republic. In particular, I wish to dedicate this medal to my brother, Dilun, and my good friend Dai Kan for their heroic deeds, for which this medal would have been more appropriate.

On the same trip, Boqun was able to raise one million yuan for Great China's next year of operating expenses. It was one of the more successful trips taken by Boqun to Chongqing. Boqun wondered whether having the high government award actually allowed him to raise more money.

On May 15, 1944, Boqun and Zhining held a birthday party for their son, Defu, who had reached his tenth birthday. It was a small affair with only a few boys from Defu's study group. Defu received many gifts from all his relatives in the compound and had a great time playing with his new toys with his study mates. Boqun had hired three tutors for Defu and four other boys about the same age from relatives and close friends. The tutors were specialists in traditional Chinese culture, world history, sciences, and mathematics. The boys studied from eight in the morning till lunch, and the afternoon would be playtime till three. The other boys would go home, and Defu would go to his father for about hour to review what he had learned in the morning. This home school routine started when Defu reached five, the same age as Boqun when he started his learning. The girls were tutored as well when each reached five but in a group with girls and with different tutors.

Wenxiang's daughter, Ruby, had given Defu an Irish setter for his birthday. Although Boqun had other dogs he used to hunt with, he

Zhining and daughters, 1944

took a particular liking to Defu's dog, Hero. A special bond developed between man and dog. Hero would sleep at Boqun's feet most of the time and was always at his beck and call. Hero was missing for a time, which caused Boqun much consternation. He advertised on billboards all around town and offered a hundred yuan for Hero's safe return. Three days later a girl brought Hero back, and Boqun was visibly happy and moved. The dog would cry every time Boqun had health issues and would only stop when Boqun recovered. The dog had spooked Zhining, and Wenxiang thought they should let the dog loose. Boqun absolutely refused and stated Hero was only doing his job, warning him when danger approached and it would be superstitious to make more out of it.

In September Boqun had his usual stomach pain, but it was more severe than the past and affected his appetite as well. The family doctor was a practitioner of Chinese medicine, and he had known Boqun since they were both in their youth and had become good friends. The problem would subside after the doctor provided some Chinese herbal treatments but would return from time to time. Zhining was worried, but Boqun assured her this would pass with time as with his past stomach problems. He continued to work just as hard as usual while the pain came and went without any discernible pattern. After consulting with several Western doctors, he completed x-rays and blood tests at the hospital, but there was no conclusive diagnosis.

At the same time, the Japanese had taken parts of Guangxi bordering Guizhou, and the Chinese defenders were in retreat. Japanese bombing at Guiyang intensified. He Yingqin telephoned Boqun and told him that Jiang Jieshi was reluctant to defend Guizhou with his best troops. Jiang wished to save them for the CCP, and he also felt the Allies would defeat Japan in time to save China. He advised Boqun to leave Guiyang for Chongqing, where Jiang would be making his last stand. Boqun decided to ask his Chinese doctor to provide his usual herb treatments to lessen his pain and bleeding, and then he worked on evacuating his family and Great China to Chongqing. He directed Great China's staff to store all valuable books, instrumentation, etc., away from populated area of Guizhou in the surrounding mountains. He sent his sister, Wenxiao, and her family back to Xingyi. He then arranged for Dilun's family and his own to be ready for relocation to Chongqing. Zhining was concerned about taking this trip with Boqun being ill and visibly weak. Boqun assured her that he had already informed Wenxiang of his medical issues and she would have the proper medical care ready for him upon the family's arrival. When they went to bed that night, Zhining realized her wedding ring was not on her finger. Boqun helped her look for it, without success. He told her not to worry about things that were replaceable if they were lost. Zhining thought it was a very bad omen.

In October when Boqun heard about Stilwell's recall, he said to Zhining,

> Stilwell's record in the field shows that he is not a great commander, but he was right about the Chinese government being corrupted and its army needing reform, particularly training, badly. He understood a good army

must be trained well and its troops motivated. He did a great job developing Sun Liren, the other officers, and men of the X force. Stilwell had the backing of Roosevelt in the beginning, and if he had pushed Jiang hard enough for army reform as the condition for the lend-lease supplies, I think he would have been more successful. His honesty and principles too often appeared to be self-serving, and his feud with Chennault was egotistical and unnecessary. The way he treated He Yingqin as though he was just a messenger from Jiang showed that after all the time spent in China, he still did not understand the Chinese political situation. It was an opportunity lost for the both America and China. Both should have gotten more out of the relationship and the money.

The Wang family departed Guiyang for Chongqing by cars in mid-December 1944. It was a cold and snowy morning, and family, friends, and students turned out to wish the party safe travels. Boqun took the time to say good-bye to most of them, and he noticed that the principal of the Great China Middle School and one of his favorite students, Wu, was shivering without a winter coat. Boqun took off his own coat and put it on Wu, who had tears in his eyes in saying thanks.

He Yingqin was in Kunming at the time, but Wenxiang, a very energetic and capable woman who was very much like her mother, had make all the arrangements for the Wang family. Zhining, her mother, Zuma, the children, and Hero would stay at the well-appointed War Ministry guesthouse across the Yangtze from the city center. Boqun would be staying at the He residence since he needed medical attention at the hospital nearby. Dilun's family would be staying at a relative's house in the city. Hero started to cry immediately after Boqun was separately from the rest of his family.

The next evening as Zhining was unpacking and settling the family into their new home, she received a call from Wenxiang that Boqun had taken a turn for the worst and had start bleeding. She advised Zhining to come to him immediately. Wenxiang sent a ferryboat, which took Zhining to Boqun, who was already in bed, but she was somewhat relieved that he was alert and looking well. Boqun seemed very happy to see her and told her that the best doctors from the army hospital had come and examined him and concluded that he had bleeding ulcers in his intestines and he needed to be hospitalized. Boqun told Zhining he did not like hospitals and did not want to go there. Zhining then spoke with Wenxiang and told her she would take care of Boqun and it was not necessary to send him to the hospital. Wenxiang told her that Boqun needed transfusions and he must be in the hospital for that and for other tests. Zhining thought to herself if Boqun was so seriously ill, he should not have traveled all this way, but she put those thought away and let Wenxiang arrange for the transfer to the hospital. On December 13, 1944, Zhining accompanied Boqun to the hospital. The next day Boqun was settled in and given several transfusions, and he then asked to see the children.

When the children arrived, Boqun spoke with Defu alone and said,

Defu, you are only ten, but I know you are ready to do what I am about to ask of you. I am sure you understand and remember all the things we talked about how to become a man and to do the work of a man. You must listen and obey your mother and your third aunt (Wenxiang) as if they were me. You must look out for your sisters, take care them, and set an example for them. Can you do all that?

Boqun spent some time with his daughters and made them feel safe about their current circumstances. He asked for Wenxiang, and Zhining left them together alone. With tears still streaming from her eyes, she told Zhining what Boqun had said.

> Zhining is young, and my children are still infants. I hope you will always be nearby to take care of them, as you would do for your own family. That was what our parents taught us. If anyone speaks ill of Zhining, do not believe them, for I know she is not capable doing anything that would dishonor me. I have left instructions for her and you to take care of my affairs. My life was dedicated to the nation, and my two sleeves are filled only with air (no graft money). My inheritance should be safeguarded for my children's upbringing, education, and career, and it should not be used for any other purpose.

Many friends and government officials came to visit Boqun at the hospital. The most notable was Jiang Jieshi, who came toward the end of the week to pay his final respects and asked Boqun for his advice. Boqun said,

> It was a great honor for me to render any assistance to our great leader, Sun Yatsen, and then to you in the formative years of our beloved republic. I know you are a patriot and Sun's principles are close to your heart. I also appreciate what a difficult task you have undertaken to defend our motherland against the Japanese. You are facing a difficult future of rebuilding

and uniting the nation after the war. Regrettably, I will no longer be able to help you. I humbly leave you with two words, *fairness* and *honesty*, to guide you in the affairs of the state.

On the night of December 20, 1944, Boqun felt extremely cold, and he asked for the doctor, who examined him and concluded that his heart was starting to weaken and there was no more that could be done medically. Knowing the end was near, Boqun expressed his regret that Zhining would be left alone to bring up the children. Not knowing what else to say in the little time they had left, she said,

Please do not be concerned about the children. I will do my best to bring them up as you would have if you were with me. Trust me to know what you would do in that regard, and trust that I will have the capacity to do that for you. When they are grown adults, I will follow you and to be together with you, wherever you may be.

Hearing this, Boqun nodded his head and let out a sigh of peace. He then asked Zhining to kiss him, and as she leaned over to kiss him, he whispered, "Live your life, and don't ever change," and died at age fifty-nine.

Boqun had died with both of eyes wide open looking at Zhining. When the doctor closed his eyes, he said to Zhining that he had seen many deaths, but Boqun's death struck him as especially poignant. Zhining was inconsolable after Boqun's death; in the thirteen years of their marriage, he was her caring teacher and best friend as well as her loving husband. They had the utmost respect for each other, helped each other in times of need, and enjoyed each other's company in the darkest times of their lives. They had a harmonious and interesting life together. Zhining's only regret was so much of her time was taken up by the care of the children's needs, and she wished she had been able to give more of herself to Boqun.

Boqun had written his last words as follows:

> I followed Sun Yatsen's revolution for over thirty years. My limited capability has rendered my accomplishments insignificant in spite my diligence and hard work. From my deathbed, I urge my comrades to continue our unfinished goals of winning the war against the invader and unite all patriots for the republic we have envisioned. I ask my friends of Great China to finish the job we began and to instill in the students to serve the country with *fairness* and *honesty*. Though I will not see our country's rebirth and world peace, my heart is tranquil knowing that the success of our revolution is at hand.

After the traditional nine-day lying in state and being visited by all the dignitaries, from Jiang Jieshi to Great China students, Boqun was buried on December 29, 1944. It was a dark and dreary day on a cliff overlooking the confluence of the great Yangtze River and surrounded by the many high mountain peaks of Sichuan. At his gravesite, Zhining paraphrased one of her favorite poems by the Sung dynasty poet Mei Yaochen.

> Heaven's already taken my son,
> Now it's also taken my husband.
> My two eyes will be dry,

My heart desires only death.
Rain falls and soaks into the earth,
A pearl sinks to the ocean's depths.
Dive in the sea, I can seek the pearl,
Dig in the earth, I can see the water.
Only people return to the source below.
For all of time, this we know.
I hold my chest and ask now to whom can I turn?
Emaciated, a ghost in the mirror.

❖ ❖ ❖

In the fall of 1944, Allied supply efforts via the Hump were steadily improving, the British increased transport of military equipment and additional troops in preparation for the defense of the approaches to India. The British, in coordination with a southern offense by Chinese Y forces army under Wei Li-huang, who was one of the few Chinese commanders who could work well with and was respected by Stilwell, launched the long-awaited invasion of northern Burma. After heavy fighting and considerable casualties, the two forces linked up in January 1945. The new Ledo Road finally reopened on February 4, 1945, and transported over fifty thousand tons of petroleum into Kunming every month. By April 1945 enough materiel had become available to the Chinese Army to equip thirty divisions with American equipment. As a result the Chinese were able to plan for a major counteroffensive. The Ledo Road was later renamed the Stilwell Road by Jiang Jieshi.

The Japanese army began preparations for the battle for western Hunan in March 1945, constructing two highways with forced Chinese labor. The Heng-Shao Highway ran from Hengyang in a northwest direction to Shaoyang, a Japanese-controlled city in central Hunan, and the Tan-Shao Highway ran from Xiangtan southwest to Shaoyang. Supplies and equipment were stockpiled near Shaoyang. The Japanese massed eighty thousand men by early April 1945 in Hunan and Guangxi.

In response, Jiang dispatched He Yingqin as the commander-in-chief of Chinese forces totaling a hundred and ten thousand men in twenty divisions. He airlifted from Kunming to Zhejiang the entire New Sixth Corps, with American-equipped troops and veterans of the Burma Expeditionary Force. Over four hundred aircraft from the combined Chinese and American air forces provided air support. The mountainous terrain was ideal for ambushes and mortar bombardment on approaching Japanese forces in the lower grounds. The Chinese also had air superiority in this battle. After some defeats, the Japanese decided to retreat. Chinese forces gave chase and inflicted heavy casualties on the Japanese. The local Chinese guerrilla forces then attacked the Japanese rear positions. Japan ended up losing a large amount of territory they had once occupied. After he had successfully driven the Japanese into retreat, He Yingqin wrote to his wife, Wang Wenxiang, about his feelings and asked her to share it with Zhining.

> I dedicate my best command success in the Western Hunan Campaign to the Wang family. To you, my wife, for always being my support, even in my darkest hours. To elder brother Boqun for his advice and kindness toward me. Even though he did not always agree with the twists and turns I had to take in my career, he always supported me. Moreover, to brother Dilun, the mentor of my humble career who gave me the opportunity to begin my career. I wish both of your brothers could have been here to help me celebrate who I really am—a simple soldier patriot who loves combat over politics.

During his time in Chongqing, Wedemeyer attempted to motivate the Jiang government to take a more aggressive role against the Japanese in the war. He was instrumental in expanding the airlift operation with additional and more capable transport aircraft and continued Stilwell's programs to train, equip, and modernize the Chinese Army. His efforts were not wholly successful, in part because of the ill will caused by Stilwell toward Jiang and his key people, as well as continuing friction over the role of the CCP forces. Wedemeyer also supervised logistical support for American air forces in China. These included the US Twentieth and Fourteenth Air Force directed by General Claire Chennault. With the Chinese army progressing well in training and equipment, Wedemeyer planned to launch Operation Carbonado in the summer of 1945 to retake Guangdong, thus obtaining a coastal port, and from there drive northward toward Shanghai.

Jiang Jieshi should have been pleased at the start of 1945 in that the Allies were wining in the Pacific and the Japanese had been defeated or stalled at several fronts; yet he was concerned about the decisions made at the Yalta Conference held on February 4 to February 11, 1945, attended by Roosevelt, Churchill, and Stalin. First Jiang was not invited, and he was not told the result officially until after four months. The Soviets promised to declare war against Japan, to invade Manchuria, and to back Jiang's GMD government. In return, it had been given ports and railway concessions in Manchuria and allowed to station troops there after the Japanese surrendered. After Roosevelt's death on April 12, Jiang was particularly concerned that the Soviets would hand over Manchuria to the CCP and Harry Truman as the new US president and Churchill would not object. Thus, Jiang sent TV Soong to Moscow to reach a deal with Stalin.

In an agreement signed in June of 1945, Jiang agreed to recognize Outer Mongolia as an independent state, to Soviet use of Port Arthur as a naval base, and to the joint control and operation of the railways in northern China. The Soviets agreed to withdraw their troops from Manchuria in three months after the Japanese surrender, and most importantly they agreed to recognize the GMD government as the government of China. As in the 1920s, Stalin did not believe the CCP could take power in China from Jiang. He kept the CCP in the dark about Yalta and chose not to consult Mao Zedong about cutting a deal with Jiang, who he felt could unify China and provide a buffer for any attack from the West.

Three months after the war ended in Europe, the United States and the Soviet Union would put an end to the Sino-Japanese War and World War II, by attacking the Japanese homeland with America's new and ever-deadly atomic bombs and an incursion into Manchuria by Soviet Army. On August 6, 1945, an American B-29 bomber, the *Enola Gay*, dropped the first atomic bomb on Hiroshima. On August 9 the Soviet Union renounced its nonaggression pact with Japan, declared war with Japan, and attacked the Japanese in Manchuria. In less than two weeks, the Japanese army in China, consisting of over a million men but lacking in adequate armor, artillery, or air support, had been destroyed by the Soviets. On August 9 a second atomic bomb was dropped on Nagasaki. Japanese Emperor Hirohito officially capitulated to the Allies on August 15, 1945, and the official surrender was signed aboard the battleship USS *Missouri* on September 2. He Yingqin was sent by Jiang as the Chinese representative.

After the Allied victory in the Pacific, General Douglas MacArthur ordered all Japanese forces within China (excluding where the Soviets already occupied, i.e., Manchuria), Formosa, and French Indochina north of 16° latitude to surrender to China, and the Japanese troops in China formally surrendered on September 9, 1945 to He Yingqin in Nanjing. Upon return home He told Zhining that how much he regretted that neither Boqun nor Dilun

**Japanese surrendered
to He Yingqin 1945**

were alive to savor the Chinese victory and its place in history. Of course, Zhining shared his pride and joy about the surrender of the Japanese and also regret that the Wang brothers were unable to be there, but she realized Boqun would have felt that China still had not achieved what Sun Yatsen had envisioned. Jiang's government is nowhere near Sun's republic with the Three People Principles.

337

AFTERWORD

After the end of the war against the Japanese, Bao Zhining, widow of Wang Boqun, returned to Shanghai in the beginning of 1947, leaving the children with her mother in Chongqing. She found the Wang house in reasonably good shape. Only minor repairs needed to be made in the greenhouse and kitchen. Apparently Wang Jingwei and his staff had taken good care of the house when it served as his residence and offices in Shanghai. Wang had served the Japanese in Nanjing as the head of state of the puppet government of the Republic of China since 1941. Upon completion of the repairs, Zhining rented the house to the British Embassy for use as its Shanghai Consulate General and British Information Offices. The rental contract provided ample living space for the Wang family to stay whenever they were in the city.

Before Zhining left Chongqing, she attempted to move Boqun's remains to Guiyang, as Boqun had wished. It was difficult to arrange the move at the time, particularly without He Yingqin. He and his family moved to the United States as the Chinese military representative to the Security Council of the United Nations in late 1946. Zhining thought she would deal with the matter later when the whole country was less frantic with dealing with after-war matters.

Nanjing became once more the capital of the GMD government. Following Boqun's wish that his family be located close to He Yingqin's family, Zhining decided to move there as well with her mother and the children. She brought a small house in the same area of the old house destroyed by the Japanese. The new house was next to General Chen Ye's house and was close to schools and shopping as well. Zhining went back to Chongqing, and accompanied her family to Shanghai and stayed at the Shanghai house for about a month. They settled in Nanjing when their house was ready.

The three older children enrolled in a private school nearby. It was the first time for the children to study in a school environment with people they did not know. Brother Johnson worked for the Ministry of Foreign Affairs; he and his wife, May, lived in their own home near Zhining's house. Channing left Guiyang in August 1944 and was now in Ithaca, New York, enrolled in a master's program for civil engineering. Gerson worked at the Nanjing mayor's office and married Soumy (Zou Zhaomei), a Guangdong native he met at his workplace. In May Soumy gave birth to the couple first son, Stanley. In 1947 the Foreign Ministry assigned Johnson as the council general in Mexico City, Mexico. Johnson and May were happy and excited to travel to their first overseas assignment.

After the Japanese had surrendered, the GMD and CCP continued armed contests. President Truman asked Patrick Hurley, the US ambassador, to arrange a meeting between Jiang Jieshi and Mao Zedong in Chongqing from the end of August 1945 to mid-October to establish the basis for a united reconstruction of China. The two sides reached an agreement in January 1946. In the meantime Stalin finally realized there was an opening for the Chinese CCP to gain the upper hand in China. In the last month of the war in East Asia, Stalin ordered a massive attack of Manchuria, completely annihilated the Japanese army, and allowed the Soviet

Patrick Hurley, Jiang, Mao, 1945.

Russia to occupy Manchuria at the end of the war. The Soviets spent the next few months dismantling the extensive industrial structure built by the Japanese and shipping it back to Russia. Stalin then turned over most of the captured Japanese weapons to the CCP. Jiang broke the truce with CCP and ordered his troops to push into Manchuria. The hostilities resumed in earnest in June 1946. The ensuing civil war raged on for more than three years before Jiang retreated to Taiwan and Mao proclaimed the People's Republic of China on October 1, 1949, at its capital, Beijing.

In December 1948, with CCP approaching Nanjing, the Wang family had to move once again to Taiwan with the He Yingqin family. He's plane only had space for three, and Zhining took Defu and Delin with her for the trip to Taipei. She left the three girls with her mother, Gerson, and Soumy in Nanjing, awaiting the next available plane. Due to the faster-than-expected moving CCP takeover of Nanjing, Soumy had to bring Grandma Bao, her son, and the girls out through Hong Kong to Taipei in early 1949, while Gerson reported for his new job in Thailand. Gerson's family then moved to Bangkok, Thailand, where Gerson worked as the administrative officer to establish the Bureau of Flood Control and Water Resources, a part of the UN Economic Commission for Asia and the Far East (ECAFE). Gerson worked at the UN until his retirement in 1978 at the highest UN profession category.

In 1949 Taiwan had an indigenous population of six million, and the GMD government and its military added two million more to the island. Grandma Bao stayed at the home of a close Bao family friend, and Zhining and her five children settled in with the He family in its spacious government residence. The children attended the local schools and generally adjusted well to their new environment. Zhining felt, however, that her children would be better educated and have a brighter future in the United States. At the time there was a limitation on Chinese immigrants by the Magnuson Act, also known as the Chinese Exclusion Repeal Act of 1943, that limited annual entry visa to

106 for Chinese, with a waiting list of tens of thousands. Through her government connections, Zhining found out that were certain exemptions, such as officials, university students, and political refugees. Political refugee status is granted to those who were stateless and homeless for two years due to political perscution. To meet the political refuge requirements, Zhining decided she would take the children to Bangkok and Lima, Peru, for the two-year period.

Zhining had several discussions with He Yingqin and Wang Wenxiang about her plan. Wang Wenxiang felt strongly that the children should not grow up in a completely different culture. Uncle CJ, now the Republic of China (Taiwan) ambassador to Peru, backed up Zhining's thinking and reminded Wenxiang that Boqun would have backed Zhining's decision as well. CJ and Boqun had discussed life in the United States, and Boqun had agreed that it might be a good alternative given the chaotic state of China. He Yingqin agreed and convinced his wife as well. Zhining thanked the couple, particularly her sister-in-law, saying how much she and her children appreciated her love and assistance over the years, without which she could not have survived the loss of Boqun. It was a tearful farewell for the two women.

Zhining and her family arrived in Bangkok, Thailand, in early 1950. They stayed with Gerson's family for about six months. Grandma Bao decided to stay with Gerson and Soumy. Zhining and the children arrived in Lima, Peru, in June 1950. Uncle CJ as the ambassador had a large residence, and Zhining's family settled into their own quarters. The children began almost immediately with lessons in both English and Spanish. Defu left for America in late August to stay with Channing's family near Camillus, New York, so he could start his third high school year in the United States, which would facilitate his admission into a university. The rest of the family followed a year later and arrived in August 1951.

Channing received his doctor of civil engineering from Cornell University, married an American named Eleanor Marks, and was the chief civil engineer at the most prestigious architecture firm in Syracuse, New York. Zhining brought a small house and settled in as the only Chinese family in town since Channing and Eleanor had children of their own and lived several miles out town. Zhining and her children adjusted well to their new lives in a completely different culture. They joined local Methodist church, and the children made friends quickly. A year or so later, the money Zhining had brought from China was all but gone. Zhining had to go to a community college to learn bookkeeping so she could secure employment as a bookkeeper for a department store in Syracuse, the "big city" near Camillus. She had to take the bus until Defu got his driver's permit and brought a used car for driving to Syracuse University, where he enrolled to study engineering in 1952. The Wangs' lives were like all the average Americans in small towns all over the United States, working hard to make a decent living.

Zhining (c), Deann, Dexiang, Dezen, Defu and grandchildren, 1989.

Over the ensuing years, all the children pursued their own dreams in the "land of opportunity," as Zhining would call America.

All of them agreed that their mother had made the right decision to bring them into a new culture where everyone had an opportunity to make something out of themselves regardless of one's family standing and connections. Zhining made the choice to leave a comfortable but restrictive life in Taiwan, with a clear understanding that it would be hard for her as a mature upper-class Chinese lady to adjust to the new world she chose to live in. The most difficult was the first years in Camillus, where her brother was the only Chinese adult around. Though she made American friends, they just could not be at the same intimate level as the friends she had left behind in China. After the children had all gone from Camillus, Zhining finally was able to move to Port Jefferson on Long Island near New York City, where some of her friends and relatives were also residing. She was able to enjoy mahjong and Chinese opera again after a long dry spell.

In 1985 Zhining and Channing returned to China for the first time since they both left in 1944 and 1949 respectively. It was a very different China than the one they had left so many years earlier. With much sadness, they visited Boqun's tomb in Chongqing and the houses in Shanghai and Guiyang, but the Culture Revolution had destroyed Dilun's tomb in Hangzhou and scattered his remains. They were respectfully welcomed by government officials as the family of a revolutionary patriot. Relatives and old friends warmly greeted them and told about their suffering under the Culture Revolution and their wish to go to the United States. Although all the family properties had been confiscated, Zhining was able to repatriate the Guiyang house on the condition that it would become the Wang Boqun Memorial Library to house all his paper and art collections. In return Zhining gave her permission to the Xingyi government to build a representative office on the grounds. Both Zhining and Channing left China glad to be Americans.

In 1990 Defu, representing the Wang family, visited Taipei for the ninetieth birthday celebration of He Yingqin. It was Defu's first time back, and many relatives and family friends he had not seen for over

He Yingqin and Wang Defu, 1990.

forty years warmly received him. He took Defu to historical sites in Taipei, such as the National Palace Museum that is located in a bombproof mountain cave and houses some seven thousand of the best pieces of Chinese art moved from the original location from the Forbidden City in Beijing. He also told many of the stories about Boqun and Dilun that are used in this book. At age ninety He Yingqin still held his military bearing when he sat. He walked briskly with his cane, spoke with the same authority, and had his quick wit of years past. When Defu said good-bye and thanked him for his kindness and hospitality of many years, He answered,

I have done nothing compared to what your family has done for me. Without your father's and uncle's mentorship and influence, I could not have achieved what I have. Let us not forget my dear wife, your aunt; I could not have survived my darkest moments without her encouragement and support. You are an American, but do not ever forget you are the progeny of a great family that I am proud to be a part of.

In 1999 Zhining died in Port Jefferson, Long Island, at age ninety. Grandma Bao died in her eighties in Bangkok. Uncle CJ died at age seventy-two after serving as ambassador to Peru, Turkey, Jordan, and Saudi Arabia. Johnson, May, Gerson, and Soumy all passed away after living full lives. Channing is still striving at age ninety-five at Syracuse, New York. As for the next generation, two of Zhining's children have died, Dexiang (Vicki) and Delin (Lily). Defu (Edward), Deann (Ann), and Dezen (Doris) remain in retirement. There are two grandsons, three granddaughters, six great-grandsons, and one great-great granddaughter.

In 2004 Defu's youngest daughter, Zenann (Alexandra), went to China and other countries for a year as a Watson fellow. While she was Kunming, Yunnan, in March 2004, hanging out with the expats at a bar, she met a young man named Liao Shiyang (Paul Leow), who was teaching English at Yunnan University and had been learning Chinese there since 2002. Paul turned out to be a great-grand-nephew or in American, a cousin thrice removed, of Liao Zongkai, a character in this book. Wang Boqun and Liao Zhongkai were studying at the same Central (Chuo) University in Tokyo for the same subject, political economics, in the same year, 1907. They belonged to the same Revolution Alliance (RA) headed by Sun Yatsen, and Liao's house was used for RA meetings. Boqun and Liao both served in the GMD government. In addition, He Yingqin was the chief instructor while Liao was the chief of the Political Bureau of the nascent Whampoa Military Academy in Guangzhou Province. If the time were turned back a century to when marriages were arranged through a matchmaker for alliances of power, such as the marriage Boqun's father and mother, Alexandra and Paul would have made a good match. Paul and Alexandra were married in 2009; the best matchmaker could not have done a better job. The Chinese would definitely call this *ming yun* (predestined fate), a most auspicious marriage indeed.

AFTERWORD

In Zhining's last entry in June 1984 in her yearly summary, she remarked:

My children have grown and are successful in their own lives, and their father would have been proud. My life was a challenge at times, but I enjoyed having the freedom to live my life as I choose, and I am satisfied that the children are now successful adults. I have to thank America as well. It is a country of freedom based on same premise of Sun Yatsen's Three People Principles. Its government is freely elected by the people. Every citizen receives free education and has the right to choose how to live his or her life. The poor will receive assistance from taxes paid by the rich. The country is strong both militarily and financially. It is respected by the rest of the world as the most powerful on earth. Boqun knows my decision to immigrate was the right one, and I am proud to be a citizen of the United States.

WANG FAMILY CREED

Written by Wang Boqun in 1943 and translated by Wang Defu

When I was a child, my father taught me that we should unite our family with filial piety and friendship, serve our nation with loyalty and righteousness, be benevolent to the people who depend on us, be kind and loving to nature and animals, and take farming and intellectual pursuits as our basic life endeavors. This is the creed of our family. Our forefather, Wang Xi, had aspirations of serving people and state, followed Marquis Jing Shuangdong, charged by an emperor of the Ming dynasty with the task of southwestern frontier pacification. The Wang family, originally from the Yangzi Delta, embarked on this assignment and settled in Guizhou Province to secure the southern frontier for the empire. There have been eight generations since Wang Xi lived here in Jingjatun (the Jing family compound), who strived through rebellions, banditry, and natural disasters and avoided the fate of decline of other more-prominent clans due the strict observance of this creed.

You, as member of our clan, must carefully follow this creed and hand it down to your descendants. When I was young, I did not understand the importance of our creed. After I matured, I found that my father and my uncle had developed such a harmonious community/clan in our region where the people were kind and considerate toward each other, and our family had great respect from all concerned. Then I, too, realized how effective our clan's creed is. When my father passed away in 1903, I was eighteen, and my brother, Dilun, was only fourteen. The next year, my uncle died as well, and he left his two sons as infants. My mother had to take over as the effective head of our clan, and she strictly observed our creed in guiding us through some tumultuous times. My own experience is a testament of the importance of the creed for future generations.

Filial piety, friendship, loyalty, righteousness, benevolence, and love can be the guidelines of our daily lives in the management of a household, administration of a state, and relationships with family, clan, and state. Among them, the most essential part is filial piety. Those who can be filial centered on respecting and following the way (Dao), as well as taking care of their parents. They will also be close to their siblings, be loyal to their nation, be benevolent to their wards, and establish relations in good faith. That is why Confucius said filial piety was the basis of morality and the origin of education. He also said filial piety was the most essential virtue and the most important principle for the ancient kings to rule. Confucian aspiration was reflected in *The Spring and Autumn Annals*, and his own life was a mirror reflection in *The Book of Filial Piety*. For his wisdom and truth, he was thought of as a paragon of virtue and learning for generations, and by the experience of history, we have seen that filial piety is indeed the most important virtue of our life's activities. Our family creed listed it first. All members of our family must observe it as the prime directive, only after which come loyalty, righteousness, benevolence, and love to serve our nation and contribute to the society.

In the past, our family's basic life revolved around farming and intellectual pursuits. Farming enhances the general economy of our community. Our country was an agricultural state since ancient times; every need of our household and clan were dependent on agriculture. With the growth of population and the progress of science, industry and commerce became more important than agriculture. After the end this great war (the Second World War), the restoration of our country will be solely dependent on industry and commerce. Descendants of our family should follow the historical trend to expand their interests beyond agriculture into industry and commerce. We live in an era of high competition for intellectual pursuits regardless of sex. All members of our family must attain the highest level of education to the limit of his or her capability. The content of their education must include all elements that will facilitate high morality, great intellectual awareness, and physical well-being and strength. Guan Zi stated:

> Only one has his granary full, would he know etiquette.
> Only one has sufficient food and clothes, would he know honor and disgrace.
> Thus, one must be well fed before one can be well bred.

It thus follows that if we want our descendants to be well bred, we must first devise the means to have a financially secure household. We are fortunate that our previous generations have already provided us with real estate and other commercial investments, but we must provide proper stewardship for conservation and growth of such investments. Our concern now must be to ensure that once we are well fed, we must be well bred. In spite of legacies, every one of our family and clan must have a suitable level of education to be financially independent and in a position to help other members in need of help. In so doing they will be worthy progeny and contributors to our family, clan, and state, thus becoming good citizens to help in the building our nation into a strong member of the international world.

Although the population and economic situation of our clan before my great-grandfather were unclear, their basic lifestyle was no doubt based on farming and intellectual pursuits. My grandfather had no brother, and he lived in troubled times. He served in the militia out of necessity to defend our community, but he did not abandon our clan's basic lifestyle. In times of relative peace, my father and uncle expanded the clan's interest in industry and commerce. Through their leadership and successes, the reputation and wealth of our clan increased. I had three brothers (one blood brother and two sons from my uncles; we always referred to cousins of this blood relation as brothers).

After the deaths of my father and uncle, I had to involve us in the greater affairs of our nation and province at the expense of our clan and community in Xingyi. As a result our community suffered decline to the extent that my youngest brother (cousin), Wenyuan, did not have the benefit of a good education as the older three brothers did. For this I feel most distressed as the head of our clan. I now have four children of my own and ten-plus offspring in the next generation. The growth of the clan population has exceeded a geometric progression. In the evolution of our society, the traditional large family is giving way to a smaller family headed by husband and wife sharing equally the responsibility of management.

I am concerned about our clan's future relative to the finite clan assets and the ever-growing population. With the war looming ever so near to our home region, we face the real problem of how to maintain our current living standards for all members of our Clan since we are extremely limited in the expansion of the clan assets. I am now approaching the age of sixty years, and my health is in rapid decline. I strongly feel that I need to clarify the ownership rights and the management of the expenditures of our various interests in Xingyi and to resolve any disputes and disagreements in my lifetime for the sake of the future generations of our family and clan. These issues must be resolved as soon as possible to strive for permanent harmony for our descendants and fulfill my responsibility as the head of the clan. Therefore, I am writing down herewith this family creed, along with the instructions on dealing with our clan properties and interests in Xingyi for all members of our clan to observe.

REFERENCES

Bao, Zhining, et al,(in Chinese) *Xingyi's Liu, Wang, and He Families.* (Guizhou, China, 1990)

Bianco, Lucien, translated by Muriel Bell, *Origins of the Chinese Revolution, 1915 – 1949.* (Stanford, 1971).

Chan, Gilbert, F., *Liao Chung-Kai and the Labor Movement in Kwangtung, 1924 -1925.* (New York, 1975).

Chen, Yatien, *Chinese Military Theory – Ancient and Modern.* (Ontario, Canada, 1992).

Dreyer, Edward L., *China at War, 1901 -1949.* (New York, 1995).

Eastman, Lloyd, *Seeds of Destruction: Nationalist China in War and Revolution, 1937 – 1949,* (Stanford, 1984).

Fairbanks, John King, *The Great Chinese Revolution 1800 – 1985.* (New York, 1987).

Fenby, Jonathan, *Chiang Kai-Shek, China's Generalissimo, and the Nation He Lost.* (New York, 2004).

Gillespie, Richard, *Whampoa and the Nanking Decade 1924 -1936.* (American University, 1971).

Harrell, Paula, *Sowing the Seeds of Change – Chinese Students, Japanese Teachers*, 1895 – 1905. (Stanford, 1992)

Isaac, Harold R., *The Tragedy of the Chinese Revolution*. (Chicago, 2010)

Kissinger, Henry, *On China*. (New York, 2011).

Lewis, John Fulton, *China's Great convulsion 1894 – 1924*. (2005).

Long Shangxue, et al. *A Hundred Year History of the Yuan Zuming Family*. (1982).

Martin, Wilbur C., *Sun Yat-sen, Frustrated Patriot*. (New York, 1976).

McCord, Edward A., *Chinese Local Elites and Patterns of Dominance. Part II, Local Elites in Transition. Chapter 6, Local Military Power and Elite Formation: The Liu Family of Xingyi County, Guizhou*. (London, 1990).

McCord, Edward A., *The Power of the Gun – The Emergence of Modern Warlordism*. (Berkley, 1993).

Pakula, Hannah, *The Last Empress – Madame Chiang Kai-Shek and the Birth of Modern China*. (New York, 2009)

Powell, Ralph L., *The Rise of Chinese Military Power, 1895 – 1912*. (Princeton, NJ, 1955).

Pye, Lucian W., *Warlord politics: conflict and coalition in the modernization of Republican China*. (1971).

Sheridan, James E., *China in Disintegration – The Republic Era in Chinese History 1912 – 1049*. (New York, 1975).

Sheridan, James E., *Chinese Warlord the Career of Feng Yu-Hsiang*. (Stanford, 1955).

Spence, Jonathan D., *The Gate of Heavenly Peace: The Chinese and Their Revolution, 1905 – 1980*. (New York, 1981).

Spence, Jonathan D., *The Search for Modern China*. (New York, 1990).

Sutton, Donald S., *Provincial Militarism and the Chinese Republic – The Yunnan Army 1905 -25*. (Ann Arbor, 1980).

Tuchman, Barbara, *Stilwll and the American Experience in China, 1911 – 1945*. (New York, 1971)

Weale, Putnam B. L., *The Fight for the Republic in China*. (Lexington, KY, 2012).

Wilbur, C. Martin, *Sun Yat-Sen, Frustrated Patriot*, (New York, 1976)

Worthing, Peter, *Toward Minjin Incident: Militarist Conflict in Guizhou, 1911 -1921*. Modern China. (April 2007).

www.ingramcontent.com/pod-product-compliance
Lightning Source LLC
Chambersburg PA
CBHW032032080426
42733CB00006B/65